外研社

IELTS SPEAKING

含MP3光盘1张

雅思名师

教你征服雅思口语

曾腾裕◎著

外语教学与研究出版社
FOREIGN LANGUAGE TEACHING AND RESEARCH PRESS
北京 BEIJING

京权图字：01-2012-1077

原著作名：《雅思口说 & 听力高分指南》
原出版社：知英文化事业有限公司
作　　者：曾腾裕

图书在版编目(CIP)数据

雅思名师教你征服雅思口语/曾腾裕著. — 北京：外语教学与研究出版社，2012.5
ISBN 978-7-5135-2027-0

Ⅰ. ①雅…　Ⅱ. ①曾…　Ⅲ. ①IELTS—口语—自学参考资料　Ⅳ. ①H319.9

中国版本图书馆 CIP 数据核字（2012）第 106703 号

出 版 人：蔡剑峰
责任编辑：陈海燕　许圆圆
封面设计：姜　凯
出版发行：外语教学与研究出版社
社　　址：北京市西三环北路 19 号（100089）
网　　址：http://www.fltrp.com
印　　刷：三河市嘉科万达彩色印刷有限责任公司
开　　本：787×1092　1/16
印　　张：18.5
版　　次：2012 年 6 月第 1 版　2012 年 6 月第 1 次印刷
书　　号：ISBN 978-7-5135-2027-0
定　　价：43.00 元（含 MP3 光盘 1 张）

*　*　*

购书咨询：(010)88819929　　电子邮箱：club@fltrp.com
如有印刷、装订质量问题，请与出版社联系
联系电话：(010)61207896　　电子邮箱：zhijian@fltrp.com

物料号：220270001

作者序 | *

本书一版初次问世后，随即被评选为“台湾出版 TOP-1 代表性图书”。

最新增订版对内容做了一定幅度的修正。最大的改变是顺应潮流，将原书的 5 张 CD 改成一张 MP3，而完整的录音内容则完全保留。

此新增订版具有以下几个特色：

1. 本书附有 MP3，以英式发音为主，新西兰、加拿大、澳大利亚口音为辅，可随时加强雅思听力。

2. 本书提供的实用表达十分丰富，涵盖衣、食、住、行等近 20 个生活化话题。

3. 本书所有问题皆附有完整的回答范例。另外，针对一般问题（general questions）部分，每一题还附有答题指导，提供考生需注意的用法或补充相关用语。

4. 本书在回答范例中，着色部分表示口语回答的句型及值得背诵的句子，可加强考生对句型的概念。

5. 本书附有雅思听力考试常见题型解析、练习及应试策略。

对于听力较弱的考生，除了做雅思听力考试练习（第五章），建议可多利用本书所附的 MP3，针对第二和第三章的内容，一边听一边动手写关键词，练习做听力笔记。若能坚持，必将有益。本书一版的读者曾表示，他就是利用这种方式，每天上班前听一小时，雅思听力成绩得到了显著提高。

感谢家人的鼓励、Stephen Browning 的协助及知英文化仲美蓝主编的支持。

祝考生　英文大跃进，雅思考试顺利！

曾騰裕

目录 | *

音标符号解说 viii

Chapter 1 考试前必知的雅思考试口语部分概况 1

雅思考试简介 2
雅思考试口语部分简介 4
雅思考试口语部分评分标准 5
雅思考试口语部分准备方针 6
对雅思考试口语部分应有的心理准备 7
实用语句 8
雅思考试常见问题集 9

Chapter 2 考试第一部分题库：日常问题对答如流 11

Part I 居家生活（Home and Family Life） 13
Part II 学习与教育背景（Study and Educational Background） 21
Part III 职业与工作经验（Job and Working Experience） 31
Part IV 兴趣与爱好（Hobbies and Interests） 40
Part V 参加雅思考试的原因（Reasons for Taking IELTS） 44
Part VI 未来的计划（Plans for the Future） 45

Chapter 3 考试第二、三部分题库：各类话题说不停 49

注意事项 51
综合分类
1. 人物篇（People） 53
同事 Colleague 54

朋友与友情 Friends and Friendship 62
2. 事物篇（Something） 73
礼物 Gift 74
商业与购物 Business and Shopping 83
3. 食物篇（Food） 91
食品与饮食习惯 Food and Eating Habits 92
4. 衣着篇（Clothes） 105
服饰与风尚 Dress and Fashion 106
5. 居住篇（Housing） 119
城市与乡镇 City and Town 120
建筑 Architecture 128
6. 交通篇（Transportation） 139
交通与运输 Traffic and Transport 140
7. 教育篇（Education） 151
语言 Language 152
同学 Co-student 165
8. 娱乐篇（Entertainment） 173
运动 Sports 174
假期与旅游 Holiday and Travel 183
9. 科技与自然篇（Technology and Nature） 193
因特网 The Internet 194
设备 Equipment 203
动物与环境 Animals and Environment 211
10. 媒体与社会篇（Media and Society） 221
媒体 The Media 222
节日 Festivals 232
宗教与文化冲击 Religion and Cultural Impact 241

Chapter 4 实战测验：仿真考场验证成效 253

IELTS Speaking Test 1 254
IELTS Speaking Test 2 257

IELTS Speaking Test 3 260
IELTS Speaking Test 4 263

Chapter 5 口语材料练听力：考生验证的彪悍听力复习法 267

Exercise 1 填表格题型 269
Exercise 2 分类题型 270
Exercise 3 完成句子的填空题型 271
Exercise 4 只写关键词的填空题型（类似笔记纲要） 272
Exercise 5 多选题题型 274
Exercise 6 简答题题型 275
听力原文（Tapescripts） 276
听力练习答案（Answer Key） 284

音标符号解说

英式英语与美式英语发音有些差异，以 /ɑr/ 中的 /r/ 音为例，英式英语把元音拖长，发成 /ɑː/，并未发出 /r/ 音；又如 /ɛr/ /ɪr/ /ʊr/ 中的 /r/ 则以 /ə/ 发音。而 KK 音标特别适用于美式发音，所以本书以国际音标（IPA，International Phonetic Alphabet）为主，KK 音标为辅。

IPA 和 KK 音标的主要差异是元音，辅音的标示并无不同，故以下仅列出元音音标对照表。

国际音标（IPA）	KK 音标	例　词	音标标示
iː	i	feel	/fiːl; fil/
ɪ	ɪ	milk	/mɪlk; mɪlk/
e	ɛ	head	/hed; hɛd/
æ	æ	bag	/bæg; bæg/
ɑː	ɑ	calm	/kɑːm; kɑm/
ɑː	ɑr	hard	/hɑːd; hɑrd/
ɒ	ɑ	clock	/klɒk; klɑk/
ɔː	ɔ	talk	/tɔːk; tɔk/
ɔː	ɔr	four	/fɔː; fɔr/
ʊ	U	foot	/fʊt; fUt/
uː	u	blue	/bluː; blu/
ɜː	ɝ	burn	/bɜːn; bɝn/
ə	ɚ	letter	/ˈletə; ˋlɛtɚ/
ə	ə	about	/əˈbaʊt; əˋbaUt/

国际音标（IPA）	KK 音标	例　　词	音标标示
ʌ	ʌ	love	/lʌv; lʌv/
eɪ	e	take	/teɪk; tek/
aɪ	aɪ	buy	/baɪ; baɪ/
aɪə	aɪr	tire	/taɪə; taɪr/
ɔɪ	ɔɪ	toy	/tɔɪ; tɔɪ/
əʊ	o	boat	/bəʊt; bot/
aʊ	aU	house	/haʊs; haUs/
aʊə	aUr	flour	/flaʊə; flaUr/
ɪə	ɪr	hear	/hɪə; hɪr/
eə	ɛr	bear	/beə; bɛr/
ʊə	Ur	tour	/tʊə; tUr/
iə	jɚ	peculiar	/pɪˈkju:liə; pɪˋkjuljɚ/

【注】：考生可能较不熟悉几个音标及读音符号，在此扼要说明：

ː　加于元音后，表示此音为长音。

ɒ　此音类似 /ɔː/ 嘴唇成圆形，但比发 /ɔː/ 时的嘴形还要稍微往下、稍大。有一些词，如 coffee, hot, stop, cod, odd 等，英国人多会念成圆嘴形的 /ɒ/，而美国人则发 /ɑ/ 音。

ɑː　有些词如 bath, pass, past, dance, plant, staff, half 等，英国人念成 /ɑː/，而美国人则发 /æ/ 音。

Chapter 1

考试前必知的

雅思考试口语部分概况

雅思考试简介

1. 何谓雅思？

国际英语语言测试系统（The International English Language Testing System，英文简称：IELTS，中文简称：雅思）是国际认可的申请赴英语国家留学、移民所需的英语能力证明。雅思亦是大多数英语国家高等学院所优先认可的英语程度标准，另一方面，因其测验内容涵盖听、说、读、写四项，故也可为应试者提供方向，改善整体英语能力。

雅思考试注重考生在专业范畴内需具备的语言能力，所以众多英语国家的学校，鼓励学生参加雅思考试。尤其为英国、澳大利亚、新西兰、加拿大及欧洲的教育系统所接受。不仅如此，现今已有愈来愈多的美国院校（超过 3000 所）接受雅思成绩为学生申请学校的英语水平衡量标准。

凡计划前往海外就读大学、研究生、专科、技术学院先修课程及其他课程，或申请英国、澳大利亚、新西兰、加拿大及欧洲移民者，都可参加雅思考试。雅思考试由剑桥大学考试委员会（University of Cambridge ESOL Examinations）、英国文化协会（The British Council）及 IDP 教育集团（IDP Education）共同举办。

2. 雅思考试方式

雅思考试分为两种类型，即学术类（A 类）和培训类（G 类）。这两类考试的听力和口语两部分使用相同的试题，阅读和写作则使用不同的试题。请先查清楚学校入学要求再决定类别。

学术类（A 类）

适用于欲申请正式课程者，如研究生、大学、专科课程或学校有要求者。

培训类（G 类）：

适用于申请移民者，及欲申请学校有要求此类别者。

雅思考试顺序如下：

听力	测试时间：40 分钟 测试方式：分为四大部分，每题给考生约 20 秒将题目浏览一次，测验完毕再留约 20 秒检查答案。 测试题数：共 40 题。
阅读	测试时间：60 分钟 测试方式：填空、选择、完成句子、配对、图表、表格、段落大纲、摘要、判断题。 测试题数：共 40 题。
写作	测试时间：60 分钟 测试方式：第一篇至少 150 个词，主要是对给出的资料、图表进行描述。第二篇至少 250 个词，以某个主题抒发自己的想法及经验。 测试题数：两篇作文。
口语	测试时间：11-14 分钟 测试方式：分三个部分，包括简介以及问答、个人陈述和双向讨论。由口试老师跟考生作一对一口试。

雅思考试口语部分简介

雅思口语考试以考生与考官展开一对一交流的方式进行（11-14 分钟），多由英籍或澳大利亚籍的考官（examiner）进行提问，口语考试分成三部分，包括简介以及问答、个人陈述和双向讨论，考试过程将被录音。

第一部分：考官问考生一些较生活化的问题，时长 4-5 分钟。

第二部分：考官会给考生一张答题任务卡，上面载有某一特定的话题，如“The person you admire most”（你最崇拜的人），并针对这个话题，附有考生在回答时需包含的要点，考生有一分钟时间准备，可以做笔记，准备时间结束，考生须作出个人陈述；这个部分，考官暂时不会插话，也不会问任何问题，直到考生无话可说，或此阶段的时间已快用尽。接着，考官会问一至二题。含给题目、准备时间，第二部分总共 3-4 分钟。

第三部分：在这个部分，考官会提出一些问题和考生讨论，问题和第二部分的话题相关，但涉及层面较广，问题也较深入，如：What factors would influence the way people choose their most admired persons?（什么因素会影响人选择他们最崇拜的对象？）这部分的问题并不会在卡片上出现，而是由考官提出来问，时长 4-5 分钟。

雅思考试口语部分评分标准

雅思口语考试以下列四项为评分标准，四项的平均分数即为考生的口语考试成绩。

1. 流畅性与连贯性（Fluency and Coherence）：

流畅性指说话的语速（rate）及连续性（continuity）；连贯性指从句或句子间的内容联结恰当；换言之，就是连接词、代名词及转折用语等使用得体。

2. 词汇多样性（Lexical Resource）：

词汇部分包含三个方面：一是词汇量的广度；二是能否用词恰当；三是遇到不知如何表达时，能否使用其他词汇来解释。

3. 语法的多样性和准确性（Grammatical Range and Accuracy）：

即会使用不同的句型结构，所说句子的语法要正确。

4. 发音（Pronunciation）：

指说话是否清晰，若考生的发音造成考官理解起来有障碍，则此项目得分必然不高。

雅思考试口语部分准备方针

针对上述评分原则，以下建议提供给各位考生参考，以便在雅思口语考试准备上有方向感。

(1) 所谓 Practice makes perfect（熟能生巧），本书所提供的练习题，若能多加练习，在流畅性上，必能进步，至少可以避免太长或太多的停顿。

(2) 至于连贯性，可参考本书第二章及第三章的回答范例着色部分，多半有适当的连接词及转折用语。

(3) 至少要熟悉本书各话题的实用词汇，以强化词汇多样性。

(4) 尽量不要只用简单句（如：主语＋动词＋名词），可用连接词、转折承接词、强调句型、虚拟语气、关系从句等，可参考本书的回答范例。

(5) 可找有经验的老师练习模考，并帮你找出最常犯的语法错误。

(6) 有些题目，如以 why 引导的问题，不要三言两语就答完，可加以扩充，多讲几点，每一点再举例子。

(7) 回答时，尽量要多说几句，发音清楚，重音要念正确。平时多朗诵口语化的文章或对话将会有帮助，不熟悉如何发音的词，一定要查阅词典。本书提供英式及美式音标对照，旨在帮助考生熟悉英式发音，能听懂英式英语，考生并无必要刻意改变原有的腔调，应以发音清晰为原则。

对雅思考试口语部分应有的心理准备

（1）雅思考试的口语考官多半来自英国、澳大利亚或新西兰，但也有可能来自南非或其他国家。

（2）考生不必担心无法说英国或澳大利亚腔调，因为考试的重点是口语表达能力。

（3）口语考试测试的并非是考生的专业知识，而是交流的有效性（effectiveness of communication），若遇到较不熟悉的话题时，以自己本身经验、所见、所闻来答题，不要说 I don't know 或不答。

（4）若考官在你回答问题时插话，不要惊慌，因为这很常见，先回答其插话的问题，答毕再问：Shall I get back to the previous question? 视考官回应再继续。千万不要因为考官插话而影响自己的情绪。

（5）若对问题不清楚，可以试着问考官，与其答非所问，不如确定问题再答。或可以试着回答，答毕再反问考官：Have I answered your question? 这样比频频询问 Pardon? 更为妥当。不过，在个人陈述的阶段，通常考官不回答或解释答题任务卡上的问题。

（6）考官会从考生回答的内容中，再问相关的问题，如考生提及：I like films. 考官可能会接着问：What is the film that you have seen most recently?

（7）回答时，考生可以呈现自然的表情及手势，一切以自然为原则。如：可以面带微笑，展现自信，目光平视考官。

实用语句

1. 对考官的问题，不是很清楚时，可用以下方法请求进一步解释：

Could you please rephrase your question?

Sorry?

Pardon?

You mean + 自己的理解?

或重复自己不懂的词，语调上升，他们通常会再加以解释。

2. 遇到较生疏的问题时，可先用以下任一方法缓冲一下，再回答：

I am not sure how to answer that question, but perhaps I can tell you a personal experience I had. ________________.

That's an interesting question, but I have never thought about it. Perhaps I can put it this way. ________________.

I don't know much about it, but it might be possible that ________________.

3. 如考生已答完某一问题，但考官还一直盯着你，考生可主动反问：

Have I answered your question?

Is there anything else you'd like to know?

Have I given you enough information?

雅思考试常见问题集

1. Q：何谓雅思？

A：是一种国际认可的英语能力测验，由剑桥大学考试委员会（University of Cambridge ESOL Examinations）、英国文化协会（The British Council）及 IDP 教育集团（IDP Education）共同负责。其全名为 International English Language Testing System。想留学英国、加拿大、澳大利亚、新西兰及欧洲大陆的教育系统，学校会要求提交雅思考试成绩证明。现今已有越来越多的美国院校（超过 3000 所）亦接受雅思考试成绩为学生申请学校的英语水平衡量标准。

2. Q：雅思考试以什么方式进行？

A：雅思考试分听力、阅读、写作及口试四大部分。阅读及写作又分为学术类和培训类两种。通常要就读大学或研究生课程者选择考学术类，要工作、移民者考培训类即可。

3. Q：雅思考试要多久？

A：考试当天早上考听力（30 分钟）、阅读（1 小时）、写作（1 小时）三部分。口语考试会根据考点情况安排在其他三部分考试之前或之后，不一定在同一天进行，每位考生为 11-14 分钟。总测验时间约为 3 小时。

4. Q：如何报名？

A：凡报考中国大陆地区雅思考试的考生须登录教育部雅思考试网上报名网站：http://ielts.etest.net.cn 进行报名和付费。各场次于距考试 12 个工作日之前截止报名；若该场次于截止日前已额满，则不再受理报名。

5. Q：成绩何时会收到？

A：在考试后第 10 个工作日，成绩单将通过 EMS 特快专递寄出，一般需 2 到 3 个工作日送达考生。

6. Q：雅思考试成绩如何解读?

A：雅思考试满分为 9 分。听、说、读、写四项之平均即为考生的分数。总平均只要小数点是 0.125 或 0.625 就不进位，0.25 或 0.75 就进位，例如四项平均是 6.125，则分数是 6；若平均是 6.625，则分数是 6.5；若平均是 6.25，则分数是 6.5；若平均是 6.75，则分数是 7。多数的大学会要求至少 6 分或 6.5 分。详细情形请向自己欲申请的学校查询。

7. Q：雅思考试可以多久重考一次?

A：只要报名之场次尚未额满，随时可再重考。

8. Q：雅思考试成绩的效力可维持多久?

A：不同学校、机构或使馆认定及接受的标准不一。一般来说，自考试之日起两年内的雅思考试成绩皆会被接受。

9. Q：哪里可进一步取得雅思考试的相关信息?

A：雅思考试中文官方网站：http://www.chinaielts.org
英国文化协会网站：http://www.britishcouncil.org.cn/zh/china.htm
教育部雅思考试网上报名网站：http://ielts.etest.net.cn

Chapter 2

考试第一部分题库：日常问题对答如流

IELTS

雅思口语考试第一部分的问题几乎都是和考生相关的一般问题（general questions），常和以下几个方面相关；考官可能从考生的回答中，挑出些许话题，再进一步询问。

I. Your home and family life
II. Your study and educational background
III. Your job and working experience
IV. Your hobbies and interests
V. Your reasons for taking IELTS
VI. Your plan for the future

为了让考生在准备雅思口语考试时，能一方面增进表达能力，一方面又兼顾真正口试时问题的多变性，本书在这一部分，尽量提供适当的辅助，如句型、用词及回答方向，而非只是固定的参考答案；回答范例中的着色部分表示可套用的句型。另外，为顾及读者背景的差异，本书提供的参考答案尽量模拟不同考生可能的情况，而非某一学科背景下的特定考生，故不同题目的回答范例并非前后一致。（考生真正应试时，要按照自己情况回答，不要前后矛盾。）

考生在练习时，要切记以下几点原则：

（1）依照自己的情况答题。
（2）回答时，尽量多说，不要总是答一句就结束。
（3）若遇到不知如何用英文表达的情况，事后要查阅汉英词典，或向人请教，以备不时之需。
（4）考生要对自己的回答，再进一步准备，如你的兴趣是旅游，则要准备谈谈自己的旅游经验、文化风俗比较及旅游趣事等。

Canada is different from China in some respects. For examples, the climate, the economy and people's lifestyle. For the climate, the winter in Canada, especially in Alberta Province is much bitterer than the one in China however I prefer living here because of the higher air quality. As far as the economy is concerned, China is a developing country while Canada is a developed country. There are also more job opportunities in Canada. In terms of people's lifestyle, Canadian are under less working pressure they have more free time to study or relax.

PART 1 居家生活

(Home and Family Life)

1. Where are you from?

I'm from Shenzhen, Guangdong Province. I've been living in this city for about ten years.

I'm from China, and I've been living here for about one year.

你从何处来？

我来自广东省的深圳市，我在这个城市已经住了约十年。

答题指导

注意使用现在完成进行时（I have been living…）（我已住了……）。

2. Where's your hometown?

I was originally from Jinan, which is to the south of Beijing.

你的籍贯在哪？

我原籍济南，在北京南边。

You might not know the city. It is called Shenyang, which is in northern China

答题指导

区分 to the south of Beijing　在北京南边

in southern Beijing　在北京的南部

For the climate, The winter in Canada is much bitterer than one in China. As far as lifestyle is concerned, Canadians are under less working pressure, they have more free time to do what they like. However, because of the population in China is much higher than CAN

climate, lifestyle, economic.

3. Is it very different from the place where you are living?

Yes, it is different in some respects, for example, the weather, the industry, the availability of job opportunities and even the people are different. As far as weather is concerned, Shenzhen is hotter than Jinan. Compared with people in Jinan, people in Shenzhen are probably under higher working pressure. Besides, since Shenzhen is more developed in industry and commerce than Jinan, it provides more job vacancies.

它跟你现在住的地方差异很大吗?

是的，在某些方面有差异。例如：天气、产业、工作机会，甚至连两地的人也有所不同。以天气来说，深圳比济南热。与住在济南的人比起来，深圳人的工作压力大概更大。还有，因为深圳在工商业方面比济南发展得快，提供的工作机会更多。

答题指导

本题属于比较的题型，可点出几方面，套用比较级和以下用法：

as far as 方面 be concerned　就……而言

in terms of 方面　就……来说

另外，注意 industry /'ɪndəstri; `ɪndəstrɪ/ 重音在第一个音节。

4. In which part of the city do you live?

Sommerset Station, Southern Calgary

I live in Shijingshan District, which lies in western Beijing.

你住在这个城市的哪一区域?

我住在北京西部的石景山区。

答题指导

I live in ________ District（区）, which is in northern / southern / central / south-western 城市名 .

我住在 ________ 区，它在 城市名 的北部 / 南部 / 中部 / 西南部。

词汇

district /'dɪstrɪkt; `dɪstrɪkt/ *n.* 区

5. What do you think are the features of this city?

It's famous for its seafood and being an international seaport.

你认为这个城市有什么特别的?

它以海鲜及国际海港闻名。

~~Gas~~, Calgary is famous for its production amount of Gas.

Some cities of China also keeps coorporate

答题指导

The city is famous for
- its seafood. 海鲜
- its beautiful scenery. 美景
- its being cosmopolitan. 大都会
- its being highly industrialized. 高度工业化
- its fishing industry. 渔业
- its farming industry. 农业
- its local snacks 当地小吃

（这个城市以……闻名。）

6. Do you live with your family?

I live with my parents. It's a typical nuclear family, I suppose.

你和你的家人一起住吗？

我和我父母亲一起住，算是一个典型的小家庭。

答题指导

或 I live on my own, but I visit my parents quite often.

我独居，但是我常常去探望父母。

注：extended family　大家庭

词汇

nuclear family　小家庭

7. What kind of house do you live in?

I live in a block of flats which has five levels. I live on the fourth level.

你住的房子是何种类型？

我住的是一栋五层楼的公寓，我住在四楼。

答题指导

a detached house　单门独户的房子

a block of flats　一栋公寓

a high-rise block　高楼

a terraced house　排房

a three-level house　三层楼的房子

villa /'vɪlə; `vɪlə/ ***n.***　别墅

a semi-detached house　一侧与他屋相连的房子

8. Could you tell me more about your room? What is it like?

My room is not very spacious. It's a study bedroom with some simple furniture including a bed, a desk and a wardrobe. It's decorated in light blue. The colour does however make me feel relaxed. The room has one window which overlooks a small park nearby.

你能谈谈你的房间吗？它是什么样子？

我的房间不是很大。它是卧室兼书房，里头有一些简单的家具，包括一张床、一张书桌和一个衣橱。它刷成了淡蓝色，这颜色的确让我觉得很舒服。房间还有一扇窗户，可以眺望附近的小公园。

答题指导

尽可能详细描述，包括家具（desk“桌子”，bed“床”，bookshelf“书架”，closet“橱柜”，computer“电脑”）、颜色、窗户外的景观如何等等。

词汇

spacious /'speɪʃəs; `speʃəs/ ***adj.***　空间大的

study bedroom　卧室兼书房

overlook /ˌəʊvə'lʊk; ˌovɚ`lʊk/ ***v.***　俯视，眺望

9. Could you describe your family members?

I'm from what's called nowadays a nuclear family. My father is a civil servant. My mother is a housekeeper, a kind-hearted, loving person. She used to be a high school teacher and helps me a lot with my English.

你能谈谈你的家人吗？

我来自时下所谓的小家庭。我爸是一位公务员。我妈是一位家庭主妇，善良有爱心。她曾经在高中教书，而且在英文学习方面给予我很大帮助。

答题指导

家庭描述包含成员、年龄、工作、各自的特点等。

词汇

civil servant　公务员

10. What is a typical day at your home like?

A typical day? Well, in the morning my father has breakfast at home and I usually join him at the table. But if I get up late and mother has gone out, I buy myself something simple from a 7-Eleven shop. The family members do things together in the evening or on weekends. We watch TV, the news programmes and soap operas. As the saying goes, "Home sweet home, there's no place like home." I do enjoy those moments of being together with the family, but sometimes I get a little bored and like to do things by myself.

你的居家生活通常是怎样的情形？

居家生活通常的情形？嗯，在早上，我和我爸常在家里一起吃早餐，但是如果我晚起，而且妈妈又出去时，我就自己从 7-Eleven 便利店买些简单的东西吃。我和我家人在晚上或周末时会在一起，我们一起看电视，看新闻节目及连续剧。有道是："我的家庭真可爱，没有任何东西可取代。"我喜欢和家人在一起的时光，但是偶尔会感到有点无聊，想单独做点事。

答题指导

可根据早上、晚上家庭成员互动的情况答题。

11. How would you characterize "family ties" in this country?

I consider family ties in this country strong, because most of the children here are brought up on a set of values based not on money but on family and traditional virtues.

你认为“家庭关系”在这个国家有何特色?

我觉得家庭关系在这个国家算是很紧密，因为这儿大部分的家庭在抚养孩子过程中所依据的价值观都是以人伦及传统美德为基准的，而不是以金钱为准则。

词汇

characterize /'kærɪktəraɪz; `kærɪktəˌraɪz/ *v.* 描述……的特性

family ties 家庭关系；亲情（的维系）

virtue /'vɜːtʃuː; `vɝtʃu/ *n.* 美德；品德

12. Do you think family ties nowadays are not so strong as they used to be, say, 10 years ago?

Well, yes and no! Based on my own experience, I would say “Yes”, because my parents care for me and I consider it my responsibility to look after them when they get old. So as far as my family is concerned, our family ties are just as strong as before. But I’ve heard news reports saying from time to time how badly some children treat their parents. This might be an indication that family ties are not as strong as before.

你是否认为家庭关系没有以前那么紧密了？比如和十年前比起来？

嗯，可说是，也可说不是。根据我自己的经历来看，因为我父母关心我，所以当他们年老时，我觉得我有责任要照顾他们。因此就我家来说，我们的家庭关系和以前一样紧密。但是，有时会听到新闻报道说有些孩子对待父母相当恶劣，这似乎是家庭关系渐趋式微的一种迹象。

答题指导

注：say 在口语中，用法和 for example 相同。

Yes and no 指“可说是，也可说不是”，接下来要给出原因。

词汇

indication /ˌɪndɪ'keɪʃən; ˌɪndə`keʃən/ *n.* 迹象；表示

13. Do you think family life in this country will play a less significant role in the future?

No, I don't think so, for one obvious reason. The policy of having two days off per week has been implemented in this country. This means that parents will have more time to spend with their children. Besides, couples nowadays have one child only, so they will surely be able to give them sufficient attention.

你认为，家庭生活在这个国家所扮演的角色，以后会越来越不重要吗？
不，我不这么认为，理由很明显，我国实行双休日的政策，这意味着父母将有更多的时间来陪伴孩子。此外，现代的夫妻只有一个小孩，所以，他们当然能够给予孩子更多的关注。

答题指导

针对 Do you think...?（你认为……？）的问题，答案不外乎是：Yes, I think so（是的，我赞成）；No, I don't think so（不，我不这么想）；或 Yes and no（可说是，也可说不是），然后再说明原因。

词汇

implement /'ɪmplɪment; `ɪmplə,mɛnt/ *v.* 执行
two days off per week 每周休息两日，双休日
sufficient /sə'fɪʃənt; sə`fɪʃənt/ *adj.* 足够的

14. If you had a choice, where would you prefer to live and why?

I would prefer to live near the Fragrant Hills, where the air is fresh and the views are magnificent. Living in a place like that, I might even live a longer and healthier life! Besides, I can't bear noise, so its tranquil environment suits me well.

如果可以选择的话，你比较喜欢住在哪里？为什么？
我会喜欢住在香山附近，那边的空气很新鲜，景色也很美。住在那样的地方，我可能会活得更久而且更健康！此外，我无法忍受噪音，所以那边的宁静生活非常适合我。

答题指导

I'll prefer to live near / in a place（或地名）where + 完整从句 .

我比较喜欢住在某个地方附近 / 住在某个地方，那里……

针对 why 问题，最好能提供至少两个理由。

词汇

tranquil /'træŋkwɪl; `træŋkwɪl/ ***adj.*** 宁静的

PART II 学习与教育背景
(Study and Educational Background)

1. Are you a student or do you work?

I am a student studying at Peking University.

目前你是上学还是工作？

我是大学生，在北京大学就读。

答题指导

或 I graduated last year, but I still consider myself a student as I spend much time studying English in the hope that I can do well in my IELTS test.

我去年毕业，但我仍觉得自己是学生，因为我花了很多时间来学习英语，希望雅思考试能取得好成绩。

2. What do you study?

I am doing a major in Education

你读的是什么专业？

我主修教育。

答题指导

do a major in 科目 / major in 科目　主修……

不要说：I major in Education Department.

3. Do you enjoy your study?

Yes, I do. My university education has helped me acquire knowledge in Information Management. I have learned how to think over an issue from different points of view. The more I learn, the more I realize how little I know. That's why I decided to pursue further study.

你喜爱你的学业吗?

是的，我很喜欢。我的大学课程帮助我学到了信息管理方面的知识。我也学会了如何从不同的角度去思考一个问题。学得越多，我愈发意识到自己知识浅陋，这也是我决定继续进修的原因。

答题指导

My university education has helped me acquire knowledge in 领域.

“学习……的知识”不要说 learn knowledge，这是中式英文；而应该说 acquire / gain knowledge。

4. What's your favourite subject?

My favourite subject! Well, if I had to choose just one, it would be a course called English Reading and Conversation. The reason why I like that one best is that I have benefited a lot from it. For example, I've learned some very useful reading skills, developed more efficient learning methods and improved my oral English.

你最喜欢的科目是什么?

我最喜欢的科目啊！假如只能选择一个的话，那应该就是英语阅读与会话的课程了。因为这门课程使我获益良多，举例来说，我学到了一些很有用的阅读技巧，掌握了更高效的学习方法，并提高了英语会话能力。

答题指导

点出科目，然后给原因。这类题目，考生都要依照自己的情况做好准备。

词汇

benefit from ... 从……中获益

5. How about your favourite subject when you were in primary school and in secondary school?

My favourite subject in primary school? Gosh, that's a long time ago! Let me think about it. I think it was music. I have been fond of music ever since I was little. I used to play the flute, the Chinese flute, in primary school. Then I became interested in English when I was in high school. I wasn't the best student of English in my class, but I have improved my English comprehension, vocabulary and conversational abilities a lot since then.

在小学及中学时代，你最喜爱的科目又是什么？

我在小学最喜爱的科目？啊，那可是很久远的事了！让我想想看，我想应该是音乐。从孩提时代我就很喜欢音乐，在小学我常吹笛，中国笛子。中学时代，我对英语产生了兴趣，当时我的英语并不是全班最好的，但从那时起我的英语理解能力、词汇运用及会话能力都有了显著的进步。

答题指导

有时，考官会针对某一话题，询问过去、现在、未来等情况，记得用适当的时态。

6. What is your school life like?

During the day, most of my time is spent attending lectures and doing my homework. In the evening, I sometimes join in group activities or just chat with a few of my friends. Like most students nowadays, I spend time surfing the Net. I try to find a balance between study and play. I try to be nice to myself although I have not forgotten my duty as a student.

你的学校生活如何？

白天，大多数时间在上课、做作业。晚上，有时我会参加社团活动，或跟几个朋友聊聊天。像时下的大部分学生一样，我也会去上上网。我努力平衡学业和娱乐。我努力善待自己，不过我并没有忘记做学生的本分。

答题指导

注意 spend 的用法：

spend ... doing（如：I spend much time studying in the library.）

spend ... on sth.（如：I spend some time on my study.）

不要说 spend time to do。

7. I wonder if you have the experience where you are not interested in a course but you have to study it?

Yes, I have. For example, a year ago, I had to take a course in Accounting, but I found it difficult, so difficult that I managed to achieve only a borderline grade. Maybe that's not where my potential lies.

我想知道你是否曾经有过对于某一科目不感兴趣，却又不得不学的经历？
是的，我有过这样的经历。举例来说，一年前，我必须修一门会计课程，但觉得它很难，难到我只能勉强过关而已，也许那并不是我的潜力所在。

答题指导

或：No, never. I always try my best whatever course I study. And I believe I can always learn something new from a course.
不，从来没有过。因为我总是尽力研习我所学的课程，并且相信我总可以从课程里学到一些新的知识。

词汇

potential /pə'tenʃəl; pə`tɛnʃəl/ ***n.*** 潜力

8. If you were in that situation where you felt frustrated, what would you do?（接上一题，回答 No 的人）

I would cooperate with a friend of mine who could help me. But then I would expect only to get a pass rather than achieve a high grade in the exams.

假如你遇到那种情况，感到沮丧时，你会怎么办？
我会跟能帮助我的朋友一起合作学习，但是我不会期待在这个科目上拿到高分，能够及格就行了。

答题指导

注意这种虚拟语气的问题，回答要用：I would _______ .

9. Do you join any extracurricular activities? Why?

I participate in a guitar club in my college. I play my guitar there almost every week. I joined it because I love music and I like to make friends there. Being in this club means a lot to me. It's a situation where I can play and share impressions with other music lovers. What's more, I'm learning how to communicate better.

你参加课外活动吗？为什么？

大学期间，我加入了吉他社，我几乎每周都去那儿弹吉他，我加入的原因是我热爱音乐，也想结识朋友。对我来说，待在这个社团是非常有意义的。它是一个让我既可以玩音乐，又可以与其他音乐爱好者分享感受的地方。而且，我还在学习如何更好地与他人沟通。

答题指导

可举出参加社团（club）的经历、活动频率及原因。

词汇

extracurricular /ˌekstrəkəˈrɪkjʊlə; ˏekstrəkəˋrɪkjələ˞/ ***adj.*** 课外的

10. Do you live in a dormitory?

Yes, I do. It's a building of five levels, housing about 700 students. It's built of red bricks and painted white inside. There are four students to each of the en suite rooms. Each student has a bed, a desk and a clothes closet. Overall, it's quite modern and cosy.

or

No, I live off campus. Three friends of mine and I rent a house not far from our college. It's family housing accommodation in a high-rise block. It has four single rooms with a shared kitchen, a living room and a bathroom.

你住学生宿舍吗?

是的，我住宿舍。它是一栋五层高的、可以容纳约700名学生的宿舍楼，是用红砖盖成的，内部则被粉刷成白色。在四人一间的套房里，每名学生有一张床、一张书桌和一个衣橱。大致上来说，既现代又温馨舒适。

或

不，我住在学校外面。我和三位朋友在学校附近的一栋高楼中租了一户家庭式的房子，有四个房间，共用厨房、客厅及浴室。

答题指导

若有的话，可大致描述一下宿舍外观、楼层及房间情况等。

词汇

dormitory /'dɔːmɪtəri; `dɔrmə,tɔrɪ/ ***n.*** 宿舍

en suite /,ɒn'swiːt; ,ɑn`swit/ ***adj.*** 套房式的；(卧室) 带浴室的

off campus 在校外

cosy /'kəʊzi; `kozɪ/ ***adj.*** 舒适的

11. How about student-teacher relationships you have experienced in your institute?

The relationships between the students and teachers that I know of tend to be friendly, because most of my professors are kind and accessible and willing to help. They are more than willing to discuss any problems I raise. They are good listeners. They're just like friends.

在你们学校，师生关系怎么样?

在我所认识的老师与学生里，他们的关系良好，因为我的大部分教授都很和善、很亲切，也愿意帮助我们。他们不仅愿意跟我一起讨论我所提出的问题，而且乐意聆听，就像朋友一般。

答题指导

其他形容关系的词汇：strained /streɪnd; strend/（紧张的）；warm（温馨的）；tenuous /'tenjuəs; `tɛnjʊəs/（淡薄的）。

词汇

accessible /ək'sesəbəl; ək`sɛsəbḷ/ ***adj.*** 亲切的

12. Where did you do your first degree?

I received my university education from Chongqing University.

你在哪儿读的本科？

我在重庆大学读的。

> **词汇**
>
> first degree （BrE）学士学位

13. Where is it?

It's located in Chongqing City, which is in southwestern China.

它在哪里？

它在重庆市，位于中国西南部。

> **答题指导**
>
> 其他情况，如：
>
> It's located in Tianjin, which is about half an hour's ride by train from Beijing.
>
> 它位于天津，从北京坐火车的话需要大约半个小时。
>
> It's located in Jinan, which is in the western part of Shandong Province.
>
> 它位于山东省西部的济南市。
>
> It's located in Yunnan Province, which is in southern China.
>
> 它在云南省，位于中国南部。

14. Could you please describe its campus?

The campus is spacious and green; it's really spectacular and impressive. And it's surrounded by mountains. Standing on the roof of the College of Foreign Languages, you can see a river nearby. There are several architectural styles of building: Chinese, European, and high-tech. The open planning and spaciousness of the campus makes me feel ever so close to nature.

你能描述一下校园吗?

校园开阔，绿意盎然，群山环绕，景色壮丽，令人难忘。伫立在外语学院天台上，你可以看见附近的一条河。建筑风格有好几种：中式的，欧式的，还有高科技的。校园开放式的规划设计和宽广空间常让我觉得与自然是如此的亲近。

答题指导

可包括校园的大小、建筑特色或周遭较特别的景观。可能用到的表达如：

be surrounded by　被……所环绕

overlook（主动用法）俯视

mostly red in appearance　在外观上大部分是红色的

The buildings on campus are characterized by Chinese architectural style.

校园建筑是中式风格。

The buildings on campus are of a Western style.

校园建筑是西式风格。

词汇

architectural /ˌɑːkɪˈtektʃərəl; ˌɑrkəˋtɛktʃərəl/ ***adj.***　建筑的

15. Why did you choose your major subject?

I took the college entrance examination in 2009. I chose a list of possible departments I was interested in, but in the end, it was my grade that determined which department I could enter.

你当初为何会选择这个专业?

我在 2009 年参加了高考，当时我选填了几个感兴趣的专业，但最终是我的成绩决定了我能进入哪个系。

答题指导

其他相关表达：

gain admission through application　申请入学

gain admission through recommendation by my high school　通过学校推荐入学

16. In this country, do students change their majors quite often?

Not very often. While some change their majors, others decide to minor in a different subject.

在这个国家，学生会经常改变他们所主修的专业吗？
并不是很经常，有些人会换专业，有些人则会选择不同的科目当作辅修。

答题指导

major 指主修，可以当动词或名词；minor 指辅修。

17. Could you introduce me a bit about your field of study?

Yes, certainly. I specialize in Business Administration, which is a discipline dealing with issues arising from managing a business, from both theoretical and practical viewpoints.

你能稍微介绍一下你所学的领域吗？
当然可以。我主修工商管理，它从理论及实际两个角度，探讨企业管理中产生的种种问题。

答题指导

I major in <u>科目</u>, which is a discipline dealing with <u>名词短语</u>. 或：It's a subject that investigates _______ .
尽可能使用不同句型结构，如定语从句 which is a discipline…，分词短语 dealing with…，arising from…。且考生要准备谈谈自己学习的领域。

词汇

discipline /'dɪsɪplɪn; `dɪsəplɪn/ ***n.*** 专业，科目

18. Will you continue to explore this area of study? Why or why not?

Hmm, in a sense, yes! I'd like to carry on my study in this field, but with a different focus. I plan to do my postgraduate study in E-business, which is quite a new area of research.

你将会继续钻研这个领域吗？为什么会或为什么不会？

嗯……可以这么说，我会继续在这领域钻研，但侧重点不同，我计划读电子商务的研究生课程，这是相当新的领域。

答题指导

若尚未决定，可点出几个可能的领域，如：I have not decided yet which subject to specialize in. I have several in mind; they are _______ , _______ and _______ . They are related, but with slightly different directions. After I find out more information about these courses, I'll make a final decision.

我还没决定要专攻的科目。我想到了几个：它们是 _______，_______及 _______。它们算是相关，但方向上仍有细微的差异，在进一步了解了这些课程后，我将会作出最后的决定。

词汇

postgraduate /ˌpəʊst'grædjuət; ˌpost`grædʒuɪt/ ***adj.*** 研究生的 ***n.*** 研究生

PART III 职业与工作经验
(Job and Working Experience)

1. Do you work? Or are you still a student?

I work as a secretary at a food processing company, which exports canned food to Japan, Europe and America.

你现在工作了吗？或者你还是个学生？
我在一家食品加工企业当秘书，这家公司的业务是出口罐装食品到日本、欧洲和美国。

答题指导

I work as a 职位 at ________ Company, which sells（或 imports / exports / manufactures）产品.
我在一家卖（或进口 / 出口 / 制造）产品 的________公司当 职位 。
或：No, I do not work at present.
我目前没在工作。
I quit my job this summer.
今年夏天我辞去了工作。
I have been devoted to preparing for this IELTS test.
我一直在全心准备雅思考试。

2. What is your present job about?

I do some administration work, and I'm also responsible for storing relevant information on computer.

你目前做什么工作？
我做些行政方面的工作，也负责在电脑上储存相关资料。

答题指导

可详加描述工作性质，如：

I am {in charge of / responsible for} + <u>工作性质</u>（如：marketing “营销”）.

我负责 / 主管……（工作）。

词汇

administration /ədˌmɪnɪˈstreɪʃən; ədˌmɪnə`streʃən/ ***n.*** 行政

3. How do you like it?

I like it tremendously, because it serves my interest and I've learned much from it.

你觉得这份工作怎么样？

我非常喜欢这份工作，因为它符合我的兴趣，而且从中我也学到了很多东西。

答题指导

此问题是问对工作的态度，而非喜不喜欢工作，故答案不是 Yes 或 No，而可能是：

I like the job a lot / tremendously.

我非常喜欢这份工作。

I think it's all right.

我觉得还可以，普通而已。

I don't like it at all.

我一点也不喜欢它。

另外，可再说明原因：

… because it serves my interest and I've learned much from it.

因为它符合我的兴趣，而且从中我也学到了很多东西。

… because I can handle it well, but it is not very interesting.

因为我可以胜任这份工作，但是它并不是很有趣。

… because it requires long hours of working, sometimes even in the evening, and it does not correspond with my university training. I don't feel well placed there.

因为它所需要的工作时数长，有时甚至要工作到晚上，而且与我在大学所受的专业训练不对口，我觉得这个岗位并不适合我。

词汇

tremendously /trɪˈmendəsli; trɪ`mɛndəslɪ/ ***adv.*** 很多地，极其地

4. Do you find it interesting or challenging?

I find it interesting, because I can meet different people and learn something new almost every day. But in a sense, it is challenging, too, as I have to ensure that my performance meets the expectation of my boss.

你认为这份工作有趣或是富有挑战性吗？

我认为这是一份很有趣的工作，因为我可以遇到各种各样的人，几乎每天都可以学到新的东西。但是从某种意义上来说，它也具有挑战性，因为我必须确保我的表现能达到老板的期望。

答题指导

对于大多数的问题，回答时要尽量给出原因。不要只回答 Yes 或 No 就结束。

find it interesting = think it interesting

（在“find + 名词或代词 + 形容词”这一结构中，find 意思是“认为”，不是“发现”。）

词汇

ensure /ɪnˈʃʊə; ɪnˋʃʊr/ *v.* 确保

5. What do you think is the most difficult part of your job?

Although I always give my best efforts, the outcome is beyond my control. For example, no matter how hard I try, I still fail to hold some of my students' attention in my classes. But if they lack the motivation to study, there's little I can do except by encouraging them one-to-one from time to time.

你认为工作中最困难的部分是什么？

即使我尽最大的努力，结果还是在我的掌控之外。举个例子来说，无论我多努力去尝试，在课堂上，我仍然无法让某些学生专心，但是如果他们缺乏学习的动力，除了不时给予一对一的鼓励，我什么忙也帮不了。

答题指导

使用 although，要避免受到中文思维的影响（虽然……，但是……），使用 although 引导从句时，不要说 although... but...。并无必要用 but，因为 although 即是连接词。

6. Do you think your working experience is rewarding?

Absolutely! My working experience has enabled me to deal efficiently with many tasks that I used to find difficult. For example, I wasn't a well-organized person, but now I've learned how to make the best of my time. Besides, my working experience has somehow transformed me into a responsible person—an image quite different from what I used to be like.

你认为你的工作经验使你受益良多吗？

确实如此！我的工作经验能让我有效地处理很多过去我觉得困难的工作。举例来说，以前的我不懂得有条理地去安排各项事情，但是现在我已经知道如何统筹利用时间。除此之外，我的工作经验已经使我变成一个负责任的人，一个和以往截然不同的人。

答题指导

提及过去和现在的差异时，记得要用正确的时态。现在完成时表示过去某件事持续到现在，或这件事的影响持续到现在。

词汇

Absolutely!　常用于英式口语，表示绝对的肯定。

rewarding /rɪ'wɔːdɪŋ; rɪˋwɔrdɪŋ/ ***adj.*** 受益良多的

transform /træns'fɔːm; trænsˋfɔrm/ ***v.*** 使转变

7. Would you consider changing your job?

Yes, I would. That's why I sit this IELTS test. I would consider changing my job, not because I dislike it, but because I've come to a point in my life when I feel like becoming a student again and fully exposing myself to a field of knowledge that I'm interested to explore.

你是否考虑换工作？

是的，这就是我参加雅思考试的原因。我会考虑换工作，并不是我不喜欢这份工作，而是因为我到了人生的某个阶段，我想要重新做回学生，完全沉浸在我想探索的知识国度里。

词汇

sit the IELTS test = take the IELTS test　参加雅思考试

consider doing sth.　考虑做某事（不可用 consider to do）

expose oneself to sth.　沉浸在……之中

8. Is this the only job you have ever had?

This is the only full-time position I've ever had. Before this I had one part-time job.

这是你唯一做过的工作吗？

这是我唯一做过的全职工作，在之前我曾做过一份兼职工作。

答题指导

视本身情况回答，若以往做过其他工作，记得用过去时。

9. Could you talk about your past working experiences?

I worked as a waitress in a restaurant. It was an interesting job, because I met different people every day. Some of them talked to me and treated me like a friend. On the other hand, it was exhausting, especially on weekends when the restaurant was fully packed. I worked there for about half a year.

可以谈谈你过去的工作经历吗？

我在一家饭店当过服务员，这是一份很有趣的工作，因为每天可以遇见形形色色的人。有些人跟我说话、待我就像朋友一样。但另一方面，这也是份累人的工作，尤其在周末饭店爆满的时候。我在那儿工作了大约有半年之久。

答题指导

其他句型，如：

My first（或 previous）job was with 公司名称. I was in charge of 工作内容.

I stayed there for about half a year.

be packed = be crowded　人很多

10. Why did you move from your former job to the present one?

Well, for several reasons, I suppose. First and foremost, I'd like to develop skills in a different field. Also, I believed my shift to my present job would provide me with a better working environment.

为什么你辞去先前的工作而任职于目前的工作？

嗯，我认为有几个原因。第一，也是最重要的原因是我想学习不同领域的技能。再者，我相信目前的工作能给我提供一个更好的工作环境。

11. How do you feel about the change of job?

I find the work more fulfilling, because my present job is reasonably well paid and my colleagues are very friendly. Whenever I feel a bit down in the dumps they encourage me and cheer me up.

换了工作之后你有什么感受？

我觉得这份工作更令人满意，因为目前的工作待遇很好，我的同事也很友善，每当我情绪低落时，他们总是鼓励我，给我打气。

答题指导

I find the work { more fulfilling / tremendously rewarding / satisfactory / slightly disappointed } because ＋从句 .

我觉得这份工作 { 更有成就感， / 让人受益良多， / 让人满意， / 有点令人失望， } 因为……。

词汇

feel down in the dumps　情绪低落

fulfilling /fʊl'fɪlɪŋ; fʊl`fɪlɪŋ/ ***adj.***　令人满意的，令人有成就感的

I feel fulfilled.　我对一切满意，别无所求。

12. Did you have to work hard to make the transition from a job you were familiar with to the new and unfamiliar one?

I usually manage to settle in well whenever I move to a new environment, so I didn't have much difficulty in making this move. But I did need a bit of time to sort things out, especially in getting to know the people I had to work with.

从熟悉的工作转换到全新、陌生的工作环境，你必须很努力来适应这样的转变吗？

我到任何新的环境，通常都能适应得很好，所以在转换过程中，我不会有什么困难，但是，我的确需要一点时间来理出头绪，尤其是去认识我的工作伙伴。

词汇

make a transition from ... to ...　从……转换到……

settle in well　适应良好

sort things out　解决事情；理出头绪

13. Does your work sometimes cause you stress?

Yes, it does. For example, when my customers complain about my service or when my manager says something discouraging.

你的工作是否有时会让你感到有压力？

是的，有这种情况。例如，当客户对我的服务有抱怨，或经理对我说些令人沮丧的话时。

词汇

cause sb. sth.　对某人造成某事（如：cause me lots of problems）

discouraging /dɪsˈkʌrɪdʒɪŋ; dɪsˋkɝɪdʒɪŋ/ *adj.*　令人沮丧的

14. How do you usually cope with problems of this kind?

If I need to perk myself up, I do a workout in a local fitness club or play a game of Ping-Pong or talk to my best friends. They are quite jolly persons and always make me laugh. Experience has also shown me the benefits of looking on the bright side of things. And then again, even when things seem really difficult, I find that the frustration can give me the energy to make a breakthrough.

你通常都怎么处理这类问题?

如果我要使自己恢复信心，就会去当地的健身中心健身，或者打打乒乓球，跟好朋友聊聊天，他们都是很风趣的人，总能逗我开心。经验也告诉我，凡事往好处想，往往能有所收获。甚至当事情变得很棘手时，我发现挫折可以给我突破困境的能量。

词汇

perk sb. up　使某人恢复信心，打起精神

do a workout　健身

jolly ***adj.***　风趣的

look on the bright side of things　看到事情积极的一面

make a breakthrough　突破

15. What is your ideal job?

Oh, this is an interesting question! My ideal job would be working at something which always interested me and inspired me and helped others too, and where my professional knowledge could be applied and … my pay was adequate.

你理想中的工作是怎么样的?

喔，这真是一个有趣的问题！我理想中的工作是自己既感兴趣，又能得到启发的工作，而且能帮助他人，跟我的专业知识也对口，还有，待遇优厚。

词汇

professional /prə'feʃənəl; prə`fɛʃənl̩/ ***adj.***　专业的

adequate /'ædɪkwət; `ædəkwət/ ***adj.***　充足的

16. What qualities do you think one should develop in order to have a successful career in your profession?

If you want to be a top executive manager, you have to have vision. Only if you've got vision and imagination can you look ahead and make valid decisions. Another important quality is the possession of good interpersonal and communication skills. As you know, a manager has to supervise many employees. Good communication skills can avoid misunderstanding.

在你的职业领域中，你认为要培养哪些特质才能获得成功？

如果你想要成为一位顶尖的行政经理，你必须有独到的眼光。只有具备独到的眼光和想象力，你才能放眼未来，作出正确的抉择。另一个重要的特质就是良好的人际沟通技巧。如你所知，一位经理必须管理许多员工，好的沟通技巧能避免误会的产生。

答题指导

依个人领域，可选以下几种特质来回答，并说明原因。

You should be patient, honest, and most importantly, enthusiastic.

你应该有耐心、诚实，最重要的是，热忱。

You should have vision, ambition, creativity, and ability to persuade people.

你应该有眼光、抱负、创造力和说服力。

You should have good interpersonal and communication skills.

你应该有良好的人际沟通技巧。

PART IV 兴趣与爱好 (Hobbies and Interests)

1. What do you do in your spare time?

In my spare time, I enjoy surfing the Net and listening to music. Over the Net, I can further explore my interest in classical music. For example, I join a discussion group on classical music. Through that I can exchange my ideas with like-minded people. I also enjoy reading.

你业余都做些什么？

业余时间，我喜欢上网和听音乐。通过网络，我可以对我感兴趣的古典音乐做更深入的探索。举例来说，我可以加入古典音乐的讨论区。在那里我可以和一些志同道合的人交换意见。我也喜欢阅读。

答题指导

类似兴趣、爱好的问题，还有其他问法，如：

Do you have any interests or hobbies?

你有什么兴趣或爱好吗？

What would you like to do in your leisure time?

你喜欢在空闲的时间做些什么事？

2. Could you please be more specific? For example, what kind of books or magazines do you like to read?

I enjoy reading computer magazines. To be frank with you, I'm a technophile. I'm crazy about the latest hi-tech developments. I'm better equipped and better qualified to climb the corporate ladder if I keep up with modern technology.

你可以说得更具体一点吗？例如，你喜欢读哪种书或杂志？

我喜欢阅读电脑杂志。老实说，我是一个技术爱好者。我非常痴迷于高科技的前沿发展。如果我能紧跟现代科技发展的步伐，我就更有资格、更有能力在职场上步步高升。

答题指导

若上一题你的回答不够明确，如你只说喜欢阅读、音乐或电影，但未说是哪一种书或哪一种音乐、电影，则考官会问这类问题。故回答时，越具体越好。建议考生对自己的兴趣及相关问题做好准备。如你的兴趣是阅读时尚杂志（reading fashion magazines），那么可以准备谈谈服饰的流行趋势。

常见的爱好有：

pop music　流行音乐	folk music　民谣
classical music　古典音乐	musical　歌舞剧
opera　歌剧	jazz　爵士乐
romantic comedy　浪漫喜剧	New Age music　新世纪音乐
sitcom　情境喜剧	soap opera　肥皂剧
science-fiction film　科幻片	action film　动作片
ballroom dancing　交际舞；国标舞	animation　动画片
country music　乡村音乐	

词汇

technophile /'teknəˌfaɪl; `teknəˌfaɪl/ ***n.*** 爱好科技的人，技术爱好者

corporate /'kɔːpərət; `kɔrpərɪt/ ***adj.*** 企业的

climb the corporate ladder　在职场步步高升

3. When did you first become interested in it?

I first became interested in classical music when I was a senior high school student. It appealed to me then really strongly. I found that when I really gave my full attention to it, if I could be fully immersed in the melody, I was able to relax deeply. So amongst other things, it served as a release from the psychological pressure caused by my schoolwork. Nowadays, I still listen to classical music. I like Bach in particular. His music makes me feel as if I were soaring into the sky or on some sort of elevated sphere.

你何时开始对古典音乐感兴趣的？

我开始对古典乐感兴趣是在上高中的时候。之后我就深深地被古典音乐所吸引着。我发现当我专注地聆听古典音乐，或者完全陶醉在音乐的旋律中时，我就能完全放松。除此之外，它还能帮我释放学业所造成的心理压力。现在我仍旧在听古典音乐；我特别喜欢巴赫的音乐，他的音乐让我感觉仿佛在天空翱翔或处于某种升华的境界。

答题指导

配合问题，回答时要用过去时。

词汇

appealed to (someone)　吸引（某人）

be immersed in　陶醉在，沉浸在

melody /'melədi; `mɛlədɪ/ ***n.***　旋律

a relase from　抒发；免除

elevated /'elɪveɪtɪd; `ɛlə,vetɪd/ ***adj.***　架高的；升高的

sphere /sfɪə; sfɪr/ ***n.***　领域；球体

4. How about your holidays? Do you do anything special?

I sometimes take trips abroad when I have a long holiday. I've been to France and New Zealand. Travelling may be exhausting physically but it inspires me spiritually. It broadens my horizon of knowledge and enables me to experience foreign culture first-hand. For example, my trip to France made me more aware of the importance of the artistic and cultural dimensions of humanity. Just seeing those works of art, those beautifully built cathedrals and those cultural landmarks was so inspiring. And my trip to New Zealand raised my awareness of issues vital to all of us concerning protection to the environment.

你的假期是如何过的？有什么特别的活动吗？

放长假的时候，我有时会到国外去旅行。我曾经去过法国和新西兰。旅行可能会使我疲惫不堪，不过在精神上，却给我不少灵感。旅行可以丰富我的见闻，还可以让我亲身体验异国文化。举例来说，法国之旅让我更了解人类艺术和文化的重要性。光看看那些艺术品、建筑华丽的大教堂和充满文化色彩的地标就会让人心旷神怡！而那趟新西兰之旅让我提高了环保意识，有关环保的种种问题对于我们所有人来讲都是很重要的。

词汇

enable sb. to do sth.　使某人能做某事

work of art　艺术品

cathedral /kə'θiːdrəl; kə`θidrəl/ ***n.***　大教堂

landmark /'lændmɑːk; `lænd,mɑrk/ ***n.***　地标

vital /'vaɪtl; `vaɪtḷ/ ***adj.***　重要的；生死攸关的

PART V 参加雅思考试的原因
(Reasons for Taking IELTS)

1. Why do you want to take IELTS?

I'm taking the IELTS test because I plan to do a Master's degree in Marketing in Australia. I want to achieve at least a band 6 so as to qualify for a place to study there.

你为何想要参加雅思考试？

我参加雅思考试是因为我计划在澳大利亚攻读市场营销硕士学位。我希望至少能达到 6 分，这样我才有机会取得入学许可。

答题指导

place 在此处指入学许可或就读机会；若考雅思，是为了移民（如：I plan to emigrate to New Zealand.），则要准备解释为何喜欢那个国家。

词汇

a Master's = a Master's degree 硕士学位

PART VI 未来的计划
(Plans for the Future)

1. Do you have any plan for the future?

Yes, certainly. I've thought a lot about my future. My short-term goal is to qualify for a place to study in a British university and receive some solid training in my field. If everything goes well, I hope eventually to become a university lecturer or to do research in a research institute.

你对未来还有什么计划吗?

是的。关于我的未来，我想了很多。我的短期目标是希望能够取得英国大学的入学许可，并能在我所学的领域受到扎实的训练。如果一切都顺利的话，我希望最后我能够成为一位大学教师，或者能在研究机构中做研究。

答题指导

可以分短期目标（short-term goal）和长远目标（long-term goal）两部分来答题。

2. What do you plan to study?

I would like to pursue advanced study in a business-related subject, possibly MBA or Hotel Management or Economics. I will make up my mind after I've reflected more on the information I have about these courses.

你打算学什么?

我希望在与商业相关的领域继续进修，可能会读工商管理硕士、酒店管理或是经济学专业。我会在对有关那些课程的信息进行进一步考虑之后，再决定读什么。

答题指导

若已决定，则按自己情况回答。若还在考虑，可说出几个可能的专业。

词汇

pursue further study; pursue advanced study　进修

reflect on　思考

3. If everything goes well, what would you like to do after you complete your study or training abroad?

I would come back to China and contribute what I've learned to the development of my country. I'll do whatever I can to put my training and study to good use. So I'm hoping to be able to find a job in which I can put my professional training into practice.

如果一切顺利，在国外完成学业或培训之后你想要做什么？

我将会回到中国并将我所学到的贡献给国家，促进祖国发展。我会竭尽所能，学以致用。因此我希望找到一个能让自己发挥所学的工作。

答题指导

配合问题的时态来回答。

词汇

contribute … to … 将……贡献给……

put my training and study to good use 学以致用

put … into practice 发挥，把……运用到实践中

4. If you could not pursue your goal in that particular direction for some unexpected reason, what would you do?

I would face the music and try again. Nothing is impossible to a willing mind. I am not expecting my first job to be perfect. In the first place, I am looking simply for something that holds my interest and something that promises to enrich my practical experience. As long as I stick to my long-term goal, I'm sure I'll make it someday. You know, human beings are adaptable, because we dream and we try to bring at least some of those dreams down to earth.

假如有一些始料未及的因素，使你不能继续追求在这方面的理想，你会怎么做？

我会面对现实，然后卷土重来。有志者事竟成。我并不期望我的第一份工作一定符合我的理想。我只要先找到一个能符合我的兴趣且可以丰富我的经历的工作。只要能够坚持我的长远目标，相信总有一天会实现理想。要知道，人类的适应性

很强，因为我们有梦想，并且会努力去实现至少一部分的梦想。

答题指导

注意要用虚拟语气：I would … 若考生会使用关系从句，记得要用，以便展现语法能力，这是口语考试的评分标准之一。

词汇

face the music　面对现实

in the first place　首先；一开始

hold my interest　符合我的兴趣

stick to　坚持

make it　成功；达成目标

bring … down to earth　实现

Chapter 3

考试第二、三部分题库：

各类话题说不停

IELTS

本书在此章节以下列十大类编排，包含近 20 个话题：

人物（People）
事物（Something）
食物（Food）
衣着（Clothes）
居住（Housing）
交通（Transportation）
教育（Education)
娱乐（Entertainment）
科技与自然（Technology & Nature）
媒体与社会（Media & Society）

由于雅思考试口语部分的第二部分及第三部分的问题，有一定的相关性，故本书将其放在一起。考生在准备时，可先练习第二部分的问题，也可选择将第二部分及第三部分的问题一起练习。每道题目均附有回答范例，且针对某一话题，本书提供相关的词汇及用语。答案范例中用特别色突出的部分，表示是回答此类问题时，可套用的句型、佳句或转折承接词，考生要多练习，才可熟能生巧。

注意事项

一、雅思考试口语部分的第二部分注意事项

（1）这一部分，考官会给考生一张答题任务卡，上面写着考生要陈述的话题及需要在陈述中包含的要点。通常考官在此阶段不会回答考生任何问题，若对题目不确定，还是要尽量回答。

（2）题目一定要看清楚，如：Talk about a famous person you admire. 则要谈你仰慕的名人，不能谈你的中学里的一位普通老师。

（3）要当机立断，选定心里最先想到的来准备。

（4）考生只有约 1 分钟的准备时间。

（5）准备时，若对某一问题胸有成竹，则不必要写笔记。若要做笔记，最好只写要点而非整句。

（6）这部分有三到四个要点，只有 1 ~ 2 分钟时间回答（不含准备时间），回答时要针对卡上列出的要点回答，且要全部涉及，千万不要把所有时间用于详细回答某一要点而其他要点全然未提及。

（7）回答时，不一定要按照要点在答题任务卡上被列出的顺序作答，但要全部回答。

二、雅思考试口语部分的第三部分注意事项

（1）此部分的题目由第二部分的话题延伸出来，故有一定相关性。

（2）此部分的问题较广且较难，故考生要有心理准备。

（3）常见题型为：

What do you think of …?

Do you think …?

What are the advantages and disadvantages of …?

How would you compare … and …?

What impact do you think … has on you / on this country?

（4）考生要利用此部分的问题，展现出能扩充话题的能力，故回答要尽量周全。

（5）有些问题，常会以考生的国家或城市为背景来发问，如：What do you think of the transport in Beijing / China?

（6）考官在此阶段所用的语言，会根据考生程度，做一定调整。对程度较弱的考生，考官说话速度会变慢；对于口语对答相当流畅的考生，考官说话速度会较快、用词较难。

（7）考官也有可能问一些即兴的问题，不见得和讨论的话题相关，特别是对于口语相当流利的考生，考官有可能在这部分以此方式问一些较多样性或突如其来的问题。

Chapter 3

考试第二、三部分题库：各类话题说不停

综合分类

1. 人物篇 (People)

Colleague

同事

USEFUL EXPRESSIONS 实用表达

1. first and foremost 首要地；首先
2. appreciate doing = enjoy doing 喜欢做……
   I ***appreciate working*** with her. 我喜欢与她共事。
3. a sales representative 业务员，销售代表
4. when I encounter difficulty = when I run into difficulty 当我遇到困难
5. learn tremendously from … 从……学了很多
6. team /tiːm; tim/ ***n.*** 团队
7. (be) responsible for … 负责……
   We belong to the same ***team responsible for*** marketing.
   我们属同一营销团队。
8. prefer to do 较喜欢……
   I ***prefer to work*** independently. 我较喜欢单独工作。
9. subjective /səb'dʒektɪv; səb`dʒɛktɪv/ ***adj.*** 主观的；subjectivity /ˌsʌbdʒek'tɪvəti; ˏsʌbdʒɛk`tɪvətɪ/ ***n.*** 主观
   When I work by myself, I can become quite ***subjective***.
   我自己独自工作时，有可能会相当主观。
10. carry the can for … 负担……责任
    When working by myself, I have to ***carry the can for*** the consequences of my subjectivity.
    单独工作时，我必须为自己的主观性所带来的后果承担责任。
11. Two pairs of shoulders carry responsibility more lightly than one pair.
    两人共同承担总比一人轻松。
12. at my own pace 依自己的步调
    I can handle a task ***at my own pace***. 我可依自己的步调来处理任务。

13. interpersonal relationship 人际关系
14. drawback /ˈdrɔːbæk; ˋdrɔˏbæk/ ***n.*** 缺点
15. time-consuming ***adj.*** 费时的
16. frame of reference 思维方式
It can be difficult to work with someone different in his educational background or ***frame of reference***.
和一个教育背景或思维方式不同的人共事，可能会有困难。
17. tolerant /ˈtɒlərənt; ˋtɑlərənt/ ***adj.*** 包容的；tolerance /ˈtɒlərəns; ˋtɑlərəns/ ***n.*** 包容
18. a greater sense of responsibility 有更强烈的责任感
19. generate /ˈdʒenəreɪt; ˋdʒɛnəˏret/ ***v.*** 产生
A greater sense of responsibility needs to be ***generated***.
得有更强烈的责任感。
20. mutual understanding and tolerance 相互的了解与包容
21. teamwork /ˈtiːmˌwɜːk; ˋtimˏwɝk/ ***n.*** 团队合作，团队精神
22. collaboration /kəˌlæbəˈreɪʃən; kəˏlæbəˋreʃən/ ***n.*** 合作
Collaboration is the key to success. 合作是成功的关键。
23. As the saying goes, "Two heads are better than one."
俗话说："三个臭皮匠胜过一个诸葛亮。"
24. profession /prəˈfeʃən; prəˋfɛʃən/ ***n.*** 行业
25. biotechnology /ˌbaɪəʊtekˈnɒlədʒi; ˏbaɪotɛkˋnɑlədʒɪ/ ***n.*** 生物科技
26. a sense of job security 对工作有安全感（即"铁饭碗"）
The company I work for gives me ***a sense of job security***.
我的工作单位让我对工作有安全感。
27. be made redundant 被裁员
28. at the drop of a hat = at once; without hesitation 立刻；毫不犹豫地
29. an incentive scheme 奖励方案，激励机制
30. regular perk 定期的额外补助津贴（如：交通费、租房补贴等）
31. sickness benefit 医疗补助
It's important that the company offers ***a*** generous ***incentive scheme***, such as ***regular perks*** and ***sickness benefit***.
重要的是，公司要提出丰厚的奖励方案，如定期的额外补助津贴和医疗补助。

32. work unsocial hours　在非正常时间上班（即上早班、上夜班等）

I don't like to ***work unsocial hours***.　我不喜欢在非正常时间上班。

33. on a voluntary basis　自愿地

I do extra work ***on a voluntary basis***.　我自愿去做额外的工作。

34. be well organized　组织得好的，有条理的

35. procrastinate　/prəˈkræstɪneɪt; proˋkræstəˌnet/　***v.***　做事拖延

36. climb the corporate ladder　在职场上步步高升

It's important not to ***procrastinate*** if you want to ***climb the corporate ladder***.

如果想在职场上步步高升，做事就不要拖拖拉拉。

QUESTION DATABASE 题库练习

个人陈述 (Individual Long Turn)

考官 Now please have a look at this card. This is your topic. I want you to talk about someone you like to work with. You have one minute to prepare.

Talk about someone you like to work with. You should say:

who this person is
how old this person is
when you first met each other
why you like to work with the person.

INSTRUCTIONS
You will be asked to talk about the topic for one to two minutes.
You have one minute to think about what you are going to say.
You can make some notes to help you if you wish.

谈谈你喜欢一起工作的某个人。你应该谈到：

这个人是谁
这人年纪多大
你们第一次相遇在什么时候
为什么你喜欢跟这个人一起工作。

【说明】：
针对这个话题作出一至两分钟的陈述。
你有一分钟的时间去思考你的陈述内容。
假如需要的话，你可以写下要点以帮助你组织陈述。

Sample Response

The person I enjoy working with is a colleague of mine called David. He is about 40 years old. I first met him a year and a half ago when I started my present position as a sales representative at Sun Company. I really appreciate working with him for several reasons. First and foremost, he is a very pleasant, friendly, interesting person to work with. Another reason is that he never hesitates to offer help when I encounter difficulty. Last but not least, I learn tremendously from him, especially his ways of organizing things and his skill in setting a reasonable deadline for a task. I'm pleased that I have such a lovely colleague.

回答范例

我喜欢共事的人叫戴维，他是我的一位同事，大约 40 岁。一年半前我在旭日公司开始从事业务员的工作时，第一次遇见了他。我喜欢与他共事的原因有好几个。首先，他是一个和蔼可亲、友善又有趣的人，和他一起工作很愉快。其次，当我遇到困难时，他总是毫不犹豫地伸出援手。最后还有一个重要的原因就是：我从他那里学到很多东西，尤其是他组织事情的方式以及他合理安排任务期限的技巧。能有这么好的同事，我感到很高兴。

◎ **How often do you work together?**

Very often indeed, as we are working in the same office and we belong to the same team—the one responsible for marketing.

你们多久合作一次?

实际上，我们合作的机会很多！因为我们在同一间办公室工作，而且我们同属市场营销团队。

双向讨论 (Two-way Discussion)

◎ **Do you prefer to work independently or with someone else?**

As a matter of fact, I prefer to work with someone else, because when I am by myself, I cannot be really sure if I am just being subjective, and then I have to carry the can for the consequences of my subjectivity. In any case, two pairs of shoulders carry responsibility more lightly than one pair.

你比较喜欢单独做事还是跟别人一起工作？

事实上，我比较喜欢跟别人一起工作，因为在单独工作的时候，我不能确定是否我会变得主观，于是我必须为自己的主观所带来的后果担负责任。不论怎样，两个人共同承担责任总比一个人轻松。

◎ **What are the advantages and disadvantages of working independently?**

I'd like to mention the advantages first. For example, you have the freedom to do your job. Another advantage is that you can handle a task at your own pace. Most importantly, you don't have to suffer from the emotional problems caused by unhappy interpersonal relationships. As to the disadvantages, I'd like to point out several drawbacks. You know, it's more time-consuming when one works by oneself. Another is that the responsibility for the quality of your work rests entirely on your own shoulders when the burden of decision-making is not shared.

独自做事的优缺点是什么？

首先，我要谈谈独自工作的优点。举例来说，你可以随心所欲去做。另一个优点是，可依自己的步调来处理事情。最重要的是，你不会为不愉快的人际关系而遭受情绪波动。至于缺点方面，我想指出几点。你知道，独自工作较耗时。另外，由于独自作决断而非群策群力，那么你就要为工作的质量负全责。

◎ **What might be the difficulty of working with someone else?**

The major difficulty lies in having to communicate with people of very different temperaments. You see—each individual is unique in terms of personality. One might work quite well with this person, but run into difficulties when working with another person because of his different educational background or frame of reference, which can lead to mutual incomprehension. Then again, you might be very tolerant yourself, but what of the other person? Also, different attitudes toward work could further complicate the whole thing.

跟别人一起工作可能会有什么困难?

最主要的困难是必须去和不同性情的人沟通。我们都知道，每个人个性不同。一个人或许能跟某个人合作愉快，可是跟另外一个人，则可能由于教育背景或思维方式不同而无法相互理解，所以处不来。而且，你自身或许有包容心，但别人呢？此外，工作态度的不同，也可能使事情更加复杂。

◎ **Do you think teamwork is always essential?**

Well, I would say teamwork is important in those cases where collaboration is the key to success. As the saying goes, "Two heads are better than one." Therefore, teamwork is essential in professions such as biotechnology and computer technology. However, working as an artist or a musician does not necessarily involve teamwork.

你认为团队合作总是必要的吗?

嗯，我要说的是，在某些情况，当合作是成功的关键时，那么团队合作很重要。俗话说：“三个臭皮匠胜过一个诸葛亮。”因此，对于有些行业如生物科技及计算机科技，团队合作绝对有必要。然而，对于艺术家或音乐家来说，就不一定需要团队合作了。

◎ **What can a company do to improve its employees' motivation to work hard?**

Perhaps I can answer this question from my own experience. There are several things I can think of. For example, the company I work for should give me a sense of job security so that I don't have to worry that I might be made redundant at the drop of a hat and without pay. Also, it's important that the company offers a generous incentive scheme, such as regular perks and sickness benefit. And … yes, a company should not force me to work unsocial hours. If such work is really necessary, it's best that I do it on a voluntary basis, from my own sense of responsibility and that I receive extra pay for it.

为了增强员工的工作动力，公司可以做些什么？

也许我可以用自己的经验来回答这个问题。我倒是想到几点。例如，我的工作单位应该给我工作上的安全感，这样一来，我就不用担心随时会被裁掉，没有薪水可领。此外，重要的是，公司应提出丰厚的工作奖励方案，如定期的额外津贴和医疗补助。而且，公司不应该强迫我在非正常工作时间上班；如果必要的话，最好是我出于自愿和责任感而接受此工作，并且另计酬劳。

◎ **How can one become an efficient worker?**

To be honest, I'm still learning how to be an efficient worker. But from my own experience, I've come to realize the importance of being well organized. One of the ways to achieve this is always to write down the tasks one has to complete and then set a reasonable deadline for each task. Another thing to remember is never to procrastinate. As the saying goes, "Do not put off till tomorrow what you can do today." I believe these principles should help one become an efficient worker.

一个人要怎么做才能高效工作？

坦白说，我仍然在学如何高效工作。但是就我个人的经验来看，我已经认识到组织安排的重要性。一个能达到这个目标的方法就是每次都把需要完成的事写下来，然后为每一件工作定一个合理的期限。另外一件要记住的事就是绝对不要拖延。所谓"今日事，今日毕。"我相信这些原则能帮助一个人高效工作。

Friends and Friendship

朋友与友情

USEFUL EXPRESSIONS 实用表达

1. pleasant /'plezənt; `plɛzn̩t/ *adj.* 和蔼可亲的
2. a strong bond of friendship 坚固的友谊
3. bosom pal 知己

Because we spent so much time together, ***a strong bond of friendship*** started to develop and we've become ***bosom pals*** ever since.

因为我们很多时间都在一起，渐渐地建立了坚固的友谊，从此成为知己。

4. attentively /ə'tentɪvli; ə`tɛntɪvlɪ/ *adv.* 专心地

My best friend Michael always listens to me ***attentively***.

我最好的朋友迈克尔总是会专心地听我说话。

5. hesitate /'hezɪteɪt; `hɛzə,tet/ *v.* 犹豫
6. a friendly hug 友好的拥抱
7. empathize /'empəθaɪz; `ɛmpə,θaɪz/ *v.* 感同身受

If I feel upset or frustrated, she never ***hesitates*** to give me ***a friendly hug*** to ***empathize*** with me and encourage me.

当我难过或受挫的时候，她总是毫不犹豫地马上给我一个友好的拥抱，和我感同身受，并鼓励我。

8. be emotionally supportive 在精神上支持的
9. be intellectually stimulating 智力上相切磋

A good friend ***is emotionally supportive*** and sometimes ***intellectually stimulating***.

一位好朋友能给予我们精神上的支持和智力上的相互切磋。

10. profound /prə'faʊnd; prə`faʊnd/ *adj.* 有深度的
11. easygoing *adj.* 随和的
12. extrovert /'ekstrəvɜːt; `ɛkstro,vɝt/ *adj. & n.* 外向的（人）

I am an ***easygoing*** person and quite an ***extrovert***. That's probably why I have so many friends.

我是一个随和且外向的人，这可能就是我有这么多朋友的原因吧。

13. introvert /ˈɪntrəvɜːt; ˋɪntrəˏvɝt/ ***adj. & n.*** 内向的（人）

14. I don't feel shy talking to people, normally.

通常我和别人说话时不会感到害羞。

15. steal the show 出风头

I've never intended to ***steal the show***, but as it happens, I seem to be popular.

我从不会刻意想要出风头，但是我似乎就是有人缘。

16. confide in (sb.) 向（某人）倾诉；向（某人）说出心声

Everyone needs to have someone to talk to, someone to ***confide in***.

每一个人都需要有能说话和倾诉的对象。

17. genuine friend 真正的朋友

A ***genuine friend*** offers help without expecting to gain something in return.

真正的朋友提供帮助却不期望任何的回报。

18. altruistic /ˌæltruˈɪstɪk; ˏæltrʊˋɪstɪk/ ***adj.*** 利他的

An ***altruistic*** act is a sign of genuine friendship.

利他行为象征了真正的友谊。

19. unselfish /ʌnˈselfɪʃ; ʌnˋsɛlfɪʃ/ ***adj.*** 无私的

Friendship is a broader conception of love than romantic love; it's an ***unselfish*** type of love.

友情是一种比爱情更广博的爱，它是一种无私的爱。

20. lose contact with 和……失去联络

21. childhood friend 儿时玩伴

Childhood friends were relatively innocent or pure.

儿时玩伴相对比较天真、纯洁。

22. be just my wishful thinking 只是我个人的臆想

23. recollection /ˌrekəˈlekʃən; ˏrɛkəˋlɛkʃən/ ***n.*** 记忆；回忆

24. sort of 有点

I don't know whether it'***s just my wishful thinking***, but my ***recollection*** of them is that they were relatively ***sort of*** innocent or pure.

我不知道是否只是我的臆想，但是我记得他们比较天真、纯洁。

25. mature /mə'tʃʊə; mə`tʃʊr/ ***adj.*** 成熟的

College friends differ from childhood friends in being more ***mature***.

大学的朋友和儿时玩伴不同，大学的朋友比较成熟。

26. colleague /'kɒliːg; `kɑlig/ ***n.*** 同僚；同事

Those people I meet at work and my ***colleagues*** are probably in some ways different from university friends.

我在工作中所遇到的人和同事或许在某些地方不同于大学的朋友。

27. complicated /'kɒmplɪkeɪtɪd; `kɑmplə,ketɪd/ ***adj.*** 复杂的

28. unpredictable /,ʌnprɪ'dɪktəbəl; ,ʌnprɪ`dɪktəbḷ/ ***adj.*** 无法预测的

29. distant /'dɪstənt; `dɪstənt/ ***adj.*** 有距离的；有隔阂的

30. disinterested /dɪs'ɪntrɪstɪd; dɪs`ɪntrɪstɪd/ ***adj.*** 和利益无关的

The work relationships are more ***complicated***, more ***unpredictable***, sometimes more ***distant***, and less ***disinterested***!

工作上的关系往往更复杂、更无法预测，有时会更有距离感且有利益关系。

31. the factor of competitiveness 竞争的因素

There is ***the factor of competitiveness*** among colleagues, most or all of whom want to gain promotion.

大多数或所有的人都想要获得升迁，于是同事之间存在竞争因素。

32. business associate 生意上的伙伴

33. utility /juː'tɪlɪti; ju`tɪlətɪ/ ***n.*** 实际利益

Business friends are very much based on ***utility***.

商业上的朋友建立在实际利益上。

34. innermost thought 内心深处的想法

35. partial friend 交情不深的朋友

You wouldn't want to share your ***innermost thoughts*** with such ***partial friends***, would you?

你不会想要和这种没什么交情的朋友分享你内心深处的想法，不是吗？

36. I am more myself when I'm with my university or high school friends than with those friends I make at work.

我和大学或中学的朋友在一起时感觉比和工作上的朋友在一起时更自在。

37. sincerity /sɪn'serɪti; sɪn`sɛrətɪ/ ***n.*** 真诚

38. sincere /sɪn'sɪə; sɪn`sɪr/ ***adj.*** 真诚的

When it comes to real friendship, ***sincerity*** is a must.

说到真正的友情，真诚是必需的。

39. tolerance /ˈtɒlərəns; ˋtɑlərəns/ ***n.*** 宽容

40. tolerant /ˈtɒlərənt; ˋtɑlərənt/ ***adj.*** 宽容的

One important quality of friendship is ***tolerance***.

宽容是友情的重要特质之一。

41. understanding /ˌʌndəˈstændɪŋ; ˏʌndɚˋstændɪŋ/ ***adj.*** 通情达理的 ***n.*** 了解

42. A friend in need is a friend indeed. 患难见真情。

43. stand the test of time 经得起时间的考验

Genuine friendship should be able to ***stand the test of time***.

真正的友谊应能经得起时间的考验。

44. net pal 网友

45. take advantage of 利用

46. the anonymity of cyberspace communication 网上匿名的沟通方式

There are those who ***take advantage of the anonymity of cyberspace communication*** to do evil things.

有些人会利用网上匿名的沟通方式来做坏事。

47. be selective in 有所选择

48. supposed friend 表面上的朋友

You have to ***be selective in*** making friends, because there are ***supposed friends*** who are in reality confidence tricksters.

你交朋友时必须有所选择，因为有些人表面是朋友，实际上却是骗子。

QUESTION DATABASE 题库练习

个人陈述 (Individual Long Turn)

考官 Now please have a look at this card. This is your topic. I want you to talk about a good friend of yours. You have one minute to prepare.

Talk about a good friend of yours. You should say:

who the person is
how long you have known each other
how you came to know each other
why the person is special to you.

INSTRUCTIONS

You will be asked to talk about the topic for one to two minutes.
You have one minute to think about what you are going to say.
You can make some notes to help you if you wish.

谈谈你的一位好朋友。你应该谈到：

那个人是谁
你们彼此认识多久
你们怎么认识对方的
为何此人对你来说很特别。

【说明】：

针对这个话题作出一至两分钟的陈述。
你有一分钟的时间去思考你的陈述内容。
假如需要的话，你可以写下要点以帮助你组织陈述。

Sample Response

I'd like to talk about my best friend Emily. She's a really sweet and pleasant girl. I first met her when I went to university. We were doing the same course and were allocated to a double room in the student accommodation on campus. That's how we came to know each other. Because we spent so much time together, a strong bond of friendship started to develop and we've been bosom pals ever since. We've known each other for about six years. You know why she's so special to me? Well, first of all, we suit each other ever so well. I am the talkative one, in Chinese of course, and she's the quiet one: She always listens to me attentively. Also, if I feel upset or frustrated, she never hesitates to give me a friendly hug to empathize with me and encourage me. So she's very emotionally supportive. Then again, she's intellectually stimulating. She often tells me her views about a film she has seen or a book she has read. I think she is really profound. Finally, she's practical and helpful. When we were university students, we studied together and helped each other to prepare for quizzes and exams. To be perfectly frank, she's my sunshine.

回答范例

我想谈谈我最好的朋友埃米莉。她是一位非常甜美的女孩，跟她相处很愉悦。我第一次遇到她是在上大学的时候。我们修同样的课程而且住在学校学生宿舍的同一间双人房。这就是我们认识的过程。因为我们很多时间都在一起，渐渐地彼此建立了坚固的友谊，从此成为知己。我们已经认识大约有六年了。你知道为何对我来说她这么特别吗？首先，我们彼此非常合得来。我爱说话，当然是讲中文，她则安静，总会专心地听我说。除此之外，当我难过或受挫的时候，她总是毫不犹豫地给我一个友爱的拥抱，对我的遭遇感同身受，然后鼓励我。她在精神上给予我很大的支持。不仅如此，在智力上我们也有相互切磋的机会。她总会跟我说一些她对于看过的电影或书的看法。我想她真的是一位很有深度的人。最后一点，她很务实而且是位益友。上大学的时候，我们一起学习，还互相帮助对方准备各种大小考试。说真的，她是我的阳光。

◎ **Do you have many friends?**

Yes, I do. I'm never lonely. My cell phone rings ever so often. I am an easygoing person and quite an extrovert. That's probably why I have so many friends. I don't feel shy talking to people, normally.

你有很多朋友吗?

是的。我从不会感觉到寂寞。我的手机常常响个不停。我是一个随和且相当外向的人，这可能是我有这么多朋友的原因吧。通常，在和别人说话时，我不会害羞。

◎ **How do you usually make friends?**

Well, to be honest, they just come to me! I've never intended to steal the show, but as it happens, I seem to be popular. Possibly it's because I smile a lot and I am willing to help out if I can offer any help.

你通常如何结交到朋友?

好吧，老实说，都是别人来找我的。我从不会刻意想要出风头，但是，我似乎就是有人缘。可能是因为我常常笑而且又乐于助人的关系吧。

双向讨论 (Two-way Discussion)

◎ **Now, let's talk about friendship. What do you think is the significance of friendship?**

Friendship is important—well, I believe it's essential. It is significant in so many ways. First and foremost, everyone needs to have someone to talk to, someone to confide in. Imagine what it would be like if you had to bear your suffering and pains alone, or no one is there to share your joys. So I think friendship is important, because it provides emotional support. Another significant aspect of friendship is that with friends you learn why giving is more blessed than receiving. A genuine friend offers help without expecting to gain something in return. Such an altruistic act is a sign of genuine friendship. Last but not least, friendship is a form of love. It's of course a broader conception of love than romantic love; it's an unselfish type of love. With friendship we can contribute to the creation of a more harmonious society and a more peaceful world.

现在，让我们来谈谈友情。你如何看待友情的重要性？

友情是很重要的，我相信友情是必不可少的。它在很多方面有其重要性。首先，每个人都需要有说话和倾诉的对象。你能想象，你得一个人承担所有痛苦与折磨，或是没有人可以分享你的喜悦，那会是怎样的情形呢？所以我认为友情是很重要的，因为它可以给予我们精神上的支持。友情的另一个重要性在于，和朋友在一起时你可以学到为何施予比接受更令人愉快。真正的朋友帮助别人却不期望任何回报。这种利他的行为象征了真正的友情。最后一点，友情是爱的一种形式。友情是一种比爱情更广博的爱，它是一种无私的爱。通过友情我们可以创造出更和谐的社会、更和平的世界。

◎ **Everyone makes friends at different stages of his or her life. Are your childhood friends different from those you made, say, when you were a college student?**

Yes, I think so. To tell the truth, I've lost contact with nearly all my childhood friends. But so far as I remember, those friends I made in my childhood were mainly just playmates. We played games and had fun together. You know, that's what childhood is like! I don't know whether it's just my wishful thinking, but my recollection of them is that they were relatively sort of … innocent or pure, as perhaps we like to imagine most children are. But college friends are different. They are adults. So they differ from my childhood friends in being more mature; they give more intellectual and emotional feedback. Another big difference, on the negative side, is that there can be sexual tension between adult friends. You see, this sort of tension didn't exist in childhood, or at least it was not evident to me at this time.

每个人在人生的不同阶段都会结交朋友。举例来说，你的儿时玩伴和你大学的朋友有什么不同吗?

是的。老实说，我几乎和所有儿时玩伴都失去联络了。但是，在我的记忆中，小时候所交的朋友大部分只是玩伴而已。我们一起玩乐。你知道的，就是所谓童年时期的样子！我不知道那是不是只是我的臆想，但是我记忆中的他们比较天真、纯洁，就像我们想象中的大部分小孩一样。但是，大学的朋友就不一样了。他们是大人。所以大学的朋友和儿时的玩伴不同，他们更加成熟，在精神与心智上彼此更好交流。另一个很大的不同是比较负面的，就是在成人的朋友之间可能会有异性间的吸引力。你知道，这种吸引力并不会存在于童年时期，或者是说至少在我童年时期没有。

◎ **How about the friends you make at work? Are they, again, different from your university friends?**

Well, those people I meet at work and my colleagues are probably, yes, in some ways different from university friends. These work relationships are, on the whole, more complicated, more unpredictable, sometimes more distant, and less disinterested! You see, there is the factor of competitiveness among colleagues, most or all of whom want to gain promotion. So there can be a "hidden agenda" in these relationships. As for business associates, very often all they are interested in is sales. These sorts of friendship are very much based on utility. Utility—it's OK, but it's only a part of more genuine friendship. You wouldn't want to share your innermost thoughts with such partial friends, would you? Generally speaking, I am more myself when I'm with my university or high school friends … than with those I make at work.

你在工作中所交的朋友怎么样呢？同样，他们是否和你大学的朋友有所不同呢？

是的，我在工作中所遇到的人和同事或许确实在某些地方不同于大学的朋友。大致来说，工作上的关系往往更复杂、更无法预测，有时会更有距离感且有利益关系。你知道的，大多数或所有的人都想要获得升迁，所以同事之间存在着竞争因素，可能会“各怀鬼胎”。至于那些生意上的伙伴，很多时候他们只对买卖有兴趣。这种友情是建立在实际利益上的。建立在实际利益上的友情是可以的，但那些只是真正友情之中的一部分而已。你总不会想要和这种没有深交的朋友分享你内心深处的想法，不是吗？一般来说，我和大学或高中的朋友在一起时感觉……比和工作上的朋友在一起时更自在。

◎ **What qualities do you think real friendship should have?**

The qualities of real friendship? Well, first and foremost, sincerity is a must. Only a sincere friend can treat you as a friend, not as someone from whom to gain profit. Then again, another quality is tolerance. Since your genuine friends have come to know you over quite a long period, they know your weaknesses and strengths. Such friends will be understanding and tolerant, but they will also encourage your development of good qualities and discourage your bad habits. Hmm … well, there's one more thing: They are willing to help you practically. As the saying goes, "A friend in need is a friend indeed." Also, genuine friendship should be able to stand the test of time. Wherever they are and however far they are from you, they remember you.

你认为真正的友情应该有什么特质呢？

真正友情的特质？首先，必须要真诚。只有真诚的朋友才会把你当作朋友，而不是只想要从你身上获得利益而已。除此之外，还有一个特质就是包容。既然你真正的朋友已经认识你这么久了，他们应该很了解你的优缺点。这样的朋友会很通情达理而且宽容，但他们还是会鼓励你去培养一些好的品质并且改掉一些坏习惯。嗯，还有一件事就是他们很乐意实实在在帮助你。俗话说：“患难见真情。”此外，真正的友情应该能经得起时间的考验。不管他们在哪里或离你有多远，他们都会记得你。

◎ **Do you think one should be selective in making friends?**

Oh, yes, absolutely! I've heard several reports recently about teenage students who were deceived by their supposed friends whom they got to know through the Internet. It seems that people these days are much more complicated than before, so we have to be very careful, especially when making "net pals". I suppose most people are honest, but there are those who take advantage of the anonymity of cyberspace communication to do evil things.

你是否认为交朋友需要有所选择?

那是当然的！我最近听到许多关于青少年学生被他们在网上所认识的朋友欺骗的事。现在的人似乎比以前的人复杂多了。因此我们应该要特别小心，尤其是交网友的时候。我认为大部分人还是诚实的，但是有些人会利用网络匿名的沟通方式来做坏事。

Chapter 3

考试第二、三部分题库：各类话题说不停

综合分类

2. 事物篇 (Something)

Gift

礼物

USEFUL EXPRESSIONS 实用表达

1. pocket money 零用钱
2. reward sb. /rɪ'wɔːd; rɪ`wɔrd/ *v.* 给某人奖励

I had expected my mum to give me a large sum of ***pocket money*** to ***reward me*** for studying so hard.

我本期望妈妈可以给我很多零用钱以奖励我这么用功读书。

3. dog-eared *adj.* 页角卷折的（书本经常使用，以致于页角卷折）

Many years ago, I was given an English dictionary by my mum as a present when I was admitted into a senior high school. The book is very ***dog-eared*** now.

很多年前，在我考上高中的时候，妈妈给了我一本英文词典当作礼物。现在这本书已经非常破旧了，页角都卷起来了。

4. gift-giving *n.* 送礼物
5. common practice 常见的习俗

Gift-giving is a ***common practice*** in this country.

在这个国家送礼物是一种常见的习俗。

6. wedding ceremony 结婚典礼
7. housewarming /'haʊsˌwɔːmɪŋ; `haʊsˏwɔrmɪŋ/ *n.* 庆祝乔迁聚会

People give gifts to their friends or relatives when they have something special to celebrate, for example, someone's birthday or a ***wedding ceremony*** or a ***housewarming***.

人们会在朋友或亲戚有某些特别的事要庆祝的时候送他们礼物，例如，在某人生日、结婚典礼或是庆祝乔迁的时候。

8. bonus /'bəʊnəs; `bonəs/ *n.* 奖金

Some well-established companies are generous with their employees; they give gifts and a ***bonus*** to their employees towards the end of the year.

一些久负盛名的公司对他们的员工很大方；年终的时候他们会给员工发礼物及奖金。

9. It's a jolly good idea! 真是个好点子！

10. the most unforgettable gift 最令人难忘的礼物

I've come to realize ***the most unforgettable gift*** is often not money but something you use ever so often or something you grew up with.

我渐渐认识到最令人难忘的礼物通常不是钱，而是一些你常用的或伴你成长的东西。

11. It's not the value of a gift that counts but its meaning and the story behind it that matters.

礼物贵不贵重并不重要，重要的是礼物的意义和背后的故事。

12. deepen one's friendship 加深朋友间的情谊

Giving a gift to your close friends ***deepens your friendship***.

给亲近的朋友送礼物可以加深你们的友谊。

13. show affection and care 表现爱与关怀

If a parent presents a gift to a child, it is an act of ***showing affection and care***.

父母给孩子送礼物是一种爱与关怀的表现。

14. recipient /rɪ'sɪpiənt; rɪ`sɪpɪənt/ ***n.*** 接受者

The meaning of gift-giving depends on what kind of relationship you have with the ***recipient***.

送礼的意义取决于你和接受礼物者的关系。

15. a token of love 爱的象征

A gift to your beloved is ***a token of love***.

给爱人送礼物是一种爱的象征。

16. custom /'kʌstəm; `kʌstəm/ ***n.*** 风俗

17. social convention 社会习俗

Sometimes when you present a gift when you visit someone "neutral", it can be just a ***custom***, just a ***social convention***.

有时你去拜访不是很熟识的人会带份礼物，这时送礼物就可能只是一种风俗，一种社会习俗。

18. express goodwill 表现善意

In the context of business, gift-giving is intended to ***express goodwill*** and maintain good business relationships.

在商业中，送礼物是为了表现善意及维持良好的商业关系。

19. ulterior motive　动机不单纯

If I were to be given a Rolex watch by someone I did not know well, I might feel uneasy; I might suspect an ***ulterior motive*** and give it back to him.

假如一位我不熟的人送我一只劳力士表，我可能会感觉很不自在，我会怀疑他的动机不单纯，并把表还给他。

20. maintain good interpersonal relationships　维持好的人际关系

There are many ways to ***maintain good interpersonal relationships***, for example, having a meal together or inviting a friend to your home.

维持好的人际关系的方法有很多，例如，一起吃饭或是邀请朋友去家里。

21. keep a friendship in good repair　巩固友情

A telephone conversation can help ***keep a friendship in good repair***, especially between real friends.

电话聊天也可以巩固友情，特别是在真心的朋友之间。

QUESTION DATABASE 题库练习

个人陈述 (Individual Long Turn)

考官 Now please have a look at this card. This is your topic. I want you to describe a present that you own which is very important or special to you. You have one minute to prepare.

Describe a present that you own which is very important or special to you.

You should say:

what it is
when you received it
who gave it to you
why it is special or important to you.

INSTRUCTIONS

You will be asked to talk about the topic for one to two minutes.
You have one minute to think about what you are going to say.
You can make some notes to help you if you wish.

描述一个你拥有的，且对你很重要或是很特别的礼物。你应该谈到：

那是什么礼物
你何时收到这个礼物
谁送你这个礼物
为什么这礼物对你来说很重要或很特别。

【说明】：

针对这个话题作出一至两分钟的陈述。
你有一分钟的时间去思考你的陈述内容。
假如需要的话，你可以写下要点以帮助你组织陈述。

Sample Response

I am going to tell you about the best gift I've ever received. It's an English dictionary. I was given it by my mother as a present when I was admitted into the senior high school. At first, I didn't think the gift was very special. In fact, I was even a bit disappointed when I received it, because … because I had expected my mum to give me a large sum of pocket money to reward me for studying so hard; my success in my studies meant that I was able to enter one of the best high schools in Beijing. Anyway, after my high school English lessons started, I began to realize that the dictionary was very good indeed. There are several reasons why I considered it such an important gift. First and foremost, as a learner of English as a foreign language I found it really useful and still do. It always provides at least one example—sometimes there is more than one example—illustrating how a word is used in English. This greatly improved my ability to use English in speaking and writing. Then again, the dictionary gives the definitions of English words both in English and with their Chinese translations. This makes it different from most of the English-Chinese dictionaries available here. As you know, with the help of the definition in English, you can make sure if that is the right word to use. The book is very dog-eared now. I shall always remember what an important role it has played in my experience of learning English.

回答范例

我要说的是我收过的最好的礼物。那是一本英文词典。这本词典是我考上高中时妈妈送给我的。刚开始我并不认为这礼物有什么特别的地方。事实上，当我收到这份礼物时，甚至有点失望，因为……因为我所期望的是妈妈可以给我很多的零花钱以奖励我这么用功读书。我努力的成果就是能够考上北京最好的高中之一。无论如何，上了高中英语课后我才发现这本词典的确很好用。我之所以会认为这是个很重要的礼物，有几个理由。第一，对于学习英语这门外语而言，这本词典至今都对我十分实用。它对每个词至少提供了一个例句，有时甚至好几个，以说明词的用法。这对我的英语口语和写作有很大帮助。除此之外，这本词典为每个词提供了英英和英汉两种语言的释义。这就是这本词典和其他英汉词典的不同之处。如你所知，有了英文释义的帮助，你就可以确定用词是否正确了。这本词典现在已经很破旧了，页角都翘起来了。我会一直记得这本词典在我学习英语的过程中所扮演的重要角色。

◎ **Is gift-giving a common practice in this country?**

Yes, I think so, especially between good friends.

送礼物在你们国家是常见的习俗吗?

我想是的，特别是在好朋友之间。

双向讨论 (Two-way Discussion)

◎ **Right! Let's continue to talk about the exchange of gifts. On what occasions do people give presents in this country?**

People give gifts to their friends or relatives when they have something special to celebrate, for example, somebody's birthday or a wedding ceremony or a housewarming. Sometimes they do it because they want to express their thanks for the help they have received. Then again, some well-established companies are generous with their employees; they give gifts and a bonus to their employees towards the end of each year.

好吧！让我们继续来谈谈礼物交换吧。这个国家，人们在什么场合中会去送礼物呢？

当有某些特别的事要庆祝的时候，会送朋友或亲戚礼物。例如，在某人生日、结婚典礼或是新居落成的时候。有时候，他们送礼物是为了表达他们对于所受帮助的感谢之情。除此之外，一些久负盛名的公司对于他们的员工很大方；在年终的时候会发给员工礼物及奖金。

◎ **What do you think of the idea of giving someone money as a gift?**

Well, if you ask me, it's a jolly good idea! Cash is certainly welcome because you can use it for anything you choose. By way of contrast, what's the point if someone gives you something you do not need at all or hardly ever use? However, from my past experience, I've come to realize the most unforgettable gift is often not money but something you use ever so often or something you grew up with. It's not the value of a gift that counts but its meaning and the story behind it that matters.

谈谈你对于把金钱当作礼物的看法？

嗯，对我而言，这是一个非常好的主意！金钱肯定是受欢迎的，因为你可以用钱买任何你要的东西。相反，假如别人送的是你不需要或不可能用到的东西，那有何意义呢？然而，就我过去的经验来说，我渐渐认识到最令人难忘的礼物通常不是钱，而是一些你常用的或伴你成长的东西。其实，礼物贵不贵重并不重要，重要的是礼物的意义和背后的故事。

◎ **What do you think is the meaning of giving a gift?**

The meaning of giving a gift? I think it depends on what kind of relationship you have with the recipient. For example, if a parent presents a gift to a child, it is an act of showing affection and care. Giving a gift to your close friends deepens your friendship. A gift to your beloved is a token of love. Then again, sometimes when you present a gift when you visit someone "neutral", it can be just a custom, just a social convention. Sometimes I suppose it's merely an act of politeness. Oh, by the way, gift-giving between business associates is slightly different. In that context it's intended to express goodwill and maintain good business relationships.

你认为送礼物的意义是什么？

送礼物的意义？我想那要看你和礼物接受者是什么关系。举例来说，父母给孩子送礼物是一种慈爱与关怀的表现。给亲近的朋友送礼物可以加深友谊。给爱人送礼物是一种爱的象征。除此之外，有时你去拜访不是很熟识的人会带份礼物，这时送礼物就可能只是一种风俗，一种社会习俗。有时我觉得送礼物只是一种礼貌的行为。顺便说一下，商业伙伴之间送礼物的意义就有些不同。在这种情况下，送礼物是为了表达善意及维持良好的商业关系。

◎ **Is it possible that the custom of giving gifts can become something negative?**

Something negative? Well, I suppose it's possible. For example, if I were to be given a Rolex watch by someone I did not know well, I might feel uneasy; I might suspect an ulterior motive and give it back to him. You see, if a gift is inappropriate, it's not just a gift but something given in exchange for, or in expectation of "something else"; it's no longer a gift but some sort of "deal" or even a bribe. This is especially evident when a gift is associated with an election or with a business transaction. In practice, I suppose, there are always two sides to the giving of a gift. I like to think that I would be principled enough to return a gift if I considered it "impure".

送礼物的做法是否有可能变成负面的事呢？

负面的事？嗯，我想是有可能的。举例来说，假如一位与我不熟的人送我一只劳力士表，我可能会感觉很不自在，怀疑他的动机不单纯，并把表还给他。你知道的，假如送的礼物不适当的话，这礼物事实上只是用来交换别人所期待的“其他东西”而已。那就不再是礼物了，而是一种“交易”或贿赂了。这种情形在选举或商业交易时特别明显。实际上，我认为送礼物往往都会有正反两面。若我收到一份“不正当”的礼物，我希望我会保持原则，将礼物退回。

◎ **What are some other common practices which people here adopt in order to maintain good interpersonal relationships?**

Well, sometimes people just go out for a walk and a talk, or else have a meal and a drink together; this is quite common in business circles here. Inviting a friend to your home, or accepting an invitation to your friend's home is also quite common. Then again, sending out a card or a letter expressing your good wishes is also a good idea. A telephone conversation can help keep a friendship in good repair, especially between real friends.

人们还会采取什么其他常见的做法来维持良好的人际关系呢？

嗯，有时候人们只是相约出来走走、聊天或一起吃饭喝点东西而已，这样的情形在商业圈非常普遍。邀朋友去你家或接受朋友的邀约也很普遍。此外，送卡片或写信来表达你的祝福也是一个非常好的主意。电话聊天也可以巩固友情，特别是在真心的朋友之间。

Business and Shopping

商业与购物

USEFUL EXPRESSIONS 实用表达

1. have mixed feelings to… 对……感觉好坏参半（注：较正式的用法是 have mixed feelings toward …）

   I ***have mixed feelings to*** the digital camera I bought last week.

   对于上星期购买的数码相机，我的感觉是好坏参半的。

2. leave something to be desired 尚待改进

   The service of that restaurant ***leaves something to be desired***.

   那家饭店的服务尚待改进。

3. provisions /prəˈvɪʒənz; prəˋvɪʒənz/ ***n.*** 必需品；饮食供应

   I go shopping for ***provisions*** only when I have to.

   我只有在缺乏必需品时才会去购物。

4. entrepreneur /ˌɒntrəprəˈnɜː; ˌɑntrəprəˋnɝ/ ***n.*** 企业家

   The biographies of successful ***entrepreneurs*** or well-known politicians are popular here.

   成功的企业家或知名政治人物的自传在这里很受欢迎。

5. best seller 畅销书

6. the prime motivator for … ……的主要原因

   The prime motivator for its popularity is the media.

   它之所以受欢迎，主要是因为有媒体的炒作。

7. publicity /pʌˈblɪsɪti; pʌbˋlɪsətɪ/ ***n.*** 宣传

   The film *Harry Potter* based on J. K. Rowling's book has been given an enormous amount of ***publicity***.

   根据 J.K. 罗琳的书所拍摄的电影《哈利·波特》进行了铺天盖地的宣传。

8. marketing strategy 市场营销策略

9. motivate sb. to 驱使某人想要……

10. consume /kən'sjuːm; kən`sum/ *v.* 消费

Good ***marketing strategies*** would ***motivate people to consume***.

好的营销策略能刺激消费。

11. discount /'dɪskaʊnt; `dɪskaʊnt/ *n.* 打折扣

Offering a ***discount*** is quite a common marketing strategy.

折扣活动是一种常见的营销策略。

12. be tempted into sth. / doing sth. 禁不住诱惑想做某事

13. at a cheaper rate for a very large quantity 便宜又量大

14. get a bargain 赚到了，拣了个便宜

Some people ***are tempted into buying things at a cheaper rate for a very large quantity***; they believe they ***get a bargain***.

有些人禁不住诱惑想买那些便宜又量大的商品，他们觉得自己拣到了便宜。

15. endorse /ɪn'dɔːs; ɪn`dɔrs/ *v.* （在广告中）强力推荐；为……背书

Another technique is through an advert or TV commercial in which a popular celebrity ***endorses*** a product.

另一个策略是经由广告或电视，找名人为其产品代言。

16. promotional method 促销方法

Still another ***promotional method*** is giving away an apparently valuable gift of some sort free if you buy the product.

还有一种促销方法，凡是购买其产品便会得到一份看起来颇有价值的赠品。

17. voucher /'vaʊtʃə; `vaʊtʃɚ/ *n.* 代金券

A ***voucher*** is given to those consumers who spend more than a certain amount of money.

代金券会被赠送给消费超过某一额度的消费者。

18. terms and conditions 条件限制

A voucher always has certain ***terms and conditions***.

代金券在使用上都有条件限制。

19. redeem /rɪ'diːm; rɪ`dim/ *v.* 抵用

You might have to spend up to another 1,000 yuan to be able to ***redeem*** a voucher of 100 yuan.

你可能要再消费至少 1000 元才能抵用 100 元的代金券。

20. consumer /kən'sjuːmə; kən`sumɚ/ *n.* 消费者

Consumers have to watch out.

消费者必须小心留意。

21. E-shopping has become trendy.　网上消费已成一种潮流。

22. good value for money　物美价廉

The things for sale on-line seem to be ***good value for money***.

网上的商品似乎是物美价廉。

23. cable shopping　电视购物

24. cable channel　有线频道

Several ***cable channels*** here are devoted to selling and promoting products.

一些有线频道是专门推销产品的。

25. place one's order　订货；下订单

If you are interested, all you need to do is ring them and ***place your order***.

如果你有购买意愿的话，你只需打电话便能跟他们订货。

26. pay by installments　分期付款

For some pricey products, you may choose to ***pay by installments***.

对一些昂贵的产品，你可以选择分期付款。

27. one-year guarantee　一年的保修期

Expensive products usually offer a ***one-year guarantee***.

昂贵的产品通常会提供一年的保修期。

QUESTION DATABASE 题库练习

个人陈述 (Individual Long Turn)

考官 Now please have a look at this card. This is your topic. I want you to talk about something you have bought recently. You have one minute to prepare.

Talk about something you have bought recently. You should say:

what it is
where you bought it
why you bought it
how you like it.

INSTRUCTIONS
You will be asked to talk about the topic for one to two minutes.
You have one minute to think about what you are going to say.
You can make some notes to help you if you wish.

请谈一谈你最近买的某样产品。你应该谈到：

它是什么
你在哪里买的
为什么买它
你喜欢的程度。

【说明】：
针对这个话题作出一至两分钟的陈述。
你有一分钟的时间去思考你的陈述内容。
假如需要的话，你可以写下要点以帮助你组织陈述。

Sample Response

Not long ago I bought a book and set of audio CDs that accompanies it. It's entitled *Cambridge IELTS 4*, a book that contains four IELTS past papers. I got it from a bookshop in Beijing. Why did I buy it? Well, I planned to take this IELTS test, so I had to find out what the test is like. This material really helps me know the format of the test. How do I like it? To be honest, I have mixed feelings to the book. On the one hand, I find it useful, because by doing those past papers, I've come to realize the level of difficulty involved in the IELTS exam, and I have developed some skills in answering questions. On the other hand, I felt frustrated when working on the past papers, because I realized that my reading rate is a bit slow and my listening comprehension leaves something to be desired.

回答范例

不久前，我买了一本附有 CD 光盘的书籍，书名是《剑桥雅思考试全真试题解析 4》，该书包含了四套雅思真题，是我在北京的一家书店买的。至于为什么要买？嗯，我打算参加此次雅思考试，所以必须搞清楚这是什么样的考试，而这套材料确实帮助我了解了考试的形式。谈到我对它的喜欢程度，说实话，感觉好坏参半，一方面我觉得它很有用，因为做过这些真题后，我了解了雅思考试的难度，也掌握了一些回答问题的技巧。但是，另一方面，当我在做真题时，也倍感挫败，因为我发现我的阅读速度有点慢，听力也有待提高。

◎ **Do you like to go shopping?**

Not really. My real interests are reading and music, so I go to the bookshops and CD stores much more often than I go to supermarkets. I don't think of buying books and CDs as quite the same as shopping for food, but I suppose you could think of them as food for the mind.

你喜欢购物吗？

我不是很喜欢。我真正的兴趣是阅读和音乐，所以我去书店和唱片店的次数远超过去超市。我觉得买书或唱片与买食物不太一样，不过，我想你可以把它们想成是在买心灵的粮食。

双向讨论 (Two-way Discussion)

◎ **What kinds of books are currently the most popular in China?**

Biography is popular, especially the biographies of successful entrepreneurs or well-known politicians. Another best seller is *Harry Potter*. The prime motivator for its popularity is the media. The film based on the book has been given an enormous amount of publicity.

在中国，最近哪一类书最畅销？

自传类很受欢迎，尤其是成功的企业家或知名政治人物的自传。《哈利·波特》也十分畅销。它之所以受欢迎，主要是因为有媒体的炒作，根据此书所拍摄的电影《哈利·波特》早已进行了大肆宣传。

◎ **Let's talk about consumption. What marketing strategies would motivate people to consume?**

Marketing strategies? You mean ... strategies used to sell a product? Hmm, let me think about it. Well, for example, offering a discount is quite a common one. You know, some people are tempted into buying things at a cheaper rate for a very large quantity; they believe they get a bargain. Another technique is through an advert or TV commercial in which a popular celebrity endorses a product. Still another promotional method is giving away an apparently valuable gift of some sort free, if you buy the product, which perhaps you don't really want or need. Or a voucher is given to those consumers who spend more than a certain amount of money.

让我们来谈谈消费吧，什么样的市场营销策略能刺激消费？

市场营销策略？你指的是……用来促销商品的策略吗？嗯，让我想一想。噢，举例来说，折扣活动是常见的策略之一。你也知道，有些人禁不住诱惑想买那些价格便宜分量又大的商品，他们觉得拣到了便宜。另一个策略是经由广告或电视，找名人为其产品代言。还有一种促销手法，凡是购买其产品便会得到一份看起来颇有价值的赠品，其实你也许不想要或根本不需要这件产品。也有商家会赠送代金券给那些消费超过某一额度的消费者。

◎ **What do you think of them?**

Well, they do work sometimes. Take me for example. I'll buy something I'll definitely use, say, Lipton's Yellow Label tea bags, if they are sold cheaper. However, I don't normally buy something just because I am given a free gift or just because a movie star endorses it. Then again, a voucher is not always what it seems; it may have certain terms and conditions. For example, you might have to spend up to another 1,000 yuan to be able to redeem a voucher of 100 yuan. So I think consumers have to watch out.

你对于这些策略有什么看法呢？

嗯，有时候的确奏效。拿我当例子吧，我会买我确实需要的东西，像降价的立顿黄牌茶包。但是，我通常不会因为有附赠品或明星代言而买其产品。再说，代金券并非总是那么简单就能使用，而可能会有条件限制。例如，你也许要再消费超过1000元才能抵用100元的代金券，所以我觉得消费者还是小心为妙。

◎ **Has technology changed the way people buy things?**

Oh, yes! Definitely! For example, e-shopping has become trendy. You order an item on the Net without having to go to a shop. This really saves time for consumers. And in most cases, the things for sale are good value for money. Then again, cable shopping is another trend in China. Products are shown and clearly introduced on a cable channel. If you are interested, all you need to do is to ring them and place your order. For some pricey products, you may choose to pay by installments.

科技是否已经改变了人们的购物方式？

当然，这是绝对的！例如，网上购物已经是一种潮流了。无须亲身到商店，你就可以在网上直接订购商品。对消费者而言，这真的是很省时。而且，绝大多数商品都是物美价廉的。此外，在中国，电视购物也是一种潮流。商家在有线频道上展示产品，并进行详细介绍，你若有兴趣的话，只需打电话便能跟他们订货。对一些昂贵的产品，你也可以选择分期付款。

◎ **How do you compare these new trends of shopping with traditional ways of shopping?**

Well, they are different in some respects. One big difference is that e-shopping and cable shopping are more convenient and less time-consuming, because you can place your order at home. Another difference is that you can see and touch a product before buying it if you go to a shop, but you cannot if you do it through the Net or TV. However, the different ways of shopping are similar in that one-year guarantees are frequently offered via the Net in just the same way as in a conventional shop.

你觉得新的购物方式和传统的购物有何异同?

噢，在某些方面它们是不同的。最大的不同点在于网上购物和电视购物更方便和省时，因为你可以直接在家里订货。另一个不同点是，在商店里，购买之前你可以亲眼看到并触摸到商品，但是用网络或电视购物就不能这么做了。然而，这些不同的购物方式有一点是相似的，即不论是网上订购或传统的购物，产品常常都一样享有一年的保修期。

Chapter 3

考试第二、三部分题库：各类话题说不停

综合分类

3. 食物篇 (Food)

Food and Eating Habits

食品与饮食习惯

USEFUL EXPRESSIONS　实用表达

1. my favourite dish　我最喜爱吃的菜
2. chow mein　炒面

   My favourite dish is ***chow mein***.　我最喜欢吃炒面。
3. serve　/sɜːv; sɝv/　***v.***　供应

   Chow mein is now quite commonly ***served*** in English-speaking countries.

   炒面现在是英语国家里很常见的一道菜。
4. home-made　***adj.***　家里做的；自制的

   I prefer ***home-made*** food.　我喜欢家里做的菜。
5. oily　/'ɔɪli; `ɔɪlɪ/　***adj.***　油腻的
6. fatty　/'fæti; `fætɪ/　***adj.***　高脂肪的

   Oily or ***fatty*** food doesn't lie easily on my stomach.

   油腻的或高脂肪的食物会使我的胃不舒服。
7. suit my palate　合我的口味

   Stir-fried rice ***suits my palate***.　炒饭合我的口味。
8. ingredient　/ɪn'griːdiənt; ɪn`gridɪənt/　***n.***　成分；原料
9. visual delight　视觉上的乐趣

   The combination of colours and ***ingredients*** even offers ***visual delight***!

   色泽和食材的组合甚至可增加视觉上的乐趣。
10. culinary art　烹饪的艺术

    Chow mein is a good example of Chinese ***culinary art***.

    炒面很好地体现了中国的烹饪艺术。
11. texture　/'tekstʃə; `tɛkstʃɚ/　***n.***　质感；质地
12. nutritional value　营养价值

Chinese food pays equal attention to the colour, smell, taste, ***texture*** and ***nutritional value*** of food.

中餐强调食物色、香、味、口感及营养价值俱全。

13. barbecued spare rib　烤猪排

14. spring roll　春卷

15. with satay sauce　加沙茶酱

I enjoy stir-fried rice ***with satay sauce***.　我喜欢沙茶炒饭。

16. won ton　馄饨

17. entertain　/ˌentəˈteɪn; ˏɛntɚˋten/　***v.***　娱乐；款待

18. eat out　外出就餐，下馆子

I cook only when I have to ***entertain*** my friends or when I am tired of ***eating out***.

我只在必须款待朋友或当我厌倦在外就餐时才下厨。

19. stir-fried vegetable　炒蔬菜

20. black bean sauce　豆豉酱

I am good at making ***stir-fried vegetables*** in ***black bean sauce***.

我的拿手菜是豆豉酱炒蔬菜。

21. noodles in soup　汤面

22. bean sprout　豆芽

23. minced meat　肉末

24. dried mushroom　香菇

25. fast food restaurant　快餐店

There are many ***fast food restaurants***.

现在有许多快餐店。

26. calorie　/ˈkæləri; ˋkælərɪ/　***n.***　卡路里

27. cholesterol　/kəˈlestərɒl; kəˋlɛstəˏrol/　***n.***　胆固醇

Hamburgers and fried chicken are high in ***calories*** and ***cholesterol***.

汉堡和炸鸡都是高热量及高胆固醇的食物。

28. with increased awareness about ...　越来越有……的意识

Some people are thinking ***with increased awareness about*** healthy food.

有些人的健康饮食意识越来越强。

29. vegetarian　/ˌvedʒɪˈteəriən; ˏvɛdʒəˋtɛrɪən/　***adj.***　素食的　***n.***　素食者

30. block the walls of the arteries　阻塞血管

More and more people are becoming ***vegetarian***, because eating too much meat can ***block the walls of the arteries*** and even cause heart problems.

有越来越多的人开始吃素，因为食用过量的肉类会引起血管阻塞，甚至导致心脏疾病。

31. ethical issue　道德问题

32. slaughter /'slɔːtə; `slɔtɚ/ ***n. & v.***　屠宰

More people are becoming sensitive to the ***ethical issues*** concerning the ***slaughter*** of animals.

有越来越多的人开始对有关屠宰动物的道德问题变得敏感起来。

33. organic /ɔː'gænɪk; ɔr`gænɪk/ ***adj.***　有机的

34. raw /rɔː; rɔ/ ***adj.***　生的；未经过处理加工的

A growing number of people here eat ***raw organic*** foods.

这里食用生鲜有机食品的人的数量在不断增加。

35. blender /'blendə; `blɛndɚ/ ***n.***　搅拌器；榨汁机

Using a ***blender***, they just mix organic fruits and vegetables.

他们用榨汁机，就可以榨取有机果蔬汁。

36. healing effect　治疗功效

Certain diets are believed to have ***healing effects***.

某些饮食据说是有治疗功效的。

37. be overweight　超重的

38. be alert to …　对……有所警觉

39. a balanced diet　均衡的饮食

40. food group　食物种类

41. protein /'prəʊtiːn; `protin/ ***n.***　蛋白质

42. mineral /'mɪnərəl; `mɪnərəl/ ***n.***　矿物质

43. fibre /'faɪbə; `faɪbɚ/ ***n.***　纤维素

44. vitamin /'vɪtəmɪn; `vaɪtəmɪn/ ***n.***　维生素

We ***are*** becoming more ***alert to*** the need for ***a balanced diet***, with sufficient quantities of different ***food groups*** such as ***protein***, ***minerals***, ***fibre***, ***vitamins***, etc.

我们变得更加重视均衡的饮食，从不同的食物类群里摄取足够的营养，如蛋白质、矿物质、纤维素和维生素等。

45. health shop 健康食品店

46. dietary supplement 膳食补充剂

There are an increasing number of "***health shops***" selling organic foods, raw ingredients and all sorts of ***dietary supplements***.

现在提供有机食品、天然食材和各种膳食补充剂的"健康食品店"在不断地增加。

47. genetically modified food; GM food 转基因食品

GM foods are definitely not 100% natural.

转基因食品绝对不是完全天然的。

48. alter /'ɔːltə; `ɔltɚ/ ***v.*** 改变；改造

49. the composition of the plant cell 植物细胞的构成

The naturally-evolved ***composition of the plant cell*** over long periods of time is then suddenly ***altered*** by scientific means.

长久以来自然进化形成的植物细胞结构就此突然被人们用科学手段改造了。

50. soya milk 豆浆

51. soya bean 黄豆

52. label /'leɪbəl; `lebl̩/ ***n. & v.*** 标示

A genetically modified product should be clearly ***labeled*** as such. Consumers should at least be informed of that so that they can choose whether or not they want to buy it.

转基因食品应该清楚地标示出其为转基因的。消费者至少应该被告知这一点，如此便可以有选择买或不买的空间。

53. seafood /'siːfuːd; `si,fud/ ***n.*** 海产食品

54. snack shop 小吃店

55. cuisine /kwɪ'ziːn; kwɪ`zin/ ***n.*** 烹饪

56. Beijing snack 北京小吃

There are numerous ***snack shops*** featuring Beijing ***cuisine***; they offer a variety of ***Beijing snacks***.

有很多小吃店推出北京菜，他们提供了丰富多样的北京小吃。

57. gourmet food 美食

58. at a reasonable price 以合理的价位

Many snack shops here provide ***gourmet foods at a reasonable price***.

这里很多的小吃店提供物美价廉的美食。

59. pea flour cake　豌豆黄（注：亦可说 Wan Dou Huang）
60. exotic restaurant　具异国风味的餐厅
61. having a hankering for …　想要……（注：口语用法）
62. something fancy　来点不一样的

A few people do go to ***exotic restaurants*** because they ***have a hankering for something fancy***.

有一些人的确因为想要来点不一样的，于是就会去具有异国风味的餐厅。

63. one's palate has become jaded　口味吃腻了
64. homely, seasonal food　家常口味、应季的食物

When ***your palate has become jaded***, you can no longer appreciate the pleasure of good traditional, ***homely*** or ***seasonal food***.

当口味吃腻了，你就不会再去珍惜美味的传统风味、家常菜或时令菜肴所带来的享受。

65. forsake /fə'seɪk; fɚ`sek/ ***v.***　舍弃

I don't see many people ***forsaking*** good traditional Chinese food for very long.

我认为很多人只是暂时舍弃美味的传统中餐。

QUESTION DATABASE 题库练习

个人陈述 (Individual Long Turn)

考官 Now please have a look at this card. This is your topic. I want you to describe your favourite food or dish. You have one minute to prepare.

Describe your favourite food or dish. You should say:

what it is
where you normally have it
how often you have it
why you like it best.

INSTRUCTIONS

You will be asked to talk about the topic for one to two minutes.
You have one minute to think about what you are going to say.
You can make some notes to help you if you wish.

描述你最喜爱的食物或菜肴。你应该谈到：

它是什么
你通常会在哪里品尝它
你多长时间吃一回
为什么你最喜爱这道菜。

【说明】：

针对这个话题作出一至两分钟的陈述。
你有一分钟的时间去思考你的陈述内容。
假如需要的话，你可以写下要点以帮助你组织陈述。

Sample Response

I'd like to tell you about my favourite dish, chow mein. The popularity of this dish is beyond any doubt; it's now quite commonly served in English-speaking countries. I often have it at home and in restaurants. But to be honest, I prefer home-made chow mein, because the product offered by restaurants is sometimes too oily. Oily or fatty food doesn't lie easily on my stomach. How often do I have it? Well, I eat it two or three times a week. There are several reasons why I enjoy it so much. First of all, it just seems to suit my palate. Also, I like its smell, especially when it is fresh from the stove. Then again, it's always reasonably priced, so I can afford to eat it as often as I like. Another reason is that I like the idea of "unity in diversity"—that everything is put together in one dish. The combination of colours and ingredients even offers visual delight! I think chow mein is a good example of Chinese culinary art, paying equal attention to the colour, smell, taste, texture and nutritional value of food.

回答范例

我很乐意与你谈谈最喜爱的一道菜，那就是炒面。这道美食受欢迎的程度是毋庸置疑的，现在是英语国家很普遍的一道菜，我经常在家里或饭店享用这道美食。但老实说，因为饭店供应的食物有时会太油腻，所以我比较喜欢吃家里做的炒面。油腻或高脂肪的食物会使我的胃不舒服。我多久吃一次呢？一个礼拜两至三次吧！我如此喜爱它的原因有几个：首先，炒面合我的口味；其次，我喜欢它的香味，特别是刚炒好时；再次，它总是价格公道，所以我能想吃就吃，不至于负担不起；还有就是我喜欢它“多样中的一致性”——也就是所有菜都放在同一个盘子上，而其色泽和食材的组合更可增加视觉上的乐趣！我认为炒面很好地体现了中国的烹饪艺术，即能够同时兼顾食物的色、香、味、口感及营养价值。

◎ **Is there any other food that you enjoy having?**

Oh, yes, absolutely. For example, I also like barbecued spare ribs, spring rolls, stir-fried rice with satay sauce, won ton, etc. I always love delicious food. My mother said when I was little, if she couldn't find me, she knew I was probably somewhere in the kitchen, no matter whose house I was in!

还有任何其他你也喜爱的食物吗?

哦，是的，当然有！比如说：烤猪排、春卷、沙茶炒饭、馄饨等。美食总是我的最爱。我母亲曾说过，在我小时候，如果她找不到我，就会想到我一定是在厨房的某个角落里，不管我是在谁家！

◎ **Do you cook by yourself?**

Yes, I do, but only occasionally. I do it only when I want to entertain my friends or when I am tired of eating out. When I cook, I normally just make something simple. For example, I make chow mein; I'm sure you would not be surprised! Also, I make stir-fried vegetables in black bean sauce. Sometimes I also make noodles in soup, with bean sprouts, minced meat and dried mushrooms.

你会亲自下厨吗?

会，但只是偶尔。我只在要款待朋友或厌倦了在外就餐时才下厨。当我下厨时，我通常都做一些较简单的，比如说，我会炒面，我想你一定不会惊讶的。另外，我会做豆豉酱炒蔬菜。有时我也会煮汤面，里面加上豆芽、肉末和香菇。

◎ **Do you enjoy cooking?**

Well, fairly, I suppose. It's good fun to cook for my friends. But it can seem tiring and time-consuming to cook just for oneself.

你喜欢下厨吗?

我觉得还好。为朋友下厨是件很有趣的事，但如果只给自己一个人做饭就会显得很乏味并且很费时间。

双向讨论 (Two-way Discussion)

◎ **Now, let's talk about eating habits. Do you think the eating habits practised in this country have changed over the years?**

Hmm … yes, I think so. One big difference is that there are many fast food restaurants. As you know, hamburgers and fried chicken are high in calories and cholesterol, but many youngsters and children just fancy them. On the other hand, I've noticed a totally different trend—some people are thinking with increased awareness about healthy food. For example, more and more people are becoming vegetarian, because eating too much meat can block the walls of the arteries and even cause heart problems. And then there's the question of compassion. More people are becoming sensitive to the ethical issues concerning the slaughter of animals. And then again, a growing number of people here eat raw organic foods. Using a blender, they just mix organic vegetables and fruits. They believe such a diet has healing effects.

现在，让我们谈谈饮食习惯。你认为这几年来这个国家里人们的饮食习惯有任何改变吗?

嗯……我想是的。其中最大的变化是现在有许多的快餐店。你知道的，汉堡和炸鸡都是高热量及高胆固醇的食物，但许多儿童和青少年就是喜欢吃这些。另一方面，我也注意到一种与之完全不同的潮流，那就是有些人的健康饮食意识越来越强。譬如，有越来越多的人开始吃素，因为食用过量的肉类会引起血管阻塞，甚至会导致心脏疾病。并且因为慈悲心，有越来越多的人开始对有关屠宰动物的道德问题变得敏感起来。此外，这里食用生鲜有机食品的人也越来越多，他们用榨汁机就可以榨取有机果蔬汁，他们相信这样的饮食是有治疗功效的。

◎ **What do you think of the change?**

Well, I have mixed feelings. I think it's a real shame that fast food is becoming so popular. I've noticed that there are more and more children who are overweight. This certainly has a lot to do with it. On the other hand, I think it's good that we are more aware of the importance of eating healthy foods such as fruits, vegetables and organic foods. At least we are becoming more alert to the need for a balanced diet, with sufficient quantities of different food groups such as protein, minerals, fibre, vitamins, etc.

你对这样的改变有什么看法？

我对这种改变的看法其实很矛盾。我认为快餐现在变得这么受欢迎实在是一件令人遗憾的事。我已经注意到现在有越来越多的小孩体重超重，这种现象当然与快餐的流行有密切的关联。另一方面，我认为，更注重对蔬果和有机食品一类的食物的摄取是很好的，至少我们变得更加重视膳食均衡，从不同的食物类群里摄取足够的营养，如蛋白质、矿物质、纤维素和维生素等。

◎ **Are organic foods popular in this country?**

They're getting popular. There are an increasing number of "health shops" selling organic foods and all sorts of dietary supplements. So yes, I think they are indeed growing popular. Though organic foods are expensive, those who can afford them consider health more important than price.

在这个国家有机食品盛行吗？

越来越流行了。"健康食品店"在不断增加，它们为人们提供了有机食品和各种膳食补充剂。所以的确，我认为有机食品越来越盛行。尽管有机食品很贵，但对那些有购买能力的人来说，健康比价钱更重要。

◎ **What do you think of genetically modified foods?**

GM foods? Well, I've got quite a lot to say about this. If I had a choice, I'd prefer not to buy them. As I see it, they are definitely not 100% natural. Plant cells have evolved through interaction with the environment—with the soil and other plants and insects and animals—over millions of years. The naturally-evolved composition of the plant cell over long periods of time is then suddenly altered by scientific means.

So how GM plants will affect the rest of life is actually unknown. And once GM seeds are planted and germinated, they are bound to spread all over the world by wind, birds, insects and so on. Though scientists claim that GM foods are "safe", they cannot really be completely sure of their effects on human, animal and plant life over a long period. And these products have already appeared on our market shelves. I think they should be clearly labeled as such. Recently a well-known soya milk product here was criticized because it used GM soya beans, but it didn't specify this detail on the package. Consumers should be at least informed of that so that they can choose whether or not they want to buy a GM food.

你对转基因食品有什么看法？

转基因食品？嗯，我对这方面倒是有很多看法。假如我能选择的话，我会尽可能不去购买。就我所知，转基因的食物绝对不会是完全天然的。植物细胞自数百万年以前就开始通过与自然环境——土壤、昆虫、动物及其他植物相互作用而不断演化，然而长久以来自然进化形成的植物细胞结构却突然被人们用科学手段改变了。

所以转基因植物会如何影响其他生物，目前仍是不得而知。而且，一旦转基因植物的种子被种植并发芽，它们就会开始借由风力、鸟及昆虫等散播至各地。虽然科学家声称转基因食品很“安全”，但他们并不能真正完全确定它们对人类和动植物的长期影响，而这些产品早已流入市场。我认为它们应该被清楚地标示出其为转基因产品。最近，这里一种很知名的豆浆产品就被批评了，因为其包装上并没有清楚地标示出其原料是转基因大豆。消费者至少应该被告知这一点，如此便有选择买或不买的空间。

◎ **Let's talk about restaurants. What types of restaurants are there in this city?**

Well, there are many types of restaurants here: Chinese, Japanese, Thai, Italian and French restaurants and even English-style tearooms. Oh, yes, I should also mention the numerous snack shops featuring Beijing cuisine; they offer a variety of Beijing snacks. They are not proper restaurants, but they do provide gourmet foods at a reasonable price. Have you ever tried pea flour cakes? It's a popular Beijing snack.

我们谈谈餐厅吧！这个城市里有哪几种餐厅？

这里有好多不同类型的餐厅：有中式、日式、泰式、意式及法式餐厅，甚至还有英式茶室。当然我也应该提到有很多小吃店推出北京菜，提供丰富多样的北京小吃。它们并不是上等的餐厅，但的确提供了物美价廉的美食。你尝过豌豆黄吗？它可是一道很受欢迎的北京小吃。

◎ **Are exotic restaurants more popular than Chinese ones?**

No, I don't think so. A few people do go to exotic restaurants. But I think it's just because they have a hankering for something fancy; they want a change just for the sake of a change. They think it will give them some undreamed-of pleasure. Perhaps their palates have become jaded and they can no longer appreciate the pleasure of good traditional, homely or seasonal food. Such places are mostly quite pricey and young people like me just could not afford to eat there very often even if we wanted to. In any case, I don't see many people forsaking good traditional Chinese food for very long. They soon return to what suits their stomachs and pockets best.

具异国风味的餐厅比中式餐厅更受欢迎吗?

不，我不这么认为。有些人的确会去具有异国风味的餐厅，但我觉得他们是因为想要来点不一样的，只是想换换口味而已。他们认为那些具有异国风味的餐厅也许会带来一些意想不到的乐趣。也许是他们已吃腻了，所以就不会再去珍惜美味的传统风味、家常菜或时令菜肴所带来的享受。具有异国风味的餐厅大多价位颇高，而像我这样的年轻人即使想去也负担不起经常去的开销。不管如何，我认为很多人只是暂时舍弃美味的传统中式菜肴，他们仍会很快回到最适合他们口味及预算的美食上。

Chapter 3

考试第二、三部分题库：各类话题说不停

综合分类

4. 衣着篇 (Clothes)

Dress and Fashion

服饰与风尚

USEFUL EXPRESSIONS 实用表达

1. dress conservatively 穿着保守

   I usually ***dress*** rather ***conservatively***, wearing a shirt with a tie.

   我的穿着相当保守，通常是一件衬衫加一条领带。

2. add variety to ... 给……添加变化

   My basic style at work doesn't change much, but the different colours of my shirts and ties ***add*** a bit of ***variety to*** it.

   我上班时的基本服装并没有多大的变化，但是不同颜色的衬衫和领带却可增添一点变化。

3. be formally dressed 穿着正式

4. business associate 商业伙伴

   We have to deal with ***business associates*** from abroad who ***are formally dressed***.

   我们必须和国外的商业伙伴打交道，而他们都穿得相当正式。

5. an act of politeness 礼貌的行为

   Dressing formally is ***an act of politeness***.

   穿着正式是一种礼貌的行为。

6. sandal /'sændl; `sændl̩/ ***n.*** 凉鞋

7. shorts /ʃɔːts; ʃɔrts/ ***n.*** 短裤（注：在美式英语中常表示男式短内裤）

8. business client 商业客户

   Imagine what would happen if I put on ***sandals*** and ***shorts*** to see a significant ***business client***!

   假如我穿一双凉鞋及一条短裤去见一位重要的客户，想想看那将会有什么后果！

9. style of dress at work 工作的服装款式

   I consider my ***style of dress at work*** is both appropriate and necessary.

   我认为我在工作时的着装风格是恰当并且必要的。

10. blouse /blaʊz; blaʊs/ *n.* 女式衬衫
11. a matching outfit 套装
12. dress /dres; drɛs/ *n.* 套裙

I often wear a ***blouse*** and a skirt, but sometimes a ***dress*** or ***a matching outfit***.

我通常穿一件衬衫搭配裙子，但有时也会穿套裙或套装。

13. neat /niːt; nit/ *adj.* 整洁的
14. graceful /'greɪsfəl; `gresfəl/ *adj.* 优雅的
15. bright and fresh 光鲜亮丽的

One thing I think is important is to look as ***neat*** and ***graceful*** and ***bright and fresh*** as possible, and to give expression to how I feel.

我认为重要的是要尽可能看起来整洁、优雅、光鲜亮丽，并能展现出自己的风貌。

16. the spice of life 生活情趣

I like to dress in all sorts of different ways—variety is ***the spice of life***.

我喜欢穿不同风格的衣服，多姿多彩的生活才有情趣。

17. all sorts of patterns and cuts 各种图案及剪裁

I combine different colours and choose ***all sorts of patterns and cuts***.

我会结合不同的颜色并选择各种图案及剪裁。

18. dress tastefully 穿着有品位

I think it's important to ***dress tastefully***.

我认为穿着有品位很重要。

19. the "total look" 整体造型

Dressing tastefully is important nowadays, especially with all this talk of ***the "total look"*** in fashion designs.

如今，有品位的穿着很重要，特别是在大家都在谈论时装设计的"整体造型"时。

20. outlandish style 奇装异服
21. avant-garde /'ævɒŋ'gɑːd; ˌævɑŋ`gɑrd/ *adj.* 前卫的
22. designer /dɪ'zaɪnə; dɪ`zaɪnɚ/ *n.* 设计师

I don't like the ***outlandish styles*** that some ***avant-garde designers*** create nowadays.

我不喜欢如今有些前卫设计师设计出的那些奇装异服。

23. be style conscious 有时尚感的

I have become more ***style conscious*** than before since I started to work.

开始工作之后，我比以前更有时尚感。

24. stylish /'staɪlɪʃ; `staɪlɪʃ/ ***adj.*** 有格调的；时髦的

I feel that wearing ***stylish*** clothes is a way of adding to the beauty in the world.

我觉得穿着有格调是一种为世界添加美感的方式。

25. dress casually 穿着随意地

26. blue jeans 牛仔裤

27. slacks /slæks; slæks/ ***n.*** 宽松的长裤；休闲裤

Sometimes I just ***dress casually***, with a T-shirt and ***blue jeans*** or ***slacks***.

有时我的穿着很随意，一件 T 恤衫加一条牛仔裤或是一条休闲裤。

28. accessory /ək'sesəri; ək`sɛsərɪ/ ***n.*** 配件；饰品

29. necklace /'nek-lɪs; `nɛklɪs/ ***n.*** 项链

30. bracelet /'breɪslɪt; `breslɪt/ ***n.*** 手镯

31. brooch /brəʊtʃ; brotʃ/ ***n.*** 胸针

Occasionally I wear ***accessories***, for example, a ***necklace***, a ***bracelet*** or a ***brooch*** and sometimes earrings.

有时我会搭配一些饰品，比如说一条项链、一只手镯或一枚胸针，有时也会戴耳环。

32. sportswear /'spɔːtsweə; `spɔrts,wɛr/ ***n.*** 运动服装

33. trainers /'treɪnəz; `trenɚz/ ***n.*** 运动鞋（注：英式英语）

34. flat shoes 平底鞋

When I was a student, I always dressed casually, with a combination of ***sportswear***, T-shirts, slacks, ***trainers***, and ***flat shoes***.

当学生的时候，我的穿着总是很随意，常是运动服搭配 T 恤衫、宽松的长裤、运动鞋或平底鞋。

35. professional /prə'feʃənəl; prə`fɛʃənḷ/ ***n.*** 专业人士

I have to dress like a ***professional***, or my colleagues might treat me like a student.

我必须穿得像是一位专业人士，否则同事可能会把我当学生看。

36. brand name 品牌

The ***brand name*** of clothes is not important to me; it's the price and style that count.

衣服的品牌对我来说并不是很重要，重要的是衣服的价钱及款式。

37. company logo　品牌标志

I don't feel obliged to spend one month's salary on a dress just to get a ***company logo*** on it.

我不需要花费一个月的薪水去买一件衣服，为的只是上面的名牌标志。

38. with poise and confidence　仪态端庄又有自信

On healthy people ***with poise and confidence***, almost anything looks good.

健康、端庄又自信的人几乎穿什么都很好看。

39. an internationally known brand name　世界知名品牌

40. a status symbol　社会地位的象征

Wearing something with ***an internationally known brand name*** has become ***a status symbol***.

穿世界知名品牌的服饰已经成为一种社会地位的象征。

41. current　/'kʌrənt; `kɝənt/　***adj.***　当前的

I pay little attention to ***current*** fashions.

我很少注意当前的流行时尚。

42. open and daring style　开放及大胆的风格

43. low-waisted trousers　低腰裤

44. come into vogue　开始流行

We've got more ***open and daring styles*** such as ***low-waisted trousers*** and short shirts ***coming into vogue***.

类似低腰裤或短上衣这样更加开放大胆的风格开始流行起来。

45. belly　/'beli; `bɛlɪ/　***n.***　腹部

Showing a bit of ***belly*** is considered sexy!

稍微露出腹部被视为性感！

46. trend　/trend; trɛnd/　***n.***　潮流

A ***trend*** that reminds me of the sixties and seventies seems to be emerging.

一股让我想起六七十年代的服装潮流似乎正在出现。

47. retro　/'retrəʊ; `rɛtro/　***adj.***　复古的

This ***retro*** style seems especially popular with the middle-aged.

这股复古风在中年人中尤其流行。

48. with-it　/'wɪðɪt; `wɪð,ɪt/　***adj.***　时髦的（注：口语用法）

49. have one's hair dyed fair　把自己的发色染淡

Those who are young and "***with-it***" here like to ***have their hair dyed*** blonde or ***fair*** or in different shades of brown.

这里那些年轻时髦的人喜欢把自己的头发染成金黄色或浅色，或是不同深浅的咖啡色。

50. glossy /ˈglɒsi; ˋglɔsɪ/ ***adj.*** 有光泽的

I rather like our natural ***glossy*** black hair.

我相当喜欢我们自然有光泽的黑发。

51. children's wear　儿童服饰

52. diversified /daɪˈvɜːsɪfaɪd; dəˋvɝsəˌfaɪd/ ***adj.*** 多样化的

Children's wear nowadays is much more stylish and more ***diversified*** than it used to be.

如今的童装比以前更为时髦，而且更多样化。

53. dress up　盛装，装扮

Children ***dress up*** for all sorts of occasions, for example, for a baseball game.

小孩子会依不同的场合而穿不同的衣服，譬如打棒球时有棒球服饰。

54. practical /ˈpræktɪkəl; ˋpræktɪkl̩/ ***adj.*** 实用的；实际的

55. impractical /ɪmˈpræktɪkəl; ɪmˋpræktɪkl̩/ ***adj.*** 不实用的；不实际的

56. wear a uniform　穿制服

57. keep up with the Joneses　与他人攀比

One of the advantages of ***wearing a uniform*** is that you don't have to try to ***keep up with the Joneses***. As you know, all too often clothes become a status symbol.

穿制服的好处之一是你不需要去与他人攀比。你知道，衣服往往是社会地位的象征。

58. surreptitiously /ˌsʌrəpˈtɪʃəsli; ˌsɝəpˋtɪʃəslɪ/ ***adv.*** 暗中地

Co-workers ***surreptitiously*** or even openly compete with one another by means of the clothes they wear.

同事之间通过衣着彼此暗中甚至公开较劲。

59. monotonous /məˈnɒtənəs; məˋnɑtn̩əs/ ***adj.*** 单调乏味的

Wearing a uniform can be ***monotonous***.

穿制服会单调乏味。

QUESTION DATABASE 题库练习

个人陈述 (Individual Long Turn)

考官 Now please have a look at this card. This is your topic. I want you to describe how you usually dress when you go to work or when you go to school. You have one minute to prepare.

Describe how you usually dress when you go to work or when you go to school. You should say:

what kind of clothes you wear
why you dress in this way
what you think about such clothes.

INSTRUCTIONS
You will be asked to talk about the topic for one to two minutes.
You have one minute to think about what you are going to say.
You can make some notes to help you if you wish.

描述在工作或上学时，你通常如何穿着。你应该谈到：

你的衣着种类
如此穿着的原因
对这种服饰的看法。

【说明】：
针对这个话题作出一至两分钟的陈述。
你有一分钟的时间去思考你的陈述内容。
假如需要的话，你可以写下要点以帮助你组织陈述。

Sample Response (for females)

I'd like to tell you the sort of styles I like to wear when I go to work. I often wear a blouse and a skirt, but sometimes a dress or a matching outfit. I don't need to dress in any particular way, but one thing I think is important is to look as neat and graceful and bright and fresh as possible, and to give expression to how I feel. I like to dress in all sorts of different ways—variety is the spice of life. I combine different colours and choose all sorts of patterns and cuts. What do I think about all this? Well, I think it's important to dress tastefully, and I believe I do. This is important nowadays, especially with all this talk of the "total look" in fashion designs. But I don't like the outlandish styles that some avant-garde designers create nowadays. I love the different forms of natural beauty we see all around us—in flowers, in plants, in ancient buildings and even in the sky and clouds. There's so much beauty and subtlety in these things. And yes, I am style conscious; I feel that wearing stylish clothes is a way of adding to the beauty in the world.

回答范例（女性）

我想要谈谈我在工作时喜欢穿的服装样式。我常常是穿一件衬衫搭配裙子去上班，但有时会穿套裙或套装。我并不需要特别的穿着，我认为重要的是要尽可能看起来整洁、优雅、光鲜亮丽又能展现出自己的风貌。我喜欢穿不同风格的衣服，因为多姿多彩的生活才有情趣。我会结合不同的颜色并选择各种图案和剪裁。我是如何想的呢？我认为有品位的穿着很重要，而我相信自己做到了这一点。如今这点很重要，特别是在大家都在谈论时装设计的“整体造型”时。但我不喜欢时下一些前卫设计师所设计出的奇装异服，我喜爱周围所看到的不同形式的自然美——在花丛中，在树木里，在古老的建筑物里，甚至是在天空与云层中。这些地方都蕴藏着太多的美与奥妙。当然，我还是具有时尚感的，我觉得穿着有格调是一种为世界增添美的方式。

Sample Response (for males)

I'm going to tell you how I normally dress for work. I usually dress quite conservatively, wearing a shirt with a tie. I don't normally wear a suit unless it's cold, or when I have to attend, say, an important event such as an office reception party. My basic style at work doesn't change much, but the different colours of my shirts and ties add a bit of variety to it. Why do I dress this way? Well, it's a practice encouraged and adopted by my company. We have to deal with business associates from abroad who are formally dressed. And I think it's important to show them that we care about their visits by dressing in a way that's not too different from theirs. In any case I think dressing formally is an act of politeness. Imagine what would happen if I put on sandals and shorts to see a significant business client! He might imagine I wasn't taking him seriously. So I consider my style of dress at work is both appropriate and necessary.

回答范例（男性）

我将要告诉你我上班通常是如何穿着的。我的穿着相当保守，经常是一件衬衫加一条领带。通常我不穿西装，除非天气寒冷，或必须出席正式的场合，如公司的招待会。我上班时的基本着装并没有多大的变化，但是不同颜色的衬衫和领带却可为我的衣着增添一点变化。为什么我会如此穿着？因为我所在的公司鼓励且采用这样的穿法。我们必须和国外的商业伙伴往来，他们都穿得相当正式。我认为衣着与他们差异不大，能显现出我们对其来访的重视。不管怎么样，我认为正式的穿着是一种礼貌的行为。想想看，假如我穿了一双凉鞋及一条短裤去见一位重要的客户，那将会有什么后果！他可能会猜想我并没有把他放在眼里。因此，我认为我在工作时的着装风格是恰当并且必要的。

◎ **How about when you go out with friends?**

Well, unless it's a special occasion, I just dress casually, with a T-shirt and blue jeans or slacks. I just want to make myself feel comfortable.

那你跟朋友出去时又会如何选择自己的衣着呢?

嗯，除非是特别的场合，要不然我也只是穿类似 T 恤、牛仔裤或宽松的长裤等休闲服出门。我只是想要让自己觉得舒适。

◎ **Do you normally wear any accessories?**

Occasionally I wear a necklace or a bracelet or a brooch and sometimes earrings.

你通常会佩戴一些饰品吗?

偶尔我会搭配一些饰品，比如说一条项链、一只手镯或一枚胸针，有时也会戴耳环。

双向讨论 (Two-way Discussion)

◎ **Is your dress style different from the way you looked when you were a college student?**

Oh, yes, very different! When I was a student, I always dressed casually, with combinations of sportswear, T-shirts, slacks, trainers, and flat shoes. At that time, I really had to watch out for the price when I shopped for clothes. I always bought the cheapest I could find. But nowadays I can afford to be more conscious about style and fashion, although money is always something that needs to be considered. Then again, I'm no longer at college; I have to dress like a professional. Otherwise, my colleagues and clients might treat me like a student.

你现在的打扮跟大学时代的穿着有什么不一样的地方吗？

是的，非常不一样！当学生的时候，我的穿着总是很随意，通常是运动服、T恤、宽松的长裤、运动鞋及平底鞋之间的搭配。那时买衣服，我不得不注意价钱的问题，我总是尽量买最便宜的。但是现在自己已有一定的经济能力，尽管价钱仍是需要考虑的因素，但是我可以稍微注意衣服的款式及流行与否。再者，我已经离开学校了，我必须穿得职业一些，否则同事可能会把我当学生看。

◎ **Do you think the brand name of clothes is important?**

Well, yes and no. Speaking for myself, it's not all that important. It's the style and the price that count. I don't feel obliged to spend one month's salary on a dress just to get a company logo on it, because there are so many other reasonably priced clothes without well-known brand names. Besides, on healthy people with poise and confidence, almost anything looks good. But yes, the brand name is certainly important to some people—movie stars, television personalities, politicians, business tycoons and so on, as you know. Wearing something with an internationally known brand name has become a status symbol; some people think they can acquire status without having to take the trouble to develop a sense of style.

你认为衣服的品牌重要吗？

这得看情况而定。以我自己来说，衣服的品牌并不那么重要，重要的是款式及价钱。我觉得并不需要花费一个月的薪水去买一件衣服，为的只是上面的品牌标志，因为还是有很多其他的衣服，虽然品牌并不响亮，但价钱却合理。除此之外，健康、端庄又自信的人几乎穿什么都很好看。不过也没错，“名牌”对一些人的确很重要，你知道的，如那些电影明星、电视名人和政商名流等。穿着国际名牌服饰已经成为一种社会地位的象征，有些人认为借此就不用那么麻烦去培养时尚感，一下子就可以获得社会地位。

◎ **Can you describe the current fashion designs?**

Current fashion designs? There seems to be an interesting contrast in current fashions. Perhaps it has to do with age. On the one hand, we've got the more open and daring styles such as low-waisted trousers and short shirts coming into vogue. This style is particularly popular with women in their early twenties. Showing a bit of belly is considered sexy! On the other hand, a trend that reminds me of the sixties and seventies seems to be emerging. This retro style seems especially popular with the middle-aged. I suppose it makes them feel more like ladies and gentlemen. Oh, by the way, I must at least mention the latest hair fashions in this country. Those who are young and "with-it" here like to have their hair dyed blonde or fair or in different shades of brown. Obviously the West is influencing us. I think this is a pity—I rather like our natural glossy black hair. Anyway, this is how I see things.

你能够描述一下时下的流行设计吗？

时下的流行设计？现在的流行似乎有着有趣的对照，或许是与年龄有关吧。一方面，类似低腰裤或短上衣这样更加开放大胆的风格开始流行起来。这种款式在20出头的年轻女性间甚受欢迎，稍微露出腹部被视为带点性感！另一方面，一股让我想起六七十年代的服装潮流似乎正在出现，这股复古风尤其受到中年人的欢迎。我想他们应该是认为这种款式能让他们变得更像淑女或绅士。啊，对了，我至少得提一下这里颇为风行的美发潮流。那些年轻时髦的人喜欢把自己的头发染成金黄色或浅色，或是不同深浅的咖啡色。很显然，我们正受西方流行的影响，我认为这是相当可惜的，我比较喜欢我们自然有光泽的黑发。无论如何，这是我个人的看法。

◎ **How about children's wear nowadays? How does it compare to children's wear, say, ten years ago or when you were little?**

Children's wear? My goodness! I am not married yet. I don't have any children, so I pay little attention to children's clothing. Hum… well, perhaps I can put it this way. My very, very general impression is that children's wear nowadays is much more stylish and more diversified than it used to be. There is a wider range of choices. They dress up for all sorts of occasions, for example, for a baseball game. Then again, they can dress up like someone they fancy, a prince or a princess, or a football star, Harry Potter or a cartoon figure. When I was little, I simply didn't have so many choices. My parents would not spend any money on a piece of clothes that they considered "impractical". I think there are so many choices nowadays that people just get confused; they hardly know why they buy one thing rather than another.

那时下的童装呢？童装跟以往有什么差异吗？比如说，十年前或在你小的时候？

小孩子的穿着？我的天啊！我还未婚。因为没有小孩，所以我很少注意到童装。嗯……也许我可以这么说，在我的印象中，现在的儿童服饰比以前更讲究款式、更多样化，人们有更大的选择空间。小孩子会依不同的场合穿着，譬如打棒球时会穿棒球服。再者，他们可以穿得像他们所崇拜的王子或公主、某位足球明星、哈利·波特或一位卡通人物。我小的时候，根本没有这么多选择，我的父母不会花钱买任何一件他们认为"不实用"的衣服。我认为现在有这么多的选择，都把人们搞糊涂了，他们很难说清楚为什么会买这一件而不是另外一件衣服。

◎ **What are the advantages and disadvantages of wearing a uniform?**

Let's consider the advantages first. You are saved the trouble of having to think about what to wear before going to work. Another advantage is that you don't have to try to keep up with the Joneses. As you know, all too often clothes become a status symbol. Co-workers surreptitiously or even openly compete with one another by means of the clothes they wear. So having a uniform circumvents this rather wasteful pursuit. Still another advantage is that it's easy for customers to find help if necessary. Imagine you are in a supermarket and you can't find what you want. It's easy to spot someone to help you if she's wearing a uniform bearing the shop logo. On the other hand, wearing a uniform can be monotonous. Then again, if you don't like its style or colour and you have no choice but to wear it every day at work, that's awful, isn't it?

穿制服有什么优缺点？

让我们先讨论它的优点。你可以省去在上班之前决定穿哪一件衣服的麻烦；另一个优点是你不需要去与他人攀比。你知道，衣服往往是社会地位的象征，同事之间会通过衣着彼此暗中甚至公开较劲。因此，穿制服刚好可以回避这类不必要的竞争。还有一个优点是顾客可以在必要时很容易获得帮助。试想你在超市找不到你所要的商品时，如果有人穿着有商店标志的制服，那么你能很容易寻求到相关人员的帮助。另一方面来说，穿制服也会单调乏味，而且万一你不喜欢它的颜色和款式，而又不得不每天穿着它去上班，那将会是多糟啊！不是吗？

Chapter 3

考试第二、三部分题库：各类话题说不停

综合分类

5．居住篇 (Housing)

City and Town

城市与乡镇

USEFUL EXPRESSIONS 实用表达

1. be located in 位于

   Beijing ***is located in*** northern China. 北京位于中国北方。

2. cosmopolitan /ˌkɒzməˈpɒlɪtən; ˏkɑzmə`pɑlətn̩/ ***adj.*** 大都会的，（人口）来自世界各地的

   Beijing is a ***cosmopolitan*** city. 北京是个大都市。

3. vitality /vaɪˈtælɪti; vaɪ`tælətɪ/ ***n.*** 活力

4. diversity /daɪˈvɜːsɪti; daɪ`vɝsətɪ/ ***n.*** 多样性

   Beijing is full of ***vitality*** and ***diversity***. 北京是一个充满活力与多样性的城市。

5. book fair 书展

6. exhibition /ˌeksɪˈbɪʃən; ˏɛksə`bɪʃən/ ***n.*** 展览

   There is always, always something new and interesting going on in Beijig: ***book fairs***, computer ***exhibitions***, car shows, etc.

   在北京总是会举办一些新鲜有趣的活动，例如书展、电脑展、车展等等。

7. architecturally impressive 建筑风格令人印象深刻的

8. the National stadium 国家体育场

   The National Stadium is ***architecturally impressive***.

   国家体育场的建筑风格令人印象深刻。

9. the Palace Museum 故宫博物院

10. city dweller 城市居民

11. numerous /ˈnjuːmərəs; `njumərəs/ ***adj.*** 很多的

12. county /ˈkaʊnti; `kaʊntɪ/ ***n.*** 县

13. vacancy /ˈveɪkənsi; `vekənsɪ/ ***n.*** 空位；空缺

    In terms of the job market, there are many more ***vacancies*** in cities than in small towns.

    以就业市场来说，都市比小镇提供的就业机会更多。

14. industry /ˈɪndəstri; ˋɪndəstrɪ/ ***n.*** 工业

15. disadvantage /ˌdɪsədˈvɑːntɪdʒ; ˏdɪsədˋvæntɪdʒ/ = drawback ***n.*** 缺点

16. hustle and bustle 忙碌喧闹

I don't like the ***hustle and bustle*** of the city, but I try to get used to the urban lifestyle.

我不喜欢都市的忙碌喧闹，但还是得适应都市的生活方式。

17. concrete jungle 钢筋水泥所构建的丛林

Big cities can be like ***concrete jungles***. 大都市就像钢筋水泥所构建的丛林一般。

18. amenity /əˈmiːnɪti; əˋmɛnətɪ/ ***n.*** 生活设施；便利设施

19. museum /mjuːˈziːəm; mjuˋziəm/ ***n.*** 博物馆

20. gallery /ˈgæləri; ˋgælərɪ/ ***n.*** 画廊

A city should provide plenty of ***amenities*** such as ***museums***, art ***galleries***, theatres and libraries.

城市应该提供充分的生活设施，如博物馆、画廊、剧院及图书馆。

21. concert hall 音乐厅

22. community centre 社区活动中心

23. an abundance of ... 很多的……

There should be ***an abundance of*** parks in a city.

城市里应该有很多公园。

24. vibrant /ˈvaɪbrənt; ˋvaɪbrənt/ ***adj.*** 有活力的；朝气蓬勃的

I prefer to live in a ***vibrant*** city.

我更喜欢住在朝气蓬勃的城市里。

25. high-density accommodation 高密度的住宅

26. claustrophobia /ˌklɔːstrəˈfəʊbiə; ˏklɔstrəˋfobɪə/ ***n.*** 幽闭恐惧（症）

Many city dwellers want to get away from the ***claustrophobia*** of their ***high-density accommodation***.

很多城市居民想要摆脱因高密度住宅环境所产生的幽闭恐惧感。

27. city planning 城市规划

28. venue /ˈvenjuː; ˋvɛnju/ ***n.*** 地方；地点

I hope the city will continue to attract large-scale events and activities here, making itself an internationally known ***venue*** with a good reputation.

我希望这座城市能继续吸引一些大规模的赛事及活动在此举办，使其成为享有国际盛名的地方。

QUESTION DATABASE 题库练习

个人陈述 (Individual Long Turn)

考官 Now please have a look at this card. This is your topic. I want you to describe your favourite city or town in China. You have one minute to prepare.

Describe your favourite city or town in China. You should say:

where it is
how long you have stayed there
in what way it is special or famous
why you like it best.

INSTRUCTIONS

You will be asked to talk about the topic for one to two minutes.
You have one minute to think about what you are going to say.
You can make some notes to help you if you wish.

描述一下在中国你最喜欢的城市或乡镇。你应该谈及：

那个城市或乡镇在哪里
你曾经在那里待了多久
那个地方以什么闻名
你为何喜欢那个地方。

【说明】：

针对这个话题作出一至两分钟的陈述。
你有一分钟的时间去思考你的陈述内容。
假如需要的话，你可以写下要点以帮助你组织陈述。

Sample Response

The city I like best is Beijing, the political and economic centre of China. It's located in northern China. I lived there for about four years when I studied as a university student. In what way is it famous or special? It is famous for its being cosmopolitan and full of vitality and diversity; there is always, always something new and interesting going on in Beijing: book fairs, computer exhibitions, car shows, fashion shows, you name it. I like it best for several reasons. One is that it has some architecturally impressive buildings, for example, the National Stadium and the Palace Museum. Another reason is that it has numerous large book shops where I can always get the books I want.

回答范例

北京是我最喜欢的城市，它是中国的政治、经济中心。它位于中国北方。上大学期间，我曾在那里住了约有四年的时间。北京以什么闻名呢？北京以它是国际化大都市和充满活力与多样性而著称。在那里总是会举办一些新鲜有趣的活动，例如书展、电脑展、车展和时装秀等，你所能想到的展览它都有。我喜欢北京有许多的原因，其中之一，是因为在北京有许多建筑风格令人印象深刻的建筑物，例如国家体育场与故宫博物院。另一个原因是北京有许多大型的书店，在那儿，我总是可以找到我想要的书。

◎ **Where were you originally from?**

My hometown is Zhuhai.

你的家乡在哪里？

我的家乡在珠海。

◎ **Do you prefer to live in a city or a town?**

I am a city dweller. I prefer to live in a city, because there are more jobs available and it's more convenient to live in cities. It's easier to get around when I need, for example, to go shopping, visit friends or see a doctor.

你比较喜欢住在城市还是乡镇?

我是一个城市居民。我更喜欢住在城市，因为在城市有更多的工作机会，而且生活上也比较方便。举例来说吧，当我需要逛街、拜访朋友或看医生的时候，住在城市里会比较方便。

双向讨论 (Two-way Discussion)

◎ **How would you compare your hometown with your favourite city?**

As far as the weather is concerned, Zhuhai is warmer than Beijing. In terms of the job market, there are many more vacancies in Beijing than in Zhuhai. Furthermore, their respective main industries are different. Financial services and commerce are the main industries in Beijing, while shipping and high-tech industry are the primary ones in Zhuhai.

请比较一下你的家乡与你最喜欢的城市。

就天气而言，珠海比北京暖和。以就业市场来说，北京比珠海提供了更多的就业机会。再者，它们各自的主要产业也不同。北京以金融服务及商业为其主要产业，而珠海以船运与高科技工业为其主要产业。

◎ **What are the advantages and disadvantages of living in a city?**

Let me mention the advantages first. It is convenient and there are many shops around. It is also interesting in that it provides all sorts of entertainment and culture, for example, theatres, the latest films and record albums and videos. But I can think of several disadvantages. The hustle and bustle of city life is sometimes hard to bear, and the air is not as fresh as in the countryside. Besides, big cities can be like concrete jungles.

住在城市的优点与缺点是什么？

我先谈谈住在城市的优点。在城市生活很方便，而且到处都有商店。城市的生活也比较有趣，有各式各样的娱乐和文化活动，例如，剧院、最新上映的电影或最新发行的专辑和录影带。但是，我也可以想到一些住在城市的缺点。有时候城市生活的忙碌喧闹实在令人难以忍受。而且，城市的空气不像乡村的空气那样清新。除此之外，大都市就像是钢筋水泥所构建的丛林一样。

◎ **Apart from providing a living environment, what other functions or services do you think a city or town should provide?**

I'd like to point out the following amenities that I think a city should provide. First and foremost, it should supply a good-quality learning environment where educational institutes at all levels meet the needs of its citizens. Another significant service a city should provide is an inexpensive, clean and efficient public transport system. Still another thing it should provide is space for the cultural and artistic dimension of city life, such as museums, art galleries, theatres, concert halls, community centres, book shops and so on. Finally, there should be an abundance of parks where its citizens can exercise or relax when they want to get away from the claustrophobia of their high-density accommodation.

城市或乡镇除了提供人们居住的环境之外，你认为它还应该具备什么其他功能与服务？

我认为一个城市应该具有以下生活设施。首先，它应该提供良好的学习环境，有符合市民需求的各级学校。它应该提供的另一项重要服务就是，一个价廉、干净且高效的公共运输系统。还有，城市应提供都市生活所需的文化、艺术空间，例如，博物馆、画廊、剧院、音乐厅、社区活动中心和书店等。最后，城市里应建有很多公园，当市民想要摆脱因高密度住宅环境所产生的幽闭恐惧感时，他们可以在那里做做运动，放松心情。

◎ **What changes have taken place recently in this city?**

Well, I haven't thought much about this. But now you ask, it occurs to me that this city looks more attractive than it used to. For instance, there are more flowers blooming beside the main roads. Another big change is the commissioning of the city's metro system. Then again, I find this city more vibrant than before in terms of the number of major events hosted here. We see colourful banners hanging on the sides of the major roads here more often than before, and then we know that some major event is being held.

这座城市最近有什么改变吗？

我之前没有想过这个问题，但你这一问，我突然想到，这座城市变得比以前更吸引人了。举例来说，在一些主要道路两旁有更多鲜花盛开。另一个重大的改变，就是地铁系统的建设。还有，就一些重大活动在这里举办的次数来说，我发现这座城市变得比以前更具活力。我们比以前更常看到一些五颜六色的旗帜飘扬在主要道路旁，然后我们就知道又有重大活动要在这举办了。

◎ **What do you think of these changes?**

I certainly see them as a positive sign, because they contribute to the image of the city as constantly changing, developing, convenient, pleasant and full of vitality.

谈谈你对这些改变的看法？

当然，我认为这些改变是正面的，因为这些都有助于塑造这座城市的形象：不断地改变和发展，便利、宜人且充满活力。

◎ **In what direction do you expect the city to develop in the future?**

I am not an expert in city planning, but as a citizen, I would hope to see it further developing its strength as a seaport and, at the same time, making itself an internationally known venue with a good reputation. Then again, while the local economy will remain prosperous, I hope the city will continue to attract large-scale events or activities here, whether cultural or sporting.

你期待这座城市未来朝什么方向发展？

我并不是城市规划专家，但身为市民，我希望这座城市未来能进一步发挥优势，发展成为一个港口都市，同时也发展成为一个享有国际盛名的地方。此外，当地方经济持续繁荣的同时，我希望这座城市能继续吸引一些大规模活动在此举办，不论是文化还是运动方面的。

Architecture

建筑

USEFUL EXPRESSIONS 实用表达

1. take a walk 散步

   I enjoy ***talking a walk*** in a park near my home.

   我喜欢在我家附近的公园散步。

2. square /skweə; skwɛr/ ***n.*** 广场

3. be adjacent to … 紧邻……

4. pursue outdoor activities 从事户外活动

   People of all ages like to ***pursue*** their ***outdoor activities*** in a ***square adjacent to*** the memorial hall.

   不论老少都喜欢到邻近纪念堂的广场从事户外活动。

5. inspiring /ɪn'spaɪərɪŋ; ɪn`spaɪrɪŋ/ ***adj.*** 激发灵感的

6. the traditional architectural style 传统建筑风格

7. be pleasing to look at 赏心悦目

   The traditional Chinese ***architectural style*** is ***inspiring*** and ***pleasing to look at***.

   中国传统建筑风格不仅能激发人的灵感，而且看起来赏心悦目。

8. be well constructed and maintained （建筑物）建造及维护都做得好

9. spacious /'speɪʃəs; `speʃəs/ ***adj.*** 广阔的

   Whenever I need a place to walk, reflect or even to go jogging, I go there; it's ***spacious***.

   无论何时我需要一个可以散步、沉思甚至是慢跑的地方，我都会去那儿，那里十分广阔。

10. musical performance 音乐表演

11. stage production 舞台表演

12. impressive /ɪm'presɪv; ɪm`prɛsɪv/ ***adj.*** 给人深刻印象的

    The Palace Museum is ***impressive***.

    故宫博物院令人印象深刻。

13. impress /ɪm'pres; ɪm`prɛs/ *v.* 给（人）印象深刻
The Palace Museum ***impresses*** me most.
故宫博物院最令我印象深刻。

14. elegant /'eləgənt; `ɛləgənt/ *adj.* 高雅的，优雅的

15. well-proportioned *adj.* 比例均衡的

16. imposing /ɪm'pəʊzɪŋ; ɪm`pozɪŋ/ *adj.* 庄严的

17. ponderous /'pɒndərəs; `pɑndərəs/ *adj.* 沉闷的；笨重的
The building looks ***elegant***, ***well-proportioned*** and ***imposing***, without being ***ponderous***.
这栋建筑物看起来高雅、比例均衡且庄严，但并不沉闷。

18. aesthetic /iːs'θetɪk; ɛs`θɛtɪk/ *adj.* 美学的

19. superb /sjuː'pɜːb; sʊ`pɝb/ *adj.* 一流的，上乘的
The ***aesthetic*** concept of the building, both inside and outside, is ***superb***.
这栋建筑物的美学概念，不论是内部或外观，皆是上乘。

20. of historical interest and value 有历史价值的
The Palace Museum houses things ***of*** national and ***historical interest and value***.
故宫博物院保存了具有民族和历史价值的物品。

21. modernist /'mɒdənɪst; `mɑdɚnɪst/ *adj.* 现代主义的

22. low-rise *adj.* 低层的

23. high-rise *adj.* 高层的，高耸的
The architectural styles here are quite a combination: ***modernist***, Western ***low-rise*** and ***high-rise*** and traditional Chinese.
这里的建筑风格将现代风格、西方低层和高层式及传统中式融为一体。

24. Buddhist temple 佛教寺院
Buddhist temples are mostly constructed in the traditional Chinese style.
佛教寺院大多是依照传统中国建筑风格去建造的。

25. storey /'stɔːri; `storɪ/ *n.* 楼层
When I was a child, most houses in the city were only three or four ***storeys*** high.
我小的时候，城里大部分的房子只有三四层楼高。

26. facade /fə'sɑːd; fə`sɑd/ *n.* （尤指大型或重要建筑物的）正面
Sometimes the ***facades*** of modern buildings are almost a work of art!
有时候现代建筑物从正面看几乎就是一件艺术品。

27. skyline /'skaɪlaɪn; `skaɪ,laɪn/ ***n.*** （山或建筑物在天空映衬下的）轮廓线

28. the street frontages 街道的门面，临街店铺

Both the ***skyline*** and ***the street frontages*** of the city are more diversified than ever before.

这个城市的空中轮廓线和街道的门面比以前更多样化。

29. a sure sign that +从句 无疑是象征着……

These changes are ***a sure sign that*** China is continuing to develop its economy and becoming more prosperous than ever.

这些改变无疑象征着中国的经济正不断地发展，并且比以前更繁荣。

30. accommodation /ə,kɒmə'deɪʃən; ə,kɑmə`deʃən/ ***n.*** 住宅；住宿

31. out of fashion 不再时兴

Low-rise flats are usually about five storeys high, but they are going ***out of fashion***.

低层公寓通常只有五层楼，而且已渐渐地不时兴了。

32. low-rise flat 低层公寓

33. high-rise flat 高层公寓

34. terraced house 整排式的房屋中的一栋房屋

35. high-rise office building 高层办公大楼

36. factory /'fæktəri; `fæktrɪ/ ***n.*** 工厂

37. religious institution 宗教机构

38. household /'haʊshəʊld; `haʊs,hold/ ***n.*** 户，一家人

39. accommodate /ə'kɒmədeɪt; ə`kɑmə,det/ ***v.*** 为……提供住处；容纳

A block of ***high-rise flats*** can ***accommodate*** as many as 200 ***households***.

一街区的高层公寓可以住下 200 户人家。

40. be popular with sb. 受某人的欢迎

41. resident /'rezədənt; `rɛzədənt/ ***n.*** 居民

42. the ground floor 一楼（注：英式用法；the first floor 指“二楼”）

As for terraced houses, they ***are popular with residents*** who run businesses on ***the ground floor***.

至于排屋，很受在一楼做生意的居民欢迎。

43. bungalow /'bʌŋgələʊ; `bʌŋgə,lo/ ***n.*** 平房

Some of the houses you see in the countryside are ***bungalows***.

你在乡下看到的房子，有些是平房。

44. farmhouse /'fɑːmhaʊs; `fɑrm,haʊs/ ***n.*** 农舍

45. detached house 独门独户的房子

46. villa /'vɪlə; `vɪlə/ ***n.*** 别墅

Most ***villas*** are ***detached houses***.

大部分的别墅都是独门独户的房子。

47. in a positive direction 朝积极的、建设性的方向

I hope the city will develop ***in*** a number of ***positive directions***.

我希望这个城市能朝着多方面积极的、建设性的方向发展。

48. unsightly /ʌn'saɪtli; ʌn`saɪtlɪ/ ***adj.*** 有碍观瞻的

49. storefront sign 店面的招牌

There are so many ***unsightly storefront signs*** here.

这里有这么多有碍观瞻的店面招牌。

50. jumble /'dʒʌmbəl; `dʒʌmbl̩/ ***n.*** 杂乱

51. be aligned with one another 相互对齐

If storefront signs could ***be*** better ***aligned with one another***, at least on the same block, the city streets would look less of a ***jumble*** and more of a unified vision.

如果招牌能排列得更整齐，至少是在同一街区，街道看起来就不会那么杂乱，会更整齐划一。

52. take account of 考虑

53. pedestrian /pɪ'destriən; pə`dɛstrɪən/ ***n.*** 行人

54. walkway /'wɔːkweɪ; `wɔk,we/ ***n.***; sidewalk /'saɪdwɔːk; `saɪd,wɔk/ ***n.*** 走道；人行道

More ***account*** should be ***taken of*** the ***pedestrian*** and his or her needs. Sometimes, I can't find a clear ***walkway*** or ***sidewalk*** anywhere.

应该多多顾虑到行人的需求，有时候我根本找不到一条畅通的人行道。

55. urban sprawl 城市开发

It's necessary to leave much more open space for parks and trees despite the general ***urban sprawl***.

纵然有普遍的城市开发，保留更多的空间给公园和树木还是必要的。

56. stroll /strəʊl; strol/ ***v.*** 漫步

I hope that someday ***strolling*** in the city will be as enjoyable as walking in Edinburgh or Paris.

我盼望有一天在这座城市散步，能像在爱丁堡或巴黎一样愉悦。

QUESTION DATABASE 题库练习

个人陈述 (Individual Long Turn)

考官 Now please have a look at this card. This is your topic. I want you to talk about a place that you enjoy visiting. You have one minute to prepare.

Talk about a place that you enjoy visiting. You should say:

what it is
where it is
when you last visited it
why you like to go there.

INSTRUCTIONS

You will be asked to talk about the topic for one to two minutes.
You have one minute to think about what you are going to say.
You can make some notes to help you if you wish.

请谈谈一个你喜欢逗留的地方，你应该谈到：

这是什么地方
它的地理位置
你最后一次去是在什么时候
为什么你喜欢去那里。

【说明】：

针对这个话题作出一至两分钟的陈述。
你有一分钟的时间去思考你的陈述内容。
假如需要的话，你可以写下要点以帮助你组织陈述。

Sample Response

I'd like to tell you about a memorial hall in this city; it's a place where I enjoy spending time. It's located in Zhongxin District. I went there last weekend. After doing some reading in the Central Library last Saturday, I walked across the street and took a walk there. There's a large square and a park adjacent to it and people of all ages like to pursue their outdoor activities there. Why do I like to go there? Well, there are several reasons. First and foremost, I find the building inspiring; its traditional Chinese architectural style is pleasing to look at and it's well constructed and maintained. And then whenever I need a place to walk, reflect or even to go jogging, I go there, because it's really spacious and pleasant around the hall. Last but not least, thinking of the inside of the place, I sometimes attend a musical performance or one of the stage productions held there.

回答范例

我想谈的是本市的一座纪念堂，我喜欢在那儿消磨时间，它位于中新区。上周末我去过那儿。上周六在中央图书馆看完书之后，我便穿过马路，到那里散步。纪念堂旁边有一个很大的广场和公园，不论老少都喜欢到那儿从事户外活动。为什么我喜欢去那里？有几个原因。第一，也是最重要的，我发觉这栋建筑能启发人的灵感，它传统的中国建筑风格看起来赏心悦目，而且建造和维护都做得十分好。并且无论何时我需要一个可以散步、沉思甚至是慢跑的地方，我都会去那儿，因为在纪念堂周围，有广阔、怡人的空间。最后也很重要的一点与它的内部功能有关，我有时候会到那里欣赏音乐会或舞台表演。

◎ **With whom do you usually go there?**

Usually I go there with my friends, but sometimes just by myself.

你通常是和谁去那里？

我通常都是和朋友一起去的，但是有时候只是自己一个人。

双向讨论 (Two-way Discussion)

◎ **Now, let's talk about architecture. What do you think is the most impressive building in this country?**

As far as I am concerned, the Palace Museum impresses me most. Its architectural style is traditional Chinese. It looks really elegant, well-proportioned and imposing, without being ponderous. Also, the aesthetic concept of the building, both inside and out, is superb. Then again, it has a hill for its background. Such a setting is just right for a building which houses things of national and historical interest and value.

现在，让我们来谈谈建筑吧。在这个国家，你认为哪一栋建筑物让你印象最深刻?

就我而言，故宫博物院令我印象最深，它采用了中国传统的建筑风格，看起来高雅、比例均衡，庄严但并不沉闷。并且，它的美学概念，不论是内部或外观，皆是上乘的。此外，它以山为背景，这样的景致正适合这种保存了具有民族和历史价值的物品的建筑物。

◎ **How do you characterize the architectural styles of the building in this country?**

Architectural styles? Good Lord! Well, I can offer you only my very, very general impressions. The architectural styles here are quite a combination: modernist, Western low-rise and high-rise, traditional Chinese and so on. For example, Buddhist temples are mostly constructed in the traditional Chinese style. KTV shops and hotels are mostly built in a modernist style. They are quite a contrast to our traditional style. Anyway, that's how I see the architectural styles here.

你觉得这个国家的建筑风格有何特征?

建筑风格？天啊！好吧，我只能告诉你我非常、非常笼统的印象。这里的建筑风格融合了现代风格、西式低层式和高楼式及传统中式等。举例来说，佛教寺院大多是按照传统中国建筑风格建造的。KTV 和旅馆大都是依现代建筑风格建造的，这些跟我们的传统建筑形成了鲜明对比。不管怎样，这是我对在这儿所看到的建筑风格的看法。

◎ **Do you think the skyline of this city has changed?**

Oh, yes, certainly. There are many more high-rises nowadays. When I was a child, most houses in the city were only three or four storeys high. But now there are even skyscrapers. Then again, I've noticed that builders and housing developers now pay more attention to the designs of the buildings they want to construct. Sometimes the facades of modern buildings are almost a work of art! But generally, buildings have got a lot higher than they used to be. So both the skyline and the street frontages of the city are more diversified than ever before.

你觉得这个城市的空中轮廓线有什么改变吗？

哦，当然有。现在有更多高楼大厦了。我还小的时候，这个城市大部分的房子都只有三四层楼高，但是现在甚至还有摩天大楼。再者，我注意到现在的房屋建筑商和开发商更注重建筑设计。有时候现代建筑从正面看几乎就是一件艺术品！但大体来说，建筑物已经比以前要高得多，所以城市的空中轮廓线和街道的门面比以前更多样了。

◎ **What do you think of the change?**

It's inevitable. These changes are a sure sign that China is continuing to develop its economy and becoming more prosperous than ever. Also, China's population is increasing. As you know, it would be a waste of valuable land to build just low-rise buildings covering a large area of land.

你对于这样的改变有何看法？

这是无法避免的。这些改变无疑表明中国的经济正在不断发展，并且比以前更繁荣。还有，中国的人口在不断增长。正如你所知，如果只建造低层公寓的话，就需要大面积占地，将会浪费珍贵的土地。

◎ **Let's move on and talk about types of accommodation. What are the major types of building in this country?**

The major types of building? Hum, well, there are low-rise flats and high-rise flats, terraced houses, low and high-rise office buildings, factories, temples, religious institutions, schools and colleges, farm buildings and so on. Low-rise flats are usually about five storeys high, but they are going out of fashion. High-rises are quite common these days. A block of high-rise flats can accommodate as many as 200 households. As for terraced houses, well, they are popular with residents who run businesses on the ground floor.

让我们继续谈谈住宅的样式吧，这个国家的主要建筑样式是什么？

主要的建筑样式？嗯，有低层及高层公寓、排房、低层或高层的办公大楼、工厂、寺庙、宗教建筑、学校或学院以及农舍等等。低层公寓通常只有五层楼高，但是快不时兴了，现在高楼已经相当普遍。一个由高楼组成的街区大约可以住 200 户人家。至于排屋，嗯，很受在一楼做生意的居民欢迎。

◎ **Are they different from the dominant types of building you see in the countryside?**

Yes, I think so. In some parts of the Chinese countryside, most of the houses you see are bungalows. Another difference is that in some areas, there are many farmhouses. They are detached houses and each one has its own unique design. They really look lovely. In fact, they look more like villas than what I think of as farmhouses with farmers and animals and farming implements and so on. That's peculiar, isn't it?

这些建筑和你在乡下看到的主要建筑样式有不同的地方吗？

是的，我想是这样。中国乡下的某些地方，你所见的大部分房子都是平房。另一个不同点是，在一些地区，有很多农舍。它们都是独门独户，并且每一户都有其独特的设计，看起来真的很可爱。事实上，这比我原先所想的那种有农夫、动物和农具等的农舍，看起来更像别墅。那真的是很奇特，不是吗？

◎ **In what directions do you expect this city to develop?**

Hum … this is an interesting question. As a citizen here, I hope that the city will develop in a number of positive directions. First and foremost, the appearance of the city streets could be more pleasing. For example, there are so many unsightly storefront signs. If they could be designed more imaginatively and better aligned with one another, at least on the same block, the city streets would look less of a jumble and more of a unified vision. Then again, more account should be taken of the pedestrian and his or her needs. Sometimes, I can't find a clear walkway or sidewalk anywhere, because they are all occupied by motorcycles. Hmm, yes, finally, it's necessary to leave much more open space for parks and trees despite the general urban sprawl. I hope that someday strolling in the city will be as enjoyable as walking in Edinburgh or Paris.

你期望这座城市往哪一方向发展？

噢，这是一个很有趣的问题。身为本地的市民，我希望这座城市能朝多方面积极的、有建设性的方向发展。第一，也是最重要的，城市的市容市貌可以更宜人。例如，这里有这么多有碍观瞻的店面招牌，如果能运用更丰富的想象力将其设计一番，而且排列得更整齐，至少在同一个街区，街道看起来不会那么杂乱，会更整齐划一。再者，应该多考虑到行人的需求，有时候我根本找不到一条畅通的人行道，因为它们都被机车给霸占了。嗯，对了，最后，纵然有普遍的城市开发，保留更多的空间给公园和树木还是必要的，我盼望有一天在这座城市散步，能像在爱丁堡或巴黎一样愉悦。

Chapter 3

考试第二、三部分题库：各类话题说不停

综合分类

6. 交通篇 (Transportation)

Traffic and Transport

交通与运输

USEFUL EXPRESSIONS 实用表达

1. a means of transport 一种交通工具
2. scooter /'skuːtə; `skutɚ/ *n.* 小型摩托车
   My ***scooter*** is ***a means of transport*** I use regularly.
   我的小型摩托车是我经常使用的一种交通工具。
3. motorcycle /'məʊtəˌsaikəl; `motɚˌsaɪkl̩/ *n.* 摩托车
4. go somewhere 前往某地
5. put my helmet on 戴上我的安全帽
   Whenever I need to ***go somewhere*** in the city, all I have to do is to walk a few yards outside my front door, ***put my helmet on***, start the engine, and off I go.
   不管什么时候，当我需要前往城市里的某地时，我需要做的就是走出大门几步，戴上安全帽，发动引擎，然后出发。
6. traffic congestion 交通拥堵
   Being on two wheels is not so affected by ***traffic congestion***.
   交通拥堵对骑摩托车而言，影响不大。
7. parking space 一个停车位
   It can be very difficult to find a ***parking space*** in a city centre if you drive.
   假如你开车的话，那么在市中心很难找到一个停车位。
8. cosy /'kəʊzi; `kozɪ/ *adj.* 温暖舒适的
   Riding a scooter is not so ***cosy*** as driving a car or sitting in a bus.
   骑小型摩托车不像开车或搭乘公车那样温暖舒适。
9. put up with the weather 承受天气的变化
   If you ride a motorcycle, you have to ***put up with the weather***.
   假如你骑摩托车，就必须能承受天气的变化。

10. go on a long journey　长途旅行

When I have to ***go on*** quite ***a long journey***, I usually take a train.

当我需要进行长途旅行时，通常会搭乘火车。

11. coach /kəʊtʃ; kotʃ/ ***n.*** 长途巴士

12. public transport　公共交通工具；大众运输

I think ***public transport*** here still leaves something to be desired.

我认为这里的公共交通仍然有很大的改进空间。

13. run /rʌn/ ***v.*** 行驶

Buses and trains ***run*** more frequently than before.

公共汽车和火车的班次比以前更多。

14. bus route　公车路线

There are more ***bus routes*** these days.

现在公共汽车有了更多不同的行驶路线。

15. metro /ˈmetrəu; ˋmɛtro/ ***n.*** 地铁系统

16. handy /ˈhændi; ˋhændɪ/ ***adj.*** 便利的；有用的

When I was studying in Beijing, I took the ***metro*** quite often and I found it really ***handy***.

当我在北京念书时，我时常搭乘地铁，觉得它实在是很便利。

17. vehicle /ˈviːɪkəl; ˋviɪkl̩/ ***n.*** 车辆

18. traffic density　交通密度

19. knock-on effect　间接的效果

20. make the traffic flow　使交通畅通

An efficient public transport system reduces ***traffic density***, which has the ***knock-on effect*** of ***making the*** remaining ***traffic flow*** more easily.

高效的公共运输系统能降低交通密度，从而间接使交通更为畅通。

21. polluting /pəˈluːtɪŋ; pəˋlutɪŋ/ ***adj.*** 污染的

22. exhaust emission　排放废气

Public transport is less ***polluting***, both in terms of noise and of ***exhaust emission***, than private transport.

公共交通工具不管是在噪音制造还是在废气的排放上，都比私人交通工具的污染少。

23. stand in a queue　排队

You may have to put up with ***standing in a queue*** when waiting for your bus to come.

等公共汽车时，你可能得忍受排队之苦。

24. squash up amongst others　跟别人挤在一起

25. at peak hour(s); at rush hour(s)　在高峰时段

You may have to ***squash up amongst others***, especially ***at peak hours***.

你可能必须跟别人挤在一起，特别是在高峰时段。

26. traffic jam　交通阻塞；塞车

I suppose some ***traffic jams*** are inevitable at those times.

我想在那些时段出现交通阻塞的情形是无可避免的。

27. road conditions　路况

The ***road conditions*** have improved a lot.

路况已经改善很多。

28. intolerable air and noise pollution　令人难以忍受的空气及噪音污染

Too many vehicles on the roads lead to traffic jams and ***intolerable air and noise pollution***.

路上太多的车辆会导致塞车和令人难以忍受的空气及噪音污染。

29. be subsidized　受到补贴

Public transport needs to ***be*** adequately ***subsidized***.

公共交通需要得到充分的补贴。

30. parking lot　停车场

More public ***parking lots*** should be built.

应该开辟更多的公共停车场。

31. traffic slows to a crawl　车流缓慢

Traffic slows to a crawl because drivers are looking for spaces to park their cars.

车流缓慢是因驾驶者都在寻找停车位。

32. park illegally　违规停车

When some drivers fail to find a space, they get so frustrated that they just park side by side with other cars already there on the roadside; they just ***park illegally***.

当有些司机无法找到停车位时，他们会因此泄气，于是就在路旁并排停车，而那是违规停车。

33. snarl things up　让情况更糟

34. block the roads　堵住道路

Those drivers who park illegally ***snarl things up*** and ***block the roads***.

那些违规停车的司机会让情况更糟，而且还堵住了道路。

35. stricter penalty　更严苛的处罚

36. infringement of the highway code　不遵守交通规则

One solution to the increasing number of accidents might be ***stricter penalties*** such as heavy fines for ***infringements of the highway code***.

解决车祸频发的一个方法可以是更严苛的处罚，如不遵守交通规则就处以高额罚款。

37. drunken driving = drunk driving　酒后驾车

38. speeding /'spiːdɪŋ; `spidɪŋ/ ***n.***　超速；开快车

Many accidents are caused by ***drunken driving*** and ***speeding***.

许多事故都是由酒后驾车或超速造成的。

39. one's license is suspended　驾驶执照被吊销

In many countries, if someone is caught driving with alcohol in his blood-stream, ***his license is suspended*** for a good long time.

在许多国家，假如一个人被测出开车时血液里含酒精的话，他的驾驶执照就会被吊销很长一段时间。

40. traffic-calming measure　确保交通安全的措施

41. speed bump　路面减速带

42. built-up area　居民密集之处

Traffic-calming measures such as ***speed bumps*** can slow traffic down, so they can be deployed to discourage drivers with a tendency to speed up in ***built-up areas***.

减速带等确保交通安全的措施可以使车速慢下来，所以可以被用于降低驾驶员在人口密集区加速的可能性。

43. vehicle maintenance　车辆的维修保养

44. unroadworthy vehicle　不适合上路的车子（即车况不佳的车子）

QUESTION DATABASE 题库练习

个人陈述 (Individual Long Turn)

考官 Now please have a look at this card. This is your topic. I want you to describe a means of transport you use often. You have one minute to prepare.

Describe a means of transport you use often. You should say:

what it is
how often you use it
how you like it
what you think of it.

INSTRUCTIONS

You will be asked to talk about the topic for one to two minutes.
You have one minute to think about what you are going to say.
You can make some notes to help you if you wish.

描述一种你经常使用的交通工具。你应该谈到：

它是何种交通工具
它的使用频率如何
你对它的喜爱程度
你对这种交通工具有何看法。

【说明】：

针对这个话题作出一至两分钟的陈述。
你有一分钟的时间去思考你的陈述内容。
假如需要的话，你可以写下要点以帮助你组织陈述。

Sample Response

I am going to tell you about my scooter—a means of transport I use quite regularly. I use it almost every day when I go to work or when I go shopping or in fact whenever I need to travel further than a reasonable walking distance. I don't particularly like my scooter, because of its noise and smell, but it gets me from A to B well enough. Whenever I need to go somewhere in the city, all I have to do is walk a few yards outside my front door, put my helmet on, start the engine, and off I go. What do I think of it? It's cheap to run, and I'm able to get where I want to go quickly enough, because being on two wheels, one's not so affected by traffic congestion. Then again, it's easy to find a place to park. As you know, if you drive a car, it can be very difficult to find a parking space in a city centre. So the scooter is a practical solution to my needs. On the other hand, riding a scooter is not so cosy as driving a car or sitting in a bus, because, well ... you have to put up with the weather, whether it's hot or cold or whether it's raining. Anyway, despite the relative discomfort of riding a scooter, I'm quite content to use it and will continue to do so until I can afford a car.

回答范例

我将谈谈我的小型摩托车——一种我经常使用的交通工具。几乎每天买东西或去上班时，我都会用到它，事实上只要是超出一定步行路程的目的地，我都会骑摩托车去。但因为它的噪音和难闻的气味，我并不是特别喜爱骑摩托车，不过它已足够能使我从甲地到乙地。不管什么时候，当我需要前往市里的某地时，我需要做的就是走出大门几步，戴上安全帽，发动引擎，然后出发。对它的看法如何？骑乘摩托车的开销少，并且能很快到达我想要去的地方，因为它体型小、轻巧，更不容易受到交通拥堵的影响。再者，我也能很轻易找到一个停车位。你看，假如开车的话，在市中心就很难找到停车位。所以小型摩托车对我来说是一种合乎需求的实用出行方式。但另一方面，骑摩托车并不像开车或搭乘公车那样温暖舒适，因为假如你骑摩托车，就必须要承受天气的变化，不管是酷热、严寒或下雨。不管怎么样，尽管骑乘小型摩托车有不舒适的方面，但直到我能买得起汽车之前，能有辆小型摩托车骑，我感到相当知足，并会继续使用这种交通工具。

◎ **Do you use any other means of transport?**

Yes, but only when I have to go on quite a long journey, for example when I need to go to another town or city.

你使用其他的交通工具吗?

是的，但只有在我必须进行长途旅行时，例如，当我需要前往另一个乡镇或城市时。

◎ **How about when you were a student?**

When I was a student, I used to ride a bicycle or take a bus, but now I prefer to ride my scooter.

在学生时代，你选择何种交通方式?

当我是学生时，我习惯骑自行车或搭乘公共汽车，但我现在比较喜欢骑小型摩托车。

双向讨论 (Two-way Discussion)

◎ **Right! What do you think of the public transport of this city?**

It's much better and more convenient than it used to be, because buses run more frequently than before. Also, there are more bus routes these days. However, I think public transport here still leaves something to be desired. When I was studying in Beijing, I took the metro quite often and I found it really handy. But we don't have metro in this city. It's a pity.

那么，你对这座城市的公共交通有何看法？

因为公共汽车比以前的班次多了，所以比以前好并且还便利很多，而且现在公共汽车行驶的路线比以前更多。然而我认为这里的公共交通还有很大的改进空间。我在北京念书时，时常搭乘地铁，觉得它实在是很便利，但这个城市并没有地铁，真是可惜。

◎ **What are the advantages and disadvantages of using public transport?**

Let me talk about the advantages first. It helps reduce the number of private vehicles on the road. So an efficient public transport system reduces traffic density, which has the knock-on effect of making the remaining traffic flow more easily. Another good thing I can think of is that ... it is a much cheaper means of transport than private ownership of a vehicle, at least for the individual. Then again, it is less polluting, both in terms of noise and of exhaust emission, than private transport. As to its disadvantages, well, I'd like to point out several things. First of all, it's not always comfortable or even convenient. You may have to put up with standing in a queue, or squash up amongst others, especially at peak hours. Another disadvantage is that you will often have to wait. And if you are in a hurry and have to wait, you will probably feel very restless and frustrated. This is my experience, anyway.

使用公共交通工具有何优缺点?

让我先谈谈优点。它有助于减少私人交通工具的流量。高效的公共交通能减小交通密度，从而间接使交通更为畅通。另一点我能想到的好处是……至少对个人来说它是一种比拥有一部私人轿车花费更低廉的交通方式。还有，搭乘公共交通工具不管在噪音制造或废气排放上，都比私人交通工具的污染少。至于它的缺点，我有几项要指出。首先，公共交通工具并不总是舒适的，甚至也不总是便利的。你可能得忍受排队之苦，或要跟别人挤在一块儿，特别是在高峰时段；另一项缺点是，你要经常去等待，如果你在赶时间又总等不到车，就可能会感到慌张又沮丧。但不管怎么说，这只是我的经验罢了。

◎ **How about the traffic in this city?**

The traffic in this city? Well, it's not bad. At rush hours, of course, it can be a bit of a nightmare; I suppose some traffic jams are inevitable at those times. Then again, traffic nowadays is certainly heavier than, say, ten years ago, but generally speaking it's still OK because the road conditions have improved a lot during the same period. During times other than peak hours, it generally runs pretty smoothly.

这座城市的交通状况如何?

这座城市的交通状况？噢……并不算很糟。在高峰时段，当然也会出现点儿噩梦般的糟糕状况，但我想在那个时段有一些交通堵塞是无可避免的。不过，今日的交通的确是比例如十年前的时候更拥挤了，但因为路况已经改善很多，所以大体而言，交通情况还可以，在高峰时段以外的时间，交通还是比较顺畅的。

◎ **Do you think it will be necessary to control the increase in numbers of vehicles?**

Yes, I certainly think so. Too many vehicles on the roads lead to traffic jams and intolerable air and noise pollution. So it's sensible to do something about the ever-increasing number of vehicles. For example, one measure the Japanese have taken is that if you want to purchase a car there, you have to prove that you have your own parking space. That's one possible solution to the problem.

你认为有必要去控制车辆数目的增加吗？
是的，我的确同意控制车辆数目的增加。太多的车辆在路上会导致塞车和令人难以忍受的空气及噪音污染。所以对日益激增的车辆采取一些应对之道是明智之举。例如，在日本采用的一种办法是，当你要买车时，你必须证明有个人的停车位。这便是一种可行之道。

◎ **How might the traffic conditions in this city be improved?**

First and foremost, public transport needs to be adequately subsidized. If it's convenient and cheap, more people will use it frequently. Then again, more public parking lots should be built. As you know, traffic slows to a crawl because drivers are looking for spaces to park their cars. Then when they fail to find a space, they get so frustrated that they just park side by side with other cars already there on the roadside; they just park illegally. As a result, you see, they really snarl things up and block the roads. Well, some offending vehicles are even towed away.

如何改善这座城市的交通情况呢？
首先，公共交通需要得到充分的补贴。假如它既方便又便宜的话，那么就会有更多的人更多地使用公共交通工具。再来是要设立更多的公共停车位。要知道，车流之所以缓慢，就是因为驾驶人在寻找停车位，然后当有些司机无法找到停车位时，他们会非常泄气，于是就在路旁并排停车，但那是违规停车。结果你看这些驾驶人只是把事情弄得更糟，而且还堵住了道路。其中一些违规停放的车辆甚至会被拖车拖走。

◎ **Injuries and fatalities caused by road accidents are increasing almost everywhere. What suggestions would you make that could reduce the number of accidents?**

One solution might be stricter penalties such as heavy fines for infringements of the highway code. As you know, many accidents are caused by drunken driving and speeding. Such inconsiderate drivers will just have to be shown that society will not tolerate such behaviour. In many countries, if someone is caught driving with alcohol in his blood-stream, his license is suspended for a good long time. I think it's a good idea. Hmm ... then again, traffic-calming measures such as speed bumps can slow traffic down, so they can be deployed to discourage drivers with a tendency to speed in built-up areas. This is another solution. Last but not least, regular vehicle maintenance is necessary. This would reduce the number of unroadworthy vehicles. Well, these are my recommendations.

各地因为交通事故引起的伤亡人数几乎都在不断地增加，你对减少意外事故有什么建议吗?

更严苛的处罚也许是一个办法，如：不遵守交通规则就处以高额罚款。你知道，许多意外事故都是由酒后驾车或超速造成的，像这样不顾及别人的驾驶员，应该让他们知道社会是不会容许这样的行为的。在许多国家，假如一个人被测出驾车时血液里含有酒精的话，他的驾驶执照就会被吊销很长一段时间。我认为那是一个不错的办法。此外，减速带等确保交通安全的措施可以使车速慢下来，所以可以被用于降低驾驶员在人口密集区加速的可能性，这又是另一个办法。最后不容忽视的一点是，定期的车辆保养是必要的，这样就可减少路上车况不佳的车辆的数目。这些便是我的几项建议。

Chapter 3

考试第二、三部分题库：各类话题说不停

综合分类

7. 教育篇 (Education)

Language

语言

USEFUL EXPRESSIONS 实用表达

1. pick up English 学英语
   Children can naturally ***pick up*** some ***English*** by singing and playing games.
   小孩能很自然地通过唱歌及玩游戏学会英语。
2. rewarding /rɪ'wɔːdɪŋ; rɪ`wɔrdɪŋ/ ***adj.*** 值得的，有意义的
   On the whole, I would say my experience of learning English is enjoyable and ***rewarding*** although I sometimes feel frustrated.
   尽管有时会有挫折感，但整体而言，我学习英语的经历是快乐并且有意义的。
3. regional accent 地方口音
   You have to get used to so many ***regional accents*** when learning English.
   在学习英语的过程中，你必须适应多种地方口音。
4. overcome /ˌəʊvə'kʌm; ˏovə`kʌm/ ***v.*** 克服
5. idiom /'ɪdiəm; `ɪdɪəm/ ***n.*** 习语，成语
   There are so many difficulties to ***overcome*** when you learn a foreign language. For example, we have to discover the unpredictable meanings of English ***idioms***.
   当你学一门外语时，会有许多困难必须去克服。举例来说，我们必须找出英文习语难以捉摸的含义。
6. pronounce /prə'naʊns; prə`naʊns/ ***v.*** 发音
7. pronunciation /prəˌnʌnsi'eɪʃən; prəˏnʌnsɪ`eʃən/ ***n.*** 发音
   There's the irritating fact of the ***pronunciation*** not always following the spelling.
   一个恼人的事实是发音与拼写方式往往不一致。
8. linguistic /lɪŋ'gwɪstɪk; lɪŋ`gwɪstɪk/ ***adj.*** 语言的；语言学的
   The ***linguistic*** skill I need to develop is my oral English.
   我需要加强的语言技能是我的英语口语能力。

9. be proficient in … 精通……，熟谙……

In order to do well in my IELTS test, I want to become ***proficient in*** all four aspects of language: listening, speaking, reading and writing.

为了在雅思考试中取得好成绩，我想要在听、说、读、写四方面都能够精通。

10. vocabulary /vəˈkæbjʊləri; vəˋkæbjəˌlɛrɪ/ ***n.*** 词汇

My ***vocabulary*** is not large enough.

我的词汇量并不够大。

11. acquire a language 习得一种语言

12. acquisition /ˌækwɪˈzɪʃən; ˌækwəˋzɪʃən/ ***n.*** 习得；获得

Vocabulary is essential to the development and ***acquisition*** of a foreign language.

词汇在外语的进步及习得过程里是不可或缺的。

13. adopt a variety of approaches 采取各种途径

A language learner should ***adopt a variety of approaches*** when trying to improve the various aspects of her skill in a particular language.

当语言学习者试着去加强在语言上的各方面能力时，有必要采用各种方法。

14. speech rhythm 说话节奏，语调

I practise speaking English with all my friends, and I read newspaper articles aloud to develop my ***speech rhythm*** and my fluency in speaking.

我和所有的朋友练习讲英语，并诵读英文报纸，为的是改善我的讲话节奏，提高流利程度。

15. read widely and intensively 泛读和精读相结合

I ***read widely and intensively*** to improve my reading comprehension and my reading rate.

我将泛读和精读结合起来，是为了提高阅读理解能力，加快阅读速度。

16. diction /ˈdɪkʃən; ˋdɪkʃən/ ***n.*** 措辞，用词

I read model essays carefully and analyze the elements of good writing such as ***diction***, organization, sentence variety and transitional words.

我会仔细阅读范文，并分析好文章的组成因素，例如遣词、组织、句型变化及转折承接词。

17. target language 目标语言

It's a good idea for children to learn a foreign language by introducing them as early as possible to an environment where the ***target language*** alone is spoken.

尽早引导孩子在全外语环境里去学习某门外语，是非常好的主意。

18. daunting /ˈdɔːntɪŋ; `dɔntɪŋ/ ***adj.*** 令人畏惧的

19. mother tongue 母语

Adult students at the beginner level might find it really ***daunting*** to have to speak in a situation where their ***mother tongue*** is not spoken at all.

那些属于基础级的成人学习者可能会觉得，在无母语掺杂的情况下开口说英文是非常吓人的。

20. heterogeneous /ˌhetərəʊˈdʒiːniəs; ˌhɛtərə`dʒinɪəs/ ***adj.*** 混杂的；不同质的

21. a ... lot ……的一群（注：口语用法）

Generally speaking, adult learners are quite ***a heterogeneous lot***.

一般说来，成人学习者是情况千差万别的一群人。

22. Practice makes perfect. 熟能生巧。

23. translated work 翻译作品

24. original version 原文

Reading a ***translated work*** is sometimes easier than its ***original version***.

读翻译作品有时会比原文简单。

25. source language 原文；源语言

A translator has to understand a text in the ***source language*** before translating it.

译者必须在翻译前先去理解原文。

26. ambiguity /ˌæmbɪˈgjuːɪtɪ; ˌæmbɪ`gjuətɪ/ ***n.*** 含糊不清，模棱两可

When translating, a translator might need to give a skilful interpretation in cases where ***ambiguity*** arises.

翻译时，若有含糊不清的语义出现，译者可能需要进行巧妙的诠释说明。

27. classical Chinese 文言文

28. colloquial Chinese 白话文

29. Chinese classics 中国古典文学作品

Reading some of the English translations of ***Chinese classics*** might be easier than reading them in the ***classical Chinese***.

阅读一些中国古典文学的英文译本可能比直接阅读其文言文原著更简单。

30. downside /'daʊnsaɪd; `daUn,saɪd/ ***n.*** 负面，缺点

A translated work may contain mistakes, and that's obviously a ***downside***.

译文可能会有一些错误，很明显那是不好的。

31. aesthetic /iːs'θetɪk; ɛs`θɛtɪk/ ***adj.*** 美学的

The ***aesthetic*** dimension of a literary work is often missing in a translated work.

文学作品的美感在译文中常常会遗失。

32. faithfulness to the original language 忠于原文

Faithfulness to the original language and fluency of the translated text are two important factors involved in translation.

译文对原文的忠实性和语言的通顺性是翻译的两大要素。

33. consult a dictionary 参考词典，查阅词典

It is often necessary to ***consult a dictionary*** when you are learning a language or doing translation.

当你在学语言或翻译时，查阅词典常常是必要的。

34. be well versed in … 精通……；……造诣高

It's equally important to ***be well versed in*** one's native language if one wants to be a translator or an interpreter.

假如想成为一位笔译或口译人员，译者本身对母语的精通也同样重要。

35. context /'kɒntekst; `kɑntɛkst/ ***n.*** 背景；上下文

A translator should be aware of the message of a book and of the ***context*** in which it was produced.

译者应该了解要翻译的作品本身的内容及作品的创作背景。

36. reference works 工具书；参考资料

A good translator is never tired of using ***reference works***.

好的译者会不厌其烦地去查阅工具书。

37. specialized dictionary 专业词典

38. encyclopedia /ɪn,saɪklə'piːdiə; ɪn,saɪklə`pidɪə/ ***n.*** 百科全书

39. Developing sensitivity to stylistic differences is a quality that a good language learner or translator should have.

培养对不同文体的敏感度，是一位优秀的语言学习者或译者所必须具备的素质。

QUESTION DATABASE 题库练习

个人陈述 (Individual Long Turn)

考官 Now please have a look at this card. This is your topic. I want you to describe your experience of learning a foreign language. You have one minute to prepare.

Describe your experience of learning a foreign language. You should say:

what it is
when you started learning it
how you have tried to improve it
what you think of this experience.

INSTRUCTIONS
You will be asked to talk about the topic for one to two minutes.
You have one minute to think about what you are going to say.
You can make some notes to help you if you wish.

描述你的外语学习经历，你应该谈到：

何种语言
何时开始学习
你如何试着去提高
对外语学习经历的感想。

【说明】：
针对这个话题作出一至两分钟的陈述。
你有一分钟的时间去思考你的陈述内容。
假如需要的话，你可以写下要点以帮助你组织陈述。

Sample Response

I'd like to describe my experience of learning English, which has become an international language and almost trendy to study. I started learning it when I was about 12 years old. I went to a private language school that offered English lessons for children. At that time I picked up English mostly by singing and playing games. Then I continued learning it when I went to junior high school and also in senior high school. Reading and grammar were the focus of language learning during my high school years. Later when I was at university, I completed the Freshman English course, which helped me improve my reading skills and oral English. Nowadays I listen to English-language radio programmes and watch TV programmes broadcast in English. On the whole, I would say my experience of learning English is enjoyable and rewarding although I sometimes feel frustrated—there are so many difficulties to overcome. For example, one has to get used to so many regional accents and usages, and has to discover the unpredictable meanings of English idioms. And last but not least, there's the irritating fact of the pronunciation not always following the spelling.

回答范例

我想要谈谈自己学习英语的经历。英语俨然已变成世界性的语言，学好英语也几乎变成了一种趋势。我大约在 12 岁左右开始接触英语，上的是一家私立的儿童英语补习学校。那时，我主要通过英文歌曲及游戏学英语。进入初、高中后我仍然继续着英文学习旅程，而英语语法及阅读是当时的学习重点。之后进入大学，大一的英文课程帮助我提高了阅读技巧及口语方面的能力。如今我会收听英文广播节目并且收看英文电视节目。大体而言，可以说我的英文学习过程是快乐并且有意义的，尽管有时我会感到沮丧——毕竟有太多的困难必须去克服。比如说，你必须去适应多种地方口音及用法，还必须找出英文习语难以捉摸的含义。最后不容忽视的一点是，发音往往与拼写不一致，这点很恼人。

◎ **Did you ever learn a second foreign language?**

Yes, I learned Spanish for about a year or so. But I haven't had any opportunity to use it since I graduated.

你学过第二外语吗?

是的，我学过大约一年的西班牙语，但毕业之后，我一直没有机会用它。

◎ **Why did you choose to learn Spanish?**

Well, it's mainly because it is a widely used language apart from English. I thought it would be quite useful to be able to speak the language.

你为什么选择学西班牙语?

主要因为它是除了英语之外的另一种被广泛使用的语言，所以我想如果会讲西班牙语，在未来会很有用。

双向讨论 (Two-way Discussion)

◎ **Right! Do you focus on any particular linguistic skills nowadays when you learn English?**

Not really. In order to do well in my IELTS test, I want to become proficient in all four aspects of language: listening, speaking, reading and writing. So my strategy for learning English, for instance, has to become more integrated by my paying attention to each of these four aspects of language. By the way, I don't think my vocabulary is large enough, so I spend quite a lot of time practising the new words I have learned. As you know, vocabulary is essential to the development and acquisition of a foreign language.

好！你现在学英语，是否会特别着重某些语言能力？

没有。为了在雅思考试中取得好成绩，我想要在听、说、读、写四方面都能够精通。所以我的英语学习策略必须是更加综合全面的，同时注重这四种能力。对了，我觉得自己的词汇量不够大，所以会花很多时间练习运用已学过的单词。你知道的，词汇在外语的进步及习得过程中是不可或缺的。

◎ **Do you think one should adopt a variety of approaches when trying to improve the various aspects of one's skill in a particular language?**

Adopt a variety of approaches? I assume you mean using different learning methods? Well yes, I do. I listen to English radio programmes and watch English-language DVDs to improve my listening. I practise speaking English with my friends and I read newspaper articles aloud to develop my speech rhythm and my fluency in speaking. I read widely and intensively to improve my reading comprehension and my reading rate. As for writing, well, I read model essays carefully and analyze the elements of good writing such as diction, organization, sentence variety and transitional words. And of course, I produce my own samples of writing and ask for feedback from someone good at English.

你认为语言学习者有必要采用各式各样的方法来加强一种语言的各方面能力吗?

采用各式各样的方法?我想你是指使用不同的学习方法吧?我想是的。我收听英文广播节目,看英文影片,为的是提高听力。我和朋友练习讲英语,并诵读英文报纸,为的是改善我的讲话节奏,提高流利程度。我将泛读和精读结合起来,是为了提高阅读理解能力,加快阅读速度。至于写作,我会仔细阅读范文,并分析好文章的组成因素,例如遣词、组织、句型变化及转折承接词。当然,我会自己写几篇,然后拿去请教文章写得好的人。

◎ **Should there be any difference in the ways children and adults learn a foreign language?**

If you ask me, my answer is yes! Children pick up languages quite naturally. They are able to pick up new words, intonations and speech patterns very easily. So it's a good idea for children to learn a foreign language by introducing them as early as possible to an environment where the target language alone is spoken. And their learning can well be combined with playing and singing. Speaking and listening should be the chief method of a language learning programme for children. For adults, well, things may be quite different. Take my father for example. I don't think he would succeed in learning English, and certainly wouldn't enjoy it, if he heard no explanations at all in Chinese in a language class. In terms of learning environment, adults, especially those at the beginner level, might find it really daunting to have to speak in a situation where their mother tongue is not spoken at all. Then again, the way in which adults pronounce words tends to become fixed rather early on; then they find it difficult to change their accent or pronunciation. Generally speaking, adult learners are quite a heterogeneous lot. They learn foreign languages for various reasons and with varying degrees of proficiency. For instance, some learn so that they can go sightseeing, some want to gain promotion, others want to study abroad, etc. It's hard to generalize what is the best learning strategy for them, because it depends on their purpose and on their motivation. However, I do believe that practice makes perfect. This principle applies to learners of all ages and of all levels.

成人的英语学习与儿童的英语学习有什么不同吗？

假如你问我，我的答案是肯定的。小孩学习语言是相当自然的，他们能非常容易地学到新的词汇、发音及句型，因此尽早引导孩子在全外语环境里去学习某门外语，是非常好的主意。并且他们的学习能与歌唱和游戏结合在一起，说和听则应是儿童语言学习的主要方法。至于成人，那当然是相当不同的。以我的父亲为例，假如在课堂上完全没有一点中文解释说明，我想他是学不好英文的，更别说喜欢上它了。在学习环境方面，特别是那些还属于基础级的成人们，可能会觉得在无母语的情况下开口说英文是非常吓人的。而且，他们的发音方式早已固定，所以他们会发现去改变本身的口音或发音方式是非常困难的。一般来说，成人学习者是情况千差万别的一群人，他们因为不同的动机来学习语言，程度也参差不齐。例如，有人是因为想出国观光；有人是为了职场上的升迁；有人则是为了出国念书等。所以要概括成人的最佳语言学习方法是很困难的，因为这要视他们不同的目标及动机而定。但我也确实相信“熟能生巧”，这个原则适用于各个年龄段及各个程度的学习者。

◎ **Do you think one's first language should be used in a language classroom?**

Well, if possible it should be kept to a minimum. Creating a totally new language environment for learners can force them, as it were, to use the language they're learning. On the other hand, using one's own, one's first language in a foreign language classroom helps slow learners understand the lesson better. But I still think one's mother tongue is best used only when it's absolutely necessary.

你认为母语应该在外语课堂上使用吗？

如果可以的话，应该尽可能少用。创造一个全新的语言环境或多或少可以强迫学生们去使用新的语言。从另一方面来说，在课堂上使用母语可以帮助那些程度落后的学生们更好地理解课程的内容。但我仍认为，最好只在绝对必要时才使用母语。

◎ **Let's talk about translation. What are the advantages and disadvantages of reading a translated work instead of the original work?**

Hmm ... let me think about it. I'd like to talk about the advantages first. One obvious advantage is that you don't have to master that foreign language to be able to read a book you are interested in. You see—it may take you ten years to master your first foreign language and another seven or eight years to learn a second one. But you can read immediately and with perfect ease any book you fancy that has been translated into your own language. Another benefit is that reading a translated work is sometimes easier than its original version. You know why? Let me tell you. A translator has to understand a text in the source language before translating it, so he or she might be able to give a skilful interpretation in cases where ambiguity arises. That's why reading some of the English translations of Chinese classics might be easier than reading them in classical Chinese. Classical Chinese is not as plain as colloquial Chinese. Hmm, as to disadvantages, perhaps I can put it this way. A translated work may contain mistakes, and that is obviously a down side. Also the aesthetic dimension of a literary work is often missing in a translated work. For example, once a Chinese poem is translated into English, some of its poetic qualities such as parallelism and rhythm are difficult to maintain.

让我们谈谈翻译吧！如果不读原文而只看译文，会有什么优缺点呢？

嗯……让我想想看，我想先谈优点好了。最明显的优点是你不用精通外语就可以阅读感兴趣的作品。你明白的，精通一种外语可能必须花上十年，然后又得花上七八年的时间去学习第二种外语，但是你却可以立即并且在极轻松的情况下，去阅读自己喜欢且已翻译为自己母语的书籍。另一项好处是阅读译本有时比原著还容易。你知道为什么吗？让我来告诉你。因为译者必须在翻译前先理解原文的意思，所以在翻译时，若有含糊不清的语义出现，译者可能需要进行巧妙的诠释说明。这也是为什么阅读一些中国古典文学的英译本，可能比直接阅读其文言文原著更简单。中文的文言文本身并不像白话文那么清楚易懂。嗯……至于其缺点，我应该可以这样说，译文可能会有一些错误，很明显那是不好的。另外，文学作品的美感在译文中经常会遗失。举例来说，当一首中国诗被翻译成英文时，有一些诗体特色，如对仗或押韵就很难在译文中得以保留。

◎ **Faithfulness to the original language and fluency of the translated text are two important factors involved in translation. In cases where the two are in conflict, which one do you think is more important?**

That's an interesting question! A good translator should find a balance between the two. If you ask me, I would say it depends on the type of text one is translating. For example, in the case of legal documents, faithfulness to the original meaning is more significant, because they are "sensitive" texts. Here, a change in phrasing, even sometimes a change in the position of a comma, could lead to a change in meaning and thus to misunderstanding. In the case of popular fiction or romance, well, perhaps fluency is more important. You know, clarity and fluency in expression enable readers to follow the story easily.

译文对原文的忠实性和语言的通顺性是翻译的两大要素，但当这两者产生冲突时，你会如何取舍？

这是一个相当有趣的问题，优秀的译者必须在两者之间取得平衡。但如果真要问我，我会说那必须取决于你所要翻的文章种类。举例来说，假如是法律文件，那么忠于原文的意义比较重要，因为它们是需要“谨慎处理”的文本。改变用语，有时甚至改变一个逗号的位置都有可能改变意思，进而产生误解。假如是通俗或言情小说，那么文章的流畅性可能会更重要，毕竟清晰及通顺的表达能使读者轻松地掌握故事的脉络。

◎ **What qualities should a good translator have?**

First and foremost, he or she should be very fluent in both the target language and the source language. Very often people think that being proficient in a foreign language should enable one to be a good translator, but it's equally important to be well versed in one's native language. And then again, developing sensitivity to stylistic differences is a necessary quality. Using a style equivalent to that of the source text is partly what makes a translation successful. A legal document, for instance, has a style that differs from a news report. A good translator should be aware of the style and nature of the original text, aware of the message itself, of the context in which it was produced ... hmm ... and also for whom it was intended. He should be able to communicate the spirit of that and if possible also the message as faithfully as he or she can in the "new" language. Finally, a good translator is never tired of using reference books. There are so many technical terms in different fields: economics, politics, laws, medicine, technology, etc. No translator can master them all, so it will often be necessary to consult a dictionary, or even several dictionaries, or probably a specialized dictionary or an encyclopedia.

一位优秀的翻译人员应该具备什么样的素质？

首先也是最重要的是，他（她）应该对目标语言和源语言都能运用自如。通常人们会认为，能精通外语的人，就应该能成为一位不错的翻译人才，但精通自己的母语也是同样重要的。还有，对不同文体的敏感度是一项必备素质，使用与原文相同的文体是促成一篇译文作品成功的部分因素。举例来说，法律文件就与新闻报道的文体是不一样的。优秀的译者应该了解原文的风格及性质，作品要传达出的信息及其创作背景，嗯……还要了解文章的目标读者是谁。译者也必须能够尽可能地以另一种语言忠实表达出原作的精神。最后，优秀的译者还要能不厌其烦地去查阅工具书，因为在不同的领域有各自不同的专业术语，如经济、政治、法律、医学、科技等，没有哪位译者可以事事精通，所以就得经常去查词典甚至多本词典，也可能要参考专业词典或百科全书。

Co-student

同学

USEFUL EXPRESSIONS 实用表达

1. He is the same age as me. 他和我同龄。
2. a second-year student 大二的学生（注：sophomore 是美式英语）
3. my study mate 读书良伴
4. has a real appetite for … 强烈渴望……（食物、知识或喜爱的事物等）

   He ***has a real appetite for*** knowledge, so he is always looking out for opportunities to learn new things.

   他有强烈的求知欲，所以总是在找机会学习。
5. extend my own knowledge 扩展自己的知识领域

   She encourages me to learn more and to ***extend my own knowledge***.

   她鼓励我学习并扩展自己的知识领域。
6. He reflects on and reviews all the schoolwork very thoroughly and systematically.

   对于课业，他总是深思熟虑，温故知新。
7. We are on the same course, and we enjoy each other's company.

   我们上同一门课，又很喜欢在一起。
8. solitary study 自己学习

   Some ***solitary study*** is essential, but I would say there are many advantages in studying with others.

   自己学习有其必要性，然而我还是觉得和他人一起读书有很多好处。
9. We can help each other to resolve difficulties, and we can share our inspiration.

   我们可以相互帮忙解决问题，也可以分享我们的灵感奇想。
10. pool our different experiences 综合不同的体验

    We can ***pool our different experiences*** and develop better learning methods with each other.

    我们可以综合不同的体验，然后总结出更好的学习方法。

11. alternative /ɔːl'tɜːnətɪv; ɔl`tɝnətɪv/ ***adj.*** & ***n.*** 可供选择的（事物）

I use the Internet as an ***alternative*** form of learning.

我将网络作为另一种学习模式来使用。

12. on the Net 网络上

13. acquire /ə'kwaɪə; ə`kwaɪr/ ***v.*** 获得

I can ***acquire*** an amazing amount of information and knowledge ***on the Net***.

我可以从网上获得大量的资讯与知识。

14. enhance /ɪn'hɑːns; ɪn`hæns/ ***v.*** 提高

I read books and magazines related to my major, and that helps me develop my knowledge and ***enhance*** and broaden my skills.

我会去阅读和专业相关的书籍杂志，这对扩展知识及提升技能着实有益。

15. correspondence course 函授课程

16. proactive /prəʊ'æktɪv; pro`æktɪv/ ***adj.*** 主动的

With some alternative learning methods, I can develop not only a ***proactive*** learning attitude but also critical thinking.

通过另外一些学习方法，我可以培养出更主动的学习态度及批判式思维。

17. concentration /ˌkɒnsən'treɪʃən; ˏkɑnsn̩`treʃən/ ***n.*** 集中精神；专注

I am a person who likes to have a quiet setting as a support for ***concentration***.

我这个人喜欢安静的环境，这样才有助于集中精神。

18. concentrate on 专注于

So long as the TV isn't turned on, I can ***concentrate on*** my studies uninterruptedly.

只要电视机不打开，我就可以专注于学习，不受干扰。

19. defect /'diːfekt; `difɛkt/ ***n.*** 缺点

The most obvious ***defect*** is that I can't discuss problems and difficulties with my classmates when I study alone.

最明显的缺点是，我自己一个人学习时，无法和同学讨论切磋。

20. When studying alone, I have to develop a sort of inner dialogue with myself.

自己学习时，我必须要和自己展开一种内心的对话。

21. Practice makes perfect; I keep this learning method as a fundamental principle.

熟能生巧，这是我学习的不二法则。

QUESTION DATABASE 题库练习

个人陈述 (Individual Long Turn)

考官 Now please have a look at this card. This is your topic. I want you to talk about someone you like to study with. You have one minute to prepare.

Talk about someone you like to study with. You should say:

who this person is
how old this person is
when you first met the person
why you like to study with the person.

INSTRUCTIONS
You will be asked to talk about the topic for one to two minutes.
You have one minute to think about what you are going to say.
You can make some notes to help you if you wish.

请谈一谈你的读书良伴，你应该谈到：

这个人是谁
他 / 她的年龄
你第一次遇见他 / 她是什么时候
为什么你喜欢和他 / 她一起念书。

【说明】：
针对这个话题作出一至两分钟的陈述。
你有一分钟的时间去思考你的陈述内容。
假如需要的话，你可以写下要点以帮助你组织陈述。

Sample Response

This is an interesting question. I could hardly forget my best friend and study mate—Helen. She is the same age as me and I first met her about two and a half years ago when I was a second-year student at the University. There are several reasons why I like to study with her. First of all, she has a real appetite for knowledge, so she is always looking out for opportunities to learn new things. Then again, she likes to share and discuss her knowledge with me, so this encourages me to learn more and to extend my own knowledge. Apart from that, she reflects on and reviews all the schoolwork very thoroughly and systematically and she likes to share her notes with me. So I think she is an ideal student—someone who has a very efficient method of learning—and I really get inspiration from studying with her.

回答范例

这是一个很有趣的问题，我几乎无法忘记我最好的朋友而且是读书良伴——海伦。她和我同龄，大约在两年半前，我第一次遇见了她，当时我还是个大二学生。我喜欢和她一起念书的原因如下：第一，她有强烈的求知欲，所以总是在找机会学习；其次，她喜欢和我分享、讨论她所知道的事，这鼓励了我去学习并扩展知识领域；此外，对于课业，她总是深思熟虑、温故知新，而且喜欢和我分享她的笔记。所以我认为她真的是一位很棒的学生，拥有一套非常高效的学习方法，与她一起学习，我真是得到不少启发。

◎ **How often do you study together?**

Well, since we are on the same course and have many assignments and tests, and since we enjoy each other's company, it makes sense to study together pretty often, oh, practically every day for a couple of hours.

你们在一起学习的时间多吗?

这个嘛，我们上同一门课而且有很多作业和考试，又很喜欢在一起，所以我们常常在一起学习，这很正常。嗯，几乎每天都有好几个小时呢！

双向讨论 (Two-way Discussion)

◎ **Do you prefer to study independently or with somebody else?**

I definitely prefer to study with someone else. Some people may say it is not easy to keep one's mind on the study material if you are not alone. It's true that some solitary study is essential, but I would say there are many advantages in studying with others. We can share what we have learned, we can help each other to resolve difficulties and we can share our inspiration. Furthermore, we can pool our different experiences and develop better learning methods with each other.

你比较喜欢一个人学习还是和其他人一起学习呢？

我当然喜欢和他人一起学习。有些人可能会觉得如果不是自己一个人的话，就不容易专心学习。自己学习有其必要性，然而我还是觉得和其他人一起念书有很多好处。我们可以分享所学，相互帮忙解决问题，也可以分享我们的灵感奇想。再说，我们可以综合不同的体验，然后总结出更好的学习方法。

◎ **Apart from attending lectures, what are other forms of learning you have experienced?**

Other forms of learning? Well, learning can take place in all sorts of ways. For myself, I use the Internet as an alternative form of learning. You can acquire an amazing amount of information and knowledge at any time you like on the Net. And then again I read books and magazines related to my major, and that helps develop my knowledge and enhance and broaden my skills. And then there's group learning or cooperative learning. That can be effective too; exchanging ideas and views face-to-face with my fellow students is an important source of learning for me. I have also heard about correspondence courses, but I've never tried any myself.

除了听课之外，你还有过哪些不同形式的学习经历呢？

不同形式的学习？嗯，学习是多样化的，至于我的话，网络是另一种学习模式。在网上，任何时候你都可以获得大量的资讯与知识。并且我会去阅读和专业相关的书籍杂志，这对扩展知识及提升技能着实有益。还有一种形式是在学习小组中的互助学习，这也很有效。和同学面对面交流意见想法，这对我来说是重要的学习资源。我也听说过函授课程，但是我自己没有尝试过。

◎ **Do you enjoy these alternative forms of learning? Why?**

Yeah, I enjoy these alternative forms a lot, since they mean I don't need to sit in a classroom listening to lectures all the time, good though some of the lectures are! In addition, I can choose the most efficient learning method for me in different times and situations and moods. Last but not least, with these alternative learning methods I can develop not only a more proactive learning attitude but also critical thinking.

你喜欢这些学习方法吗？为什么？

是的，我可是乐在其中呢，因为那意味着我不用老是坐在教室里听课，虽然有些课是不错的！再者，我可以依时间、情境和心情选择对我最有效的学习方法。最后还有一点也很重要，通过这些学习方法，我可以培养出更主动的学习态度及批判式思维。

◎ **What are the advantages and disadvantages of studying independently?**

Let me talk about the advantages first. A quiet environment is definitely the best for study. As I am a person who likes to have a quiet setting as a support for concentration, I tend to prefer to study alone at home where it's really peaceful. In this sort of setting, so long as the TV isn't turned on, I can concentrate on my studies uninterruptedly. However, I also realize there are some disadvantages. The most obvious defect is that I can't discuss problems and difficulties with my classmates. Besides, I have to do all the work, all the thinking, by myself. I have to develop a sort of inner dialogue with myself. It's possible but difficult.

单独学习的优点和缺点有哪些？

我先说它的优点好了。安静的环境当然最适于学习。我这个人喜欢安静的环境，这样才有助于集中精神，所以我比较喜欢一个人在家念书，家里真的很安静。在这样的环境下，只要电视机不打开，我就可以专心学习，不受打扰。但是，我知道单独学习还有些缺点。最明显的一点就是我无法和同学讨论切磋。除此之外，一切都得靠我自己完成和思考，必须要和自己展开一种内心的对话，这虽可行，但很难。

◎ **What do you think is the most efficient way of learning?**

Well, I would say practice makes perfect; that is the most efficient way of learning for me. I used to be a very slow learner and for a long time I thought the only way I could get a comprehensive understanding of a question or learn a skill was from textbooks. So I would often feel very upset and worried about whether I would make my grades. Fortunately, one of my teachers had a lot of patience. She managed to calm me down and suggested I practise with something I really wanted to learn about. Then my grades began to improve a lot. So now I keep this learning method as a fundamental principle. You learn by concentrating on what you are interested in and practising that.

你认为什么是最高效的学习方法?

这个嘛，对我而言，我会说熟能生巧是最高效的学习方法。我以前的学习速度很慢，有很长的一段时间，我认为唯有课本才能让我对一个问题有全面了解，才能教我学会一项技能，所以我常觉得苦恼且担心是否能得到好的成绩。很幸运，我的一位老师十分有耐心。她努力让我冷静下来，并建议我多练习我想学的东西。后来，我的成绩开始突飞猛进。因此现在我仍视其为学习的不二法则。专心学习你有兴趣的，并反复练习。

What do you think is the most efficient way of learning?

[illegible]

you are interested in and pursuing it.

[illegible]

Chapter 3

考试第二、三部分题库：各类话题说不停

综合分类

8. 娱乐篇 (Entertainment)

Sports

运动

USEFUL EXPRESSIONS 实用表达

1. table tennis = Ping-Pong 乒乓球
2. when it comes to sth. 要是说到某物

   When it comes to my favourite sport, I would like to mention ***table tennis***.

   说到我最爱的运动，那非乒乓球莫属。
3. I can do it indoors. 我可以在室内进行这项运动。
4. I don't have to worry about the risk of too much exposure to the sun.

   我不必担心会有晒伤的危险。
5. Overall, it's quite a mild sport. 整体而言，它算是相当温和的运动。
6. characteristic /ˌkærɪktə'rɪstɪk; ˌkærɪktə`rɪstɪk/ ***n.*** 特色
7. have a quick eye and a deft hand 眼明手快

   You do need to ***have a quick eye and a deft hand***—good hand-eye coordination—to be a good player.

   你必须眼明手快，即有良好的手眼配合，才能打得好。
8. a national passion 全国皆为之疯狂

   Football has become ***a national passion*** in England.

   足球在英国可是全民皆为之疯狂。
9. volleyball /'vɒlibɔːl; `vɑlɪˌbɔl/ ***n.*** 排球
10. badminton /'bædmɪntən; `bædmɪntən/ ***n.*** 羽毛球
11. jogging /'dʒɒgɪŋ; `dʒɑgɪŋ/ ***n.*** 慢跑
12. basketball court 篮球场

    There are plenty of ***basketball courts*** in parks and schools.

公园及学校有很多篮球场。

13. After school, almost every basketball court is crowded with people.

放学后，几乎每个篮球场都挤满人。

14. Sport teaches us how to strive and how to do our best to excel at a task.

运动教导我们如何奋力一战，如何尽其所能，出色地完成一项任务。

15. When emotions intensify, whether it is joy or frustration, players should be able to play on with equanimity.

当情绪沸腾，不管是喜悦或沮丧，球员都应能沉着应战。

16. cultivating good sportsmanship　培养良好的运动精神

Sport is important not only in terms of health but also for the sake of ***cultivating good sportsmanship***.

不仅是对健康，对于培养良好的运动精神来说，运动也十分重要。

17. Nowadays, people have become more aware of the benefits that sports activities can offer.

现代人比以前更了解体育活动可以带来的好处。

18. Yes and no.　可说是，也可说不是。

19. is well received　广受欢迎

When an athlete wins an international game, he is usually treated as a hero and ***is well received*** wherever he goes.

运动员赢得国际比赛时，总是被视为英雄，所到之处皆被人前呼后拥。

20. professional /prəˈfeʃənəl; prəˋfɛʃənḷ/ ***adj.***　职业的 ***n.***　职业选手；专业人士

21. sportsman = athlete　运动员

22. There is a stereotype that those who are good at sports usually cannot do well in school.

有一种成见认为，擅长运动的人，学业表现通常不尽理想。

23. The ancient Greeks used to think that a healthy body and a healthy mind went together.

古希腊人认为健康的身体和健康的心灵相辅相成。

24. unbiased /ʌnˈbaɪəst; ʌnˋbaɪəst/ ***adj.***　不偏不倚的

A sports commentator should be ***unbiased***.　体育评论员应不偏不倚。

25. Any comment on sport should be based on the real situation, not one's personal liking for a particular team.

体育评论的立足点应该是真实的情况，而非个人对某支参赛队伍的喜好。

26. keep up with ... 赶上，跟上（变化、潮流、想法等）

I ***keep up with*** the latest news on sports.

我会时时掌握最新的体育新闻。

27. I don't normally spend much time avidly listening to or watching the latest sporting news.

我通常不会花很多时间兴致勃勃地去收听或观看最新的体育新闻。

28. be enthusiastic about sports = be keen on sports 对体育热衷

29. (be) associated with = (be) connected with 和……联系在一起

Unfortunately, sport ***is*** sometimes ***associated with*** drugs.

很不幸，体育有时和禁药扯在一起。

30. gamble on 对……下赌注

Some people ***gamble on*** the results of the national professional football games.

有人对国内职业足球赛的结果下赌注。

31. football hooliganism 足球暴力

I've heard of ***football hooliganism*** in Europe, but that has not happened here so far.

我听过欧洲有足球暴力，但这里还不曾发生。

QUESTION DATABASE 题库练习

个人陈述 (Individual Long Turn)

考官 Now please have a look at this card. This is your topic. I want you to talk about your favourite sport. You have one minute to prepare.

Talk about your favourite sport. You should say:

what it is
when you first became interested in it
where you usually play it
why you like it best.

INSTRUCTIONS

You will be asked to talk about the topic for one to two minutes.
You have one minute to think about what you are going to say.
You can make some notes to help you if you wish.

谈谈你最喜欢的运动。你应该谈到：

那是什么运动
你何时开始对此运动感兴趣
你通常都在哪做此运动
你为何最喜欢此运动。

【说明】：

针对这个话题作出一至两分钟的陈述。
你有一分钟的时间去思考你的陈述内容。
假如需要的话，你可以写下要点以帮助你组织陈述。

Sample Response

When it comes to my favourite sport, I would like to mention table tennis. I first became interested in it when I was a senior high school student. I usually play it at school. I rarely play it after school, because there is no room for it at my home. I like Ping-Pong best for several reasons. One reason is that it is suitable for people of all sizes. You don't have to be tall or strong to be able to play it well. Apart from that, you can do it indoors, so you don't have to worry about the risk of too much exposure to the sun. And overall, it's quite a mild sport—you don't run the risk of serious injury.

回答范例

说到我最爱的运动，那非乒乓球莫属。当我念高中时，便开始对此运动产生兴趣。我通常都是在学校打乒乓球，很少在放学后进行这项运动，因为家里没有空间。我最喜欢乒乓球有几个原因。其中之一是因为这项运动适合各种体型的人玩。你不一定要长得很高或很壮也可以打得很好。除此之外，你可以在室内进行这项运动，所以不必担心有晒伤的危险。而且，整体而言，它算是相当温和的运动，你不必担心会受重伤。

◎ **Is it popular in China?**

Yes, very popular. It is kind of a national passion like football in England or baseball in Japan.

这种运动在中国流行吗？

是的，很流行。这种运动有点儿像足球在英国或棒球在日本一样，是一种全国流行的运动。

◎ **What other sports are popular in China?**

There are a number of popular sports in China, such as basketball, volleyball, badminton, swimming and jogging. I think one of the most popular sports is basketball. There are plenty of basketball courts in parks and schools of all levels. After school, they are usually crowded with people.

在中国还有什么其他运动很受欢迎呢？

在中国有许多流行的运动，例如：篮球、排球、羽毛球、游泳和慢跑。我认为最流行的运动之一是篮球，公园与各级学校都有许多篮球场。放学后，篮球场通常都挤满了人。

双向讨论 (Two-way Discussion)

◎ **What are some of the characteristics of this sport?**

First and foremost, it takes at least two to play the game. Like other sports, it requires skill. But unlike basketball, you don't have to be tall to be able to play well. You do need to have a quick eye and a deft hand—good hand-eye coordination—to be a good player. And you need to be light and fast on your feet.

这项运动有些什么特色呢?

首先，至少需要两个人才能玩。就像其他运动一样，你需要有一些技巧。不过，不像篮球，你不一定要长得高才能打得好。你必须眼明手快，有良好的手眼配合，才能打得好。而且你还必须要能轻快地移动自己的脚步才行。

◎ **What is the significance of sport?**

I consider sport a kind of entertainment. It has the same function as music and movies, helping us to relax. In addition, sport teaches us how to strive and how to do our best to excel at a task. It also teaches us how to play in a controlled mood. For example, when emotions intensify, whether it is joy or frustration, players should be able to play on with equanimity. Whatever the result is, they shake hands with each other. So sport is important not only in terms of health but also for the sake of cultivating good sportsmanship.

运动的重要性是什么?

我认为运动是一种娱乐，它和音乐、电影有同样的功能，可以帮助我们放松。除此之外，运动教导我们如何奋力一战，如何尽其所能，出色地完成一项任务。运动也可以教会我们如何控制情绪。举例来说，当情绪沸腾，不管是喜悦或沮丧，运动员都该沉着应战。不管最后的结果如何，他们都需与对方握手言和。所以不仅是对于健康，对于培养良好的运动精神来说，运动也十分重要。

◎ **In this country, do athletes enjoy high status and respect?**

Well, yes and no. The well-known ones do, especially when they win an international game. They are usually treated as heroes and are well received wherever they go. However, not every sportsman is as lucky as those sports stars. In this country, very few parents encourage their children to become professional athletes, because this is a society which emphasizes education. Unfortunately, there is a stereotype that those who are good at sports usually cannot do well in school. But it's not necessarily so. The ancient Greeks used to think that a healthy body and a healthy mind went together.

运动员在这个国家是否享有崇高的社会地位且受人尊敬呢？

可以说是，也可以说不是。对于那些有名气的运动员，特别是当他们赢得国际比赛时，的确会受到尊敬并享有崇高的社会地位。他们总是被视为英雄，所到之处皆被人前呼后拥。然而，并不是每一个运动员都像那些体坛明星一样幸运。在这个国家，鲜有父母会鼓励小孩成为职业运动员，这是因为社会的发展重心是教育，而遗憾的是，有一种成见认为，擅长运动的人，学业表现通常不尽理想。但是，事实并非如此。古希腊人曾认为健康的身体和健康的心灵是相辅相成的。

◎ **What qualities do you think a sports commentator should have?**

First of all, he should know all the rules thoroughly. And then again, his comments should be based on the real situation, not on his personal liking for a particular team. He should be unbiased.

你认为一个体育评论员应该具备什么素质？

首先，他应该详尽了解所有的体育运动规则。除此之外，他的评论应该立足于真实的情况，而非他个人对某一支参赛队伍的喜好。他应该是不偏不倚的。

◎ **How do you usually keep up with the latest news on sports?**

To be honest, I'm not very enthusiastic about sports. I don't normally spend much time avidly listening to or watching the latest sporting news. I usually hear the latest scores from my friends who are keen on sports.

通常你是如何掌握到最新的体育新闻的?

老实说，我对体育并不是很热衷。通常我不会花太多时间兴致勃勃地去收听或观看最新的体育新闻。通常我都是从那些爱好体育的朋友口中听到最新的比赛分数。

◎ **Is there any social problem particularly associated with sport in this country?**

Problem associated with sports? Let me think! Hum ... one problem I have heard about is gambling. Some people, I've heard, gambled on the results of the national professional football games. Oh yes, and I've heard that bribery is another problem. It's reported before that some players have accepted bribes and deliberately lost a game. Generally speaking, the situation here is quite different. For example, I've heard of football hooliganism in Europe, but that has not happened here so far. Well, I hope not!

在这国家有没有任何和体育扯上关系的社会问题?

和体育扯上关系的问题？让我想想！嗯……我听说过的一个问题就是赌博。听说有人对国内职业足球赛的结果下赌注。哦，我还听过的另一个问题就是贿赂。之前有报道指出，有一些参赛者接受贿赂而故意输球。一般来说，这里的情况非常不一样。举例来说，我听说欧洲出现过足球暴力，但这里还不曾发生过。哦，我希望不会!

Holiday and Travel

假期与旅游

USEFUL EXPRESSIONS 实用表达

1. explore /ɪk'splɔː; ɪk`splɔr/ ***v.*** 探索
2. custom /'kʌstəm; `kʌstəm/ ***n.*** 风俗

   I like to ***explore*** different cultures and ***customs***.

   我喜欢探索不同的文化及风俗。
3. go cycling 骑自行车
4. be into sth./doing = be interested in sth./doing 对某事物或做某事感兴趣

   I ***am into*** different ***cultures***. 我对不同的文化感兴趣。
5. one's cup of tea 喜欢的事

   A holiday abroad is ***my cup of tea***. 我喜欢到国外度假。
6. view /vjuː; vju/ ***n.*** 景观
7. fancy /'fænsi; `fænsɪ/ ***v.*** 喜欢

   When travelling alone, I can enjoy the ***views*** and stop at any place I ***fancy***.

   独自旅游时，我可以欣赏景色并随意驻足停留在我喜欢的地方。
8. leaves' whispering 树叶的低语
9. birdsong /'bɜːdsɒŋ; `bɝd,sɔŋ/ ***n.*** 鸟儿歌唱

   I like to hear the ***leaves' whispering*** and the ***birdsong***.

   我喜欢听树叶的低语及鸟儿歌唱。
10. landscape /'lændskeɪp; `lændskep/ ***n.*** 风景
11. be in the open air 在户外

    I enjoy ***being in the open air***. 我喜欢在户外。
12. the wayside flowers 路边的花朵

    In the open air, I'd be able to enjoy the smell of those beautiful ***wayside flowers***.

    在户外，我就可以享受路旁花朵的芬芳。

13. twinkling star　闪烁的星星

At night, I could lie on the beach and chat with the ***twinkling stars***.

夜晚，我可以躺在沙滩上和闪烁的星星交谈。

14. drop a hint to ...　对……（人）暗示

15. trendy /'trendi; `trɛndɪ/ ***adj.***　成为风潮的

Having a holiday abroad has become ***trendy***.

到国外度假已成风潮。

16. see and hear the sights and sounds overseas　亲身体验异国的风情

People nowadays can go and ***see and hear the sights and sounds overseas*** without straining their purses.

现在，人们可以亲身体验异国的风情而不会觉得腰包紧缩。

17. broaden our cultural horizons　扩展文化视野

By traveling abroad, we can ***broaden our cultural horizons***.

到海外旅游可以扩展我们的文化视野。

18. mountain-climbing　爬山

19. angling /'æŋglɪŋ; `æŋglɪŋ/ ***n.***　钓鱼

20. hiking /'haɪkɪŋ; `haɪkɪŋ/ ***n.***　踏青，远足

People like my parents chose ***mountain-climbing***, ***angling***, picnicking and ***hiking*** as their entertainment on holidays.

我的父辈们会选择爬山、钓鱼、郊游和踏青作为他们在假期的休闲娱乐方式。

21. commercialism and industrialization　商业主义及工业化

With ***commercialism and industrialization***, people are wealthier.

随着商业化及工业化的推进，人们变得越来越富裕。

22. travel agency　旅行社

23. package tour　跟团旅游；全包式的旅游

There are many ***travel agencies*** that arrange tours abroad; there are ***package tours*** to the UK, Europe, Japan and so on.

有很多的旅行社负责安排出国的旅程，去英国、欧洲其他国家、日本等地方可以选择跟团旅游。

24. flourishing /'flʌrɪʃɪŋ; `flɝɪʃɪŋ/ ***adj.***　欣欣向荣的

25. deteriorating /dɪ'tiəriəreɪtɪŋ; dɪ`tɪrɪə͵retɪŋ/ ***adj.***　衰退的

26. be booming 蓬勃发展中

Tourism in this country ***is booming***.

这个国家的旅游业正在蓬勃发展。

27. We have more national holidays than before. 我们现在的国家法定节假日比以前增加了。

28. boost the tourist industry of this country 促进国内的旅游业

29. place of interest 观光景点，风景名胜

30. be widely accessible 广为流传的；可轻易取得的

To ***boost the tourist industry of this country***, information about ***places of interest*** could ***be*** made more ***widely accessible*** through websites, advertisements and TV reports.

为了促进国内的旅游业，有关旅游景区的资讯可以通过网站、广告和电视报道轻松获得。

31. attraction /ə'trækʃən; ə`trækʃən/ ***n.*** 风景区

32. signpost /'saɪnpəʊst; `saɪn,post/ ***v.*** 标示

Directions to ***attractions*** should be clearly ***signposted***.

风景名胜的方向应被清楚标示出来。

33. booklet /'bʊklɪt; `bʊklɪt/ = brochure /'brəʊʃə; bro`ʃʊr/ ***n.*** 小册子

34. feature ***v.*** 呈现……的特色 ***n.*** 特色

35. handicraft /'hændikrɑːft; `hændɪ,kræft/ ***n.*** 手工艺品

36. cuisine /kwɪ'ziːn; kwɪ`zin/ ***n.*** 美食

37. traditional Chinese culture 中国传统文化

38. be given wide publicity 广为宣传

Traditional Chinese culture should ***be given wide publicity***.

应广为宣传中国传统文化。

39. backpacker = independent traveller 背包客，自助旅游者

When I go abroad, I enjoy being a ***backpacker***. While exploring and experiencing a foreign culture, I can practise my English.

当我出国时，我喜欢当一名背包客。在探索及体验异国文化时，我还可以练习英语。

40. itinerary /aɪ'tɪnərəri; aɪˋtɪnəˌrɛrɪ/ ***n.*** 行程

If I joined a package tour, I would have to follow the tour leader's ***itinerary***.

假如是跟团出游的话，我就必须遵循导游的行程安排。

41. go sightseeing 观光旅行

One of the advantages of travelling alone is that I can ***go sightseeing*** at my own pace.

自助旅行的优点之一是可以依自己的步调来观光旅行。

QUESTION DATABASE 题库练习

个人陈述 (Individual Long Turn)

考官 Now please have a look at this card. This is your topic. I want you to describe your perfect holiday. You have one minute to prepare.

Describe your perfect holiday. You should say:

where you want to spend it
when you will take the holiday
with whom you will go
why it is a perfect holiday for you.

INSTRUCTIONS

You will be asked to talk about the topic for one to two minutes.
You have one minute to think about what you are going to say.
You can make some notes to help you if you wish.

描述你理想中的假期。你应该谈到：

你想要去哪个地方
你何时会去
跟谁一起同行
为什么它会是一次理想中的假期。

【说明】：

针对这个话题作出一至两分钟的陈述。
你有一分钟的时间去思考你的陈述内容。
假如需要的话，你可以写下要点以帮助你组织陈述。

Sample Response

I'd like to spend my perfect holiday in my hometown, a coastal city, exploring every inch of the beautiful place. The time I'd like best to do it is during my summer vacation. I'd go cycling with my best friends. They like the things I'm into—we all love nature. A holiday like that would be just my cup of tea. Do you know why? Well, first, on a bike I can take my time and have fun. I enjoy the views and stop at any place I fancy—like where I can hear the leaves' whispering and the birdsong. And in the open air, I'd be able to enjoy the smell of those beautiful wayside flowers. And then at night, I could lie on the beach and chat with the twinkling stars. They seem to smile at me, you know. Some people might think a holiday like that is a bit crazy. But a little bit of craziness makes life more fun!

回答范例

我会以我土生土长的家乡——一座海滨城市——作为我度过理想假期的地点，去体验这里每一处之美。暑假是我理想中的最佳时段。我将跟我最要好朋友一起骑自行车旅行。我们志趣相投，都爱好大自然。这样的假期正是我喜欢的。你知道为什么吗？首先，因为骑自行车时，我可以很悠闲地玩，欣赏沿途的景色，当听到树叶的低语及鸟儿歌唱时，可以随意驻足停留。在户外，我可以享受路旁花朵的芬芳；夜晚，我可以躺在沙滩上和闪烁的星星交谈，它们似乎对着我微笑呢！有些人可能会认为这样的假期有一点疯狂，但是一点点的疯狂却会给生活带来更多的乐趣！

◎ **Did you ever have such a holiday?**

No, I've never had a holiday like that, though I've been thinking about it for several years. I even dropped a hint to some of my friends recently. I said, "How great it would be to go along the coastline on a bike!" But they just said, "Oh, that would be tiring!" I think it will take a lot of hard work and courage to have such an adventure. But I'm still into doing it if I can find someone to go with me.

你曾有过像这样的假期吗?

没有，虽然我已经梦想能有这般的假期好几年了，但还不曾有过。最近我甚至暗示过一些朋友，我对他们说：“假如我们能够骑自行车沿海岸线旅行的话，那将会是多么棒的一件事！”但是他们却只是说：“那得多累啊！”我想，要尝试这样的假期，会很辛苦，也需要很大的勇气，但是假如我能找到某人结伴一起去，我仍然会很有兴趣去将之付诸实践。

双向讨论 (Two-way Discussion)

◎ **Is it a common practice for people in this country to spend their holidays abroad?**

It certainly is! It's become almost trendy, especially when people have a long vacation. That's because the standard of living is much higher than it used to be here. People nowadays can go and see and hear the sights and sounds overseas without straining their purses.

对这个国家的人来说，出国度假是很普遍的做法吗？

不用说，那是当然的！它甚至几乎已成为一种风潮，特别是当人们放长假的时候。这是因为生活水平比以前高了。现在，人们可以亲身体验异国风情而不会觉得腰包紧缩。

◎ **What do you think of this trend?**

On the one hand, I see it as a positive sign. It shows that China's economy has done really well during the past 30 years. And then again, by travelling abroad, we can make friends with people in different parts of the world; we can broaden our cultural horizons. On the other hand, I think it's worth pointing out that China's scenery is amongst the best in the world. On the whole, though, I consider it's a very good thing for us to see other parts of the world and to make friends with people of other cultures.

你又如何看待这种趋势呢？

一方面来说，我认为这是一种正面的迹象，它表明中国的经济在过去 30 年来发展得非常好。而且通过到国外旅游，我们可以跟来自世界各地的人交朋友；我们也可扩展自己的文化视野。另一方面来说，我想值得一提的是，中国可是世界上风景最好的地方之一。然而，整体来看，我觉得能去看看世界不同的角落，交不同文化背景的朋友，对我们来说还是一件很棒的事。

◎ **Do you think the ways people here spend their holidays have changed, say, over the past 30 years? What changes have taken place?**

Yes, I do think so. 30 years ago, China was not as prosperous as it is now. People like my parents chose mountain-climbing, angling, picnicking and hiking as their entertainment on holidays. With commercialism and industrialization, people are wealthier, but there's less and less space for us. So more and more people think of holidaying abroad. There are many travel agencies that arrange tours abroad; there are package tours to the UK, Europe, Japan and so on. You can even make your own arrangements if you want a bit of an adventure or if you already have friends there.

你认为这里人们的度假方式已经改变了吗？好比说，过去30年来呢？出现了怎样的变化呢？

没错，我认为这里的度假方式的确已经改变了。30年前的中国并不像现在这样繁荣。我的父辈们会选择爬山、钓鱼、郊游和踏青作为他们在假期的休闲娱乐。随着商业化及工业化的推进，人们越来越富裕，但是属于自己的空间却越来越少，因此越来越多的人喜欢到国外去度假。有很多旅行社负责安排出国的旅程，去英国、欧洲其他地方、日本等地可以选择跟团旅游。如果你想要一点儿冒险或已有朋友在那里了，还可以自己来安排想要的旅程。

◎ **Do you think tourism in this country is flourishing or deteriorating?**

Well, I think it is booming. Nowadays we have more national holidays than before, so many people are able to spend their free time exploring the country.

你认为这个国家的旅游业是欣欣向荣还是在走下坡？

我认为它正蓬勃发展。现在我们国家的法定节假日比以前增加了，所以很多民众能够有空闲时间去探索我们的国家。

◎ **What could best be done to boost the tourist industry of this country?**

First of all, information about places of interest could be made more widely accessible through websites, advertisements and TV reports. Secondly, directions to attractions should be clearly signposted so that drivers can easily see how to get there. Thirdly, information about accommodation and restaurants needs to be supplied through relevant booklets or brochures. Last but not least, places that feature traditional Chinese handicrafts, cuisines or cultures should be given wide publicity.

有什么最佳的方法可以促进国内旅游业的发展呢？

首先，可以利用网站、广告和电视报道让人们更轻松地获得有关旅游景点的资讯。第二，风景名胜的方向路标要标示清楚，使驾驶者能很容易了解如何能到达目的地。第三，关于食宿方面的资讯，需要在相关的书籍或小册子中提供。最后一点不容忽视的是，一些以中国传统手工艺品、美食或文化为特色的地方，应该广为宣传。

◎ **Do you prefer to travel alone or with someone? Why?**

As a person loving nature, I prefer to travel alone. Especially when I go abroad, I enjoy being a backpacker. So then, while exploring and experiencing a foreign culture, I can practise my English.

你比较喜欢独自旅行还是与人结伴一起去？为什么？

身为一位自然爱好者，我更喜欢独自旅行。特别当我去国外时，我喜爱当一名背包客，因此在探索及体验异国文化时，我还可以练习英语。

◎ **What are the advantages and disadvantages of travelling alone?**

Well, the advantages of travelling alone are: I'm free to set off whenever I like, I can go sightseeing at my own pace, and I can visit just those places I am interested in without wasting my time. If I joined a package tour, I would have to follow the tour leader's itinerary. On the other hand, travelling alone has several disadvantages. For example, I cannot share my thoughts and feelings with fellow travellers and I have to do everything by myself. In an emergency, I might feel pretty helpless.

自助旅游的利与弊各是什么？

自助旅游的优点有：可以随意停留，依自己的步调来观光旅行，并且不用浪费时间，只参观自己有兴趣的地方就行。假如跟团出游的话，我就必须遵循导游的行程安排。但另一方面来说，自助旅游也有一些缺点，例如，我不能与同伴分享自己的想法及感受，又必须完全靠自己去处理每一件事，当有紧急状况时，我可能会觉得非常无助。

Chapter 3

考试第二、三部分题库：各类话题说不停

综合分类

9. 科技与自然篇

(Technology and Nature)

The Internet

因特网

USEFUL EXPRESSIONS 实用表达

1. log on to the Internet 连线上网
2. diversified /daɪ'vɜːrsɪfaɪd; də`vɝsə,faɪd/ ***adj.*** 多样化的
   The functions that computers serve now are ***diversified***.
   现在，电脑的功能相当多元化。
3. surf the Internet 上网
4. access /'ækses; `æksɛs/ ***v.*** & ***n.*** 取得
   The Net is the fastest and the least costly medium to ***access*** and exchange information.
   网络是获取并交换信息最快速、最经济的媒介。
5. do without ... 没有……也可以
6. Yes and no. 可说是，也可说不是。
7. up-to-date ***adj.*** 最新的
   If I am preparing for an oral presentation, the Internet helps me search for really ***up-to-date*** and relevant information.
   如果我在准备一份口头报告，网络可以帮我搜寻到最新的相关信息。
8. connect ... with 把……紧密联结
   The Internet helps me ***connect*** myself ***with*** the immense world of knowledge.
   因特网有助于让我和浩瀚的知识紧密联结。
9. I don't need to spend hours hiding myself in a great pile of books.（spend 时间 / 金钱 doing）
   我不必花上好几个小时，埋首书堆中，才能找到我要的资料。
10. impact /'ɪmpækt; `ɪmpækt/ ***n.*** 冲击
    The Internet has made a strong ***impact*** on society.
    因特网已深刻地影响了整个社会。

11. It is no exaggeration to say that ＋从句　说……一点也不夸张
12. revolutionize /ˌrevəˈluːʃənaɪz; ˌrɛvəˋluʃən-ˌaɪz/ *v.* 革命化；对于……有很大的改变
The Internet ***revolutionizes*** the way people communicate.
因特网对人际沟通方式产生了革命化的影响。
13. e-commerce /ˈiːkɒmɜːs; ˋi kɑmɚs/ *n.* 电子商务
14. affect /əˈfekt; əˋfɛkt/ *v.* 影响
The Internet has ***affected*** forms of entertainment.　因特网已影响到娱乐的形式。
15. copyright violation　侵犯版权
16. Net pornography　网络色情
17. Net prostitution　网络卖淫
18. handwriting /ˈhændˌraɪtɪŋ; ˋhændˌraɪtɪŋ/ *n.* 笔迹，字迹
The ***handwriting*** of my friend calls up the image of him when I read his letter.
看到朋友来的亲笔信函中的笔迹，脑海中就会浮现他的身影。
19. been integrated into　融入
The Internet has ***been integrated into*** our daily life.
因特网已融入我们的日常生活中。
20. digital house　数字房屋
21. wired /waɪəd; waɪrd/ *adj.* ＝ Internet-connected　数字化的；联网的
22. enable sb. to do　使某人能够去做
23. in terms of　就……而言
24. potential risk　潜在的危险
We have to be aware of some ***potential risks*** of the Internet.
我们必须注意因特网的潜在危险。
25. nuclear engineering　核工程
Nuclear engineering might lead to disasters if nuclear power plants are not properly maintained.
核电厂若维护不当，核工程可能导致浩劫。
26. genetic engineering　基因工程
27. pose all sorts of knotty ethical questions　造成种种棘手的人伦问题
The possibilities opened up by ***genetic engineering pose all sorts of knotty ethical questions***.
基因工程的发展造成了种种棘手的人伦问题。

28. virtual reality　虚拟现实

Virtual reality can be put into good use.　虚拟现实有其实用之处。

29. Virtual reality can assist psychotherapy by providing a soothing atmosphere for the mentally sick.

通过为精神病患者提供一种令人放松的气氛，虚拟现实可以辅助心理治疗。

30. draw the line　划清界限

QUESTION DATABASE 题库练习

个人陈述 (Individual Long Turn)

考官 Now please have a look at this card. This is your topic. I want you to describe your experience with the Internet. You have one minute to prepare.

Describe your experience with the Internet. You should say:

where you usually use it
when you started using it
what role it plays in your life
what you think of it.

INSTRUCTIONS
You will be asked to talk about the topic for one to two minutes.
You have one minute to think about what you are going to say.
You can make some notes to help you if you wish.

描述你的上网经验。你应该谈到：

通常上网的地点
何时开始使用网络
网络在你生活中所扮演的角色
个人对网络的看法。

【说明】：
针对这个话题作出一至两分钟的陈述。
你有一分钟的时间去思考你的陈述内容。
假如需要的话，你可以写下要点以帮助你组织陈述。

Sample Response

As a college student, I use either my notebook in my room or a PC in the computer lab of my university to log on to the Internet. I started to learn about the Net when I was a junior high school student. At that time, the computer was used simply as a tool to store information or to do secretarial work efficiently. However, the functions computers serve nowadays are much more diversified. For example, I can surf the Internet whenever I need to search for information or want to find out about current affairs. So for me the Internet does provide a lot of help and at the same time, a window from which to see the changing world. I think that in the future, people will rely on the Internet even more heavily than they do now, since it's the fastest and the least costly medium to access and exchange information.

回答范例

身为一名大学生，我会在自己的房间用笔记本电脑，要不然就是在学校电脑室里上网。我开始接触电脑是在上初中的时候。那时电脑只是储存资料的工具，或者是被用来快速执行文书之类的工作。然而，电脑现今的功用相当多元化。例如，当需要搜寻信息或想了解时事时，我会去上网。所以对我来说，因特网的确提供了很多的帮助，同时它也开启了一扇窗，让我可以看到世界的变化。我认为未来人们应该会比现在更依赖网络，因为它是获取并交换信息最快速、最经济的媒介了。

◎ **Do you prefer to use your notebook or a PC in the computer lab of your university?**

I prefer to use my notebook in my room, because sometimes the PC lab in my university is packed. Then again, I have more privacy when I use it in my room.

你更喜欢用自己的笔记本电脑还是学校电脑室里的电脑？

我更喜欢在自己的房间用自己的笔记本电脑，因为学校的电脑室有时会满座。还有，在自己的房间，我能拥有更多隐私。

双向讨论 (Two-way Discussion)

◎ **Do you think you can do without computers?**

Yes and no. As for my daily life, I can still get the news I want through newspapers and TV. But if I am preparing for a writing assignment or an oral presentation, the Internet helps me search for really up-to-date and relevant information and also to connect myself with the immense world of knowledge. I don't need to spend hours hiding myself in a great pile of books. I simply type on the keyboard or ... move the mouse forwards and backwards, and in a few moments every bit of detail I need is accessible.

你认为你可以没有电脑吗？

我想，要视情况而定。如果是在平常，我仍然可以通过报纸和电视获得新闻资讯。但假如我正准备学校的书面作业或口头报告，网络可以帮我搜寻到最新的相关信息，并且也有助于让我和浩瀚的知识紧密联结。我不必花上好几个小时，埋首书堆，才能找到我要的资料。我只要敲敲键盘或……前后动动鼠标，便可在几分钟之内获得任何需要的小细节。

◎ **What impact does the Internet have on society?**

Well, it has made a strong impact on society. First of all, in terms of communication, the Internet does make a great difference. It's no exaggeration to say that the Internet revolutionizes the way people communicate, for example, email, chat room, etc. Another influence is that e-commerce has changed the way people buy things. Still another difference is that it has affected forms of entertainment. For example, there are many on-line games, which have attracted many youngsters.

On the other hand, there are some problems arising from the Internet: copyright violation, Net pornography and Net prostitution. Well, by "Net prostitution", I mean offering sex in return for money by advertising on the Net.

因特网对社会有什么影响？

因特网已深刻地影响了整个社会。首先，从人际沟通层面来看，网络的确造成了今日与昔日社会间很大的差异，如果说网络对人际沟通产生了革命性的影响，一点也不夸张，电子邮件及聊天室便可说明这一点。另一个影响是电子商务已改变了人们购物的方式。此外，它还影响了娱乐的形式。举例来说，在网上就有很多吸引青少年的网络游戏。

但另一方面来说，一些问题也因此而产生，如：版权侵犯、网络色情及网络卖淫。呃，"网络卖淫"指的就是在网上刊登广告，说要以性交换金钱。

◎ **How do you compare emails with traditional letters?**

Well, they are different in some aspects. Basically, emails are much more practical than the traditional mail delivered by postal workers, because there is no need to use stamps or to go to a post office. Besides, emails are faster. Still another difference is that emails always arrive in good shape, while traditional mail runs the risk of being damaged or lost during delivery. However, traditional letters have one advantage that emails do not have: the feelings created by seeing the handwriting of a friend or a relative. Since emails are typed messages, they all appear to be the same. But the different styles of handwriting can call up images of the persons who write them.

你如何比较电子邮件和传统信件？

这两种通信方式的确有一些不同。基本上，电子邮件比一般由邮差寄送的传统邮件更方便实用，因为电子邮件并不需要邮票或前往邮局。除此之外，电子邮件也更快速。还有一点就是，电子邮件在被送达收信人时总能完好无损，而传统邮件可能会在途中被损坏或遗失。然而，传统的信件也有电子邮件所没有的优点：亲朋好友不同的书写笔触所传达出的情感是电子邮件所不能企及的。因为电子邮件中的文字是电脑打出来的，所以看起来大同小异，但是如果看到不同朋友写出的不同字迹，脑海中就会浮现他们的身影。

◎ **In what direction do you think the Internet will change?**

I must say that I am not an expert in this field, but if you ask me, I think the main change is that it will be even more integrated into our daily life. For example, I've heard about "digital houses" where almost everything is "wired", that is, Internet-connected. You can turn on an air conditioner or heat a bathtub through the Net while you are driving or working.

你认为因特网将来会朝哪方面改变呢？

我并不是这一领域的专家，但如果你问我的话，我想主要变革是它会更融入我们的日常生活中。例如，我曾经听说过"数字房屋"，也就是屋内几乎所有东西都是数字化的，也就是与电脑联网的。你可以在开车或工作时，通过网络将空调或热水器打开。

◎ **Do you think the development of science and technology has made our lives better?**

I think so. Modern science has at least added comfort and convenience to our lives. For example, we have various forms of entertainment such as TV, DVD, stereo, etc. The development of medical science has enabled people to live longer than before. In terms of communication and transport, it's much easier to communicate and to travel now than ever before. But we have to be aware of some potential risks. For example, nuclear engineering might lead to disasters if nuclear power plants are not properly maintained. Then again, the possibilities opened up by genetic engineering pose all sorts of knotty ethical questions. We need to make sure that we are in control of technology before technology controls us.

你认为科技的发展有助于我们的生活吗？

我想是的。至少现代科学为我们的生活增添了舒适与便利，例如：我们有电视、光碟、音响等不同形式的娱乐方式。又如医药科技的发展使人类的寿命得以延长。在通讯运输领域，我们的交流与出行也比以往更加便捷。但我们必须注意其潜在的危险。例如：核电厂若维护不当，核工程可能导致浩劫。而且，基因工程的发展也造成了种种棘手的人伦问题。所以我们必须在科技控制我们之前确保我们能掌控科技的发展。

◎ **What do you think of the idea of virtual reality?**

I have heard about it, but so far I've not seen a demonstration of it. So it's a bit hard for me to answer this question. If you really want my opinion, I believe ... it can be put to good use. For example, it is already used to help train pilots. I think it can also assist psychotherapy by providing a soothing atmosphere for the mentally sick. However, we have to be aware that virtual reality is not the true reality. It's important to draw the line.

对于虚拟现实，你有什么看法？

我曾听说过，但还没有亲身体验过，所以对我来说，回答这个问题，有点困难。假如真要我说出对它的想法的话，我相信虚拟现实有其实用之处。举例来说，它早已被拿来帮助训练飞行员。并且，我认为，通过为精神病患者提供一种令人放松的气氛，虚拟现实可以辅助心理治疗。然而，我们必须知道虚拟现实并不是真正的实际状况，划清两者的界限是很重要的。

Equipment

设备

USEFUL EXPRESSIONS 实用表达

1. utilize /'juːtəlaɪz; `jutl̩,aɪz/ *v.* 使用（= use）

I have been ***utilizing*** the computer for three years.

那台电脑我已经用了三年。

2. benefit /'benɪfɪt; `bɛnəfɪt/ *n.* 好处 *v.* 受益

Technology brings about some ***benefits***. 科技带来了一些好处。

3. provide sb. with sth. 为某人提供某物

The Internet ***provides us with the information*** we want.

因特网给我们提供所要的信息。

4. enable sb. to do 使某人能做……

Computers ***enable me to process*** data efficiently and effectively.

电脑使我能快速高效地处理资料。

5. indispensable /ˌɪndɪ'spensəbəl; ˌɪndɪ`spɛnsəbl̩/ *adj.* 不可或缺的

Email correspondence is ***indispensable***. 用电子邮件通信是不可或缺的。

6. the digital age 数字时代

7. e-commerce /'iː kɒmɜːs; `i kɑmɝs/ 电子商务

E-commerce is becoming the norm. 电子商务正成为常态。

8. facilitate /fə'sɪlɪteɪt; fə`sɪlə,tet/ *v.* 使便利

The computer really does ***facilitate*** work. 电脑能使工作更便利。

9. Huge amounts of data can be processed at great speed by computer without involving time-consuming manual and mental drudgery.

电脑可以快速处理大量资料，无须费时、劳力又劳心。

10. relieve sb. of ... 使某人从……中解放出来；解除某人的……

Computers can ***relieve the employees of*** a lot of tedium.

电脑可以舒缓员工很多的枯燥感。

11. Computers can serve as a powerful means of communication.
电脑是一种强大的沟通工具。
12. tele-conferencing /'teliˌkɒnfərənsɪŋ; `tɛlɪˏkɑnfərənsɪŋ/ ***n.*** 远程会议
13. There are often two very different sides to the story. 事情常有两面性 。
14. what's worse 更糟的是
15. chaos /'keɪ-ɒs; `keɑs/ ***n.*** 大乱；混乱
Chaos is bound to occur if important data is accidentally destroyed, altered or misused.
若有重要资料不小心被损毁、修改或误用，随之而来的必然是大乱一场。
16. inevitable /ɪ'nevɪtəbəl; ɪn`ɛvətəbl̩/ ***adj.*** 不可避免的
17. transaction /træn'zækʃən; trænz`ækʃən/ ***n.*** 交易
E-commerce serves as an efficient tool of ***transaction***.
电子商务是高效的交易工具。
18. be cautious about … 对……保持警觉
We should ***be cautious about*** the risk of relying too much on computers.
对于过度依赖电脑的潜在危险，我们要有警觉性。
19. "wired house" or "digital dream house" 数字房屋
20. Internet-connected 联网的
21. taking advantage of … 利用……
Schools at all levels are ***taking advantage of*** this new technology.
各级学校都在利用此项新技术。
22. multi-media learning resource 多媒体学习资源
Various kinds of ***multi-media learning resources*** have emerged on the market.
琳琅满目的多媒体学习资源已在市面上出现。
23. E-learning is enjoyable and diversified. 电子化的学习有趣且多样。
24. I am a bit concerned about all this obsession with technology.
对科技趋之若鹜的态度，令我有点担忧。
25. human civilization 人类文明
26. be absorbed in … 沉浸在……
27. technological gadget 科技产品
We need to remember the human touch when we***'re absorbed in*** our ***technological gadgets***.
沉浸在科技产品中时，我们不能忘记与人的实际接触。

28. alienate us from ...　将我们与……疏远
We might ***alienate ourselves from*** the human world if we were lost in technological development.　我们如果迷失在科技发展之中，则可能将自己与人类世界疏远。
29. Genuine human interaction cannot be replaced by chat-room communication.
真正的人类互动无法被聊天室的沟通取代。
30. Machines do not necessarily make the world a more harmonious and friendly place.
机器不见得使这个世界更和谐友善。
31. Machines cannot guarantee the success of interpersonal relationships.
机器无法保证良好的人际关系。
32. striking /'straɪkɪŋ; `straɪkɪŋ/ ***adj.***　明显的
33. Will nuclear bombs lead to total destruction or world peace?
原子弹将毁灭一切还是带来世界和平呢？
34. These are questions to ponder.　这些问题有待深思。
35. clone /kləʊn; klon/ ***v.*** & ***n.***　克隆；（使）无性生殖
36. biotechnology /ˌbaɪəʊtek'nɒlədʒi; ˌbaɪotɛk`nɑlədʒɪ/ ***n.***　生物科技
37. A patient who has an organ removed can be restored to health with the help of a cloned organ.
若有病人被切除某器官，可借由克隆器官来恢复健康。
38. Cloning the human embryo raises the issue of the ethics of cloning.
克隆人类胚胎会引发伦理问题。
39. It's important to know where to draw the line before the situation is out of control.
在情况失控之前，要懂得适可而止，这是很重要的。

QUESTION DATABASE 题库练习

个人陈述 (Individual Long Turn)

考官 Now please have a look at this card. This is your topic. I want you to talk about a piece of equipment which you often use at home or in your work place. You have one minute to prepare.

Describe a piece of equipment which you often use at home or in your work place. You should say:

what it is
how long you have used it until now
what you can get from it
why it is so important for you.

INSTRUCTIONS
You will be asked to talk about the topic for one to two minutes.
You have one minute to think about what you are going to say.
You can make some notes to help you if you wish.

请描述一件你在家或工作上常用的工具，你应该谈到：

这是什么
至目前为止你已使用了多久
你可以从中获取什么
为什么它对你如此重要。

【说明】：
针对这个话题作出一至两分钟的陈述。
你有一分钟的时间去思考你的陈述内容。
假如需要的话，你可以写下要点以帮助你组织陈述。

Sample Response

I'd like to describe a computer that I often use at work. I have been utilizing it for about three years. As to what I can get from it, I'd like to point out one obvious benefit: it provides me with the information I need in order to do my work well. It is important to me for several reasons. For example, it enables me to process data efficiently and effectively. You know, this really saves me lots of time. In business, time is money. Also, I use it to keep in touch with the customers of my company. Email correspondence is indispensable nowadays. Last but not least, it is an essential tool in this digital age when e-commerce is becoming the norm.

回答范例

我想谈的是我在工作上常使用的电脑，我已经用了大约有三年的时间。至于我能从中获得什么，有一项好处是显而易见的，它能提供我所要的有利于工作的信息。它对我确实很重要，原因很多。例如，它使我能快速高效地处理资料，为我节省不少时间。生意场上，时间就是金钱。再者，我可以用它来和公司的客户保持联系。现在，用电子邮件通信是不可或缺的。最后不容忽视的一点就是，电子商务现在很普遍，电脑是数字时代的必备工具。

◎ **Do you use any digital products apart from computers?**

Not really. I've heard about digital cameras and digital TV, but I haven't used them yet. I think I will. It's just a matter of time.

除了电脑外，你还使用其他数字产品吗？

没有。我听过数码相机及数字电视，但还不曾用过，以后会用到，只是早晚罢了。

双向讨论 (Two-way Discussion)

◎ **Do you think the advantages of the equipment you use often outweigh its disadvantages?**

Oh, yes, absolutely! Let me talk about the advantages first. The computer really does facilitate work. For example, huge amounts of data can be processed at great speed by computer without involving time-consuming manual and mental drudgery. In this way computers can save a tremendous amount of time and money for a company, and relieve the employees of a lot of tedium. Besides, computers can serve as a powerful means of communication. Through email or tele-conferencing, discussions, meetings and negotiations between companies become easier. However, there are often two very different sides to the story. There are several weighty disadvantages to computers. For example, relying too much on them carries a serious potential risk. The moment they stop functioning everything seems to stop. What's worse, chaos is bound to occur if important data is accidentally destroyed, altered or misused.

你常用的这项设备，你认为它的利大于弊吗？

当然，一点也不错！让我先谈谈它的好处，电脑确实可以使工作更便利。举例来说，它可以快速处理大量资料，无须费时、劳力又劳心。电脑由此可为公司节省大量的时间和金钱，并且可舒缓员工的枯燥感。除此之外，电脑是一种强大的沟通工具。通过电子邮件和远程会议，公司间的会议及协商就变得更便利。然而，事情常有两面性，电脑还是有些重大的缺点。例如，过度依赖电脑有严重的潜在危险。一旦电脑停止运作，所有工作也几近停止。更糟的是，若有重要资料不小心被损毁、修改或误用，随之而来的必然是大乱一场。

◎ **What do you think of the increase in e-commerce?**

I think this trend is inevitable. In the world of business, time is money. E-commerce is fast, so it serves as an efficient tool of transaction.

电子商务越来越普遍，对此你有什么看法？

我认为这种趋势是不可避免的。生意场上，时间就是金钱。电子商务非常快捷，因此是高效的交易工具。

◎ **What do you think of the increasing use of technology in our life?**

I think this trend is inevitable, but we should be cautious. As technology becomes more and more sophisticated and diversified, we think rather uncritically that it will bring us unlimited convenience and comfort. For example, I have heard about the "wired house" or "digital dream house", which is Internet-connected. Through the Net or a PDA, the owner of a wired house can turn its lights on or off, heat a bathtub, control an air conditioner, etc. without having to be at home. Another example is that schools at all levels are taking advantage of this new technology. Various kinds of multi-media learning resources such as interactive CD-ROMs have emerged on the market. They seem to promise that learning will automatically become more enjoyable and more diversified. However, I am a bit concerned about all this obsession with technology. Well, I mean we have to be aware that technology is not everything. Human civilization is based on healthy human beings ... meeting and ... co-operating in friendly fashion face-to-face and not on this very recent technology. We need to remember the human touch when we're absorbed in our technological gadgets; otherwise, all too easily, we alienate ourselves from the human world.

越来越多的科技被应用在我们的日常生活中，你对此有什么看法？

我认为这样的潮流是无法避免的，但是我们应该对此保持警觉。科技越来越精细，越来越多元化，我们不假思索地认为它能带给我们无限的便利与舒适。举例来说，我曾听过全屋联网的“数字房屋”，通过网络或掌上电脑，屋主不用待在家里就能开灯或关灯、将热水器打开或遥控空调等等。另一个例子是各级学校都在利用新科技，如互动光碟等琳琅满目的多媒体学习资源已在市面上出现。他们好像在断言，说学习会自动变得越来越有趣且多样化。但是，人们对科技趋之若鹜的态度令我有点担心。噢，我指的是我们必须认识到，科技并不是一切，人类文明的基础是健康的人类之间能和善地面对面接触及合作，而不是新兴的科技。当我们沉浸在科技产品中时，不能忘记与人的真实接触，否则我们很容易将自己与人类世界疏远。

◎ **You really think, all too easily, we alienate ourselves from the human world due to technology?**

Oh, yes! Well, I mean genuine human interaction simply cannot be replaced by, say, email or chat-room communication. Computers and all those other technological gadgets are simply machines. They don't possess the subtlety and complexity and richness of human beings. They do not necessarily make the world a more harmonious and friendly place. Nor do they guarantee the success of interpersonal relationships. One striking example is the invention of the nuclear bomb. Will it lead to total destruction or to world peace? Has it increased man's happiness? These are questions to ponder.

你真的认为因为科技，我们很容易将自己与人类世界疏远吗？

对，没错！我想说的是，真正的人类互动根本无法被电子邮件或是聊天室这类沟通方式所取代。电脑和其他所有的科技产品都只是机器而已，它们不像人类那么微妙、复杂及丰富，它们不见得使世界更和谐、友善，它们也无法保证良好的人际关系。原子弹的发明就是一个明显的例子，它是会毁灭一切还是带来世界和平呢？它使人类变得更幸福了吗？这些都是我们必须去深思的问题。

◎ **Let's talk about cloning. What's your view on it?**

It's yet another example of modern technology, biotechnology. The good thing about it is that cloning promises to be useful in medical treatment. For example, a patient who has an organ removed can apparently be restored to health with the help of a cloned organ. But there are so many potential dangers. What about the consequences of cloning human beings? What is the nature of the identity and parentage of a human clone? Would a human being produced by cloning still be a human being? These raise the issue of the ethics of cloning. Therefore, I think it's important to know where to draw the line before the situation is out of control.

让我们来谈谈克隆这个问题，你对它有什么看法？

这又是现代科技的另一个例子，所谓的生物科技。克隆技术的好处是它能在医学治疗上发挥作用。例如，有病人被切除某器官，克隆的器官能使他恢复健康。然而，仍有许多潜在的危险存在。克隆人类的后果会是什么？克隆人的身份和家系该怎么认定？一个被克隆出的人还能被称作是人类吗？这些引发了有关克隆的伦理问题。所以我觉得在情况失控前，懂得适可而止是很重要的。

Animals and Environment
动物与环境

USEFUL EXPRESSIONS 实用表达

1. panda /'pændə; pændə/ ***n.*** 熊猫
2. endangered species 濒临绝种的动物
3. inhabit /ɪn'hæbɪt; ɪn`hæbɪt/ ***v.*** 居住在……

   The ***panda*** is an ***endangered species*** that ***inhabits*** southern China.

   熊猫是一种濒临绝种的动物，栖息在中国南部。
4. gentle nature 温驯的本性

   I like the cat because of its ***gentle nature***.

   我喜欢猫，因为它有着温驯的本性。
5. bamboo leaf 竹叶

   The panda's favourite food is ***bamboo leaves***.

   熊猫最喜爱的食物是竹叶。
6. creature /'kriːtʃə; `kritʃɚ/ ***n.*** 生物

   Koalas are lovely ***creatures***.

   树袋熊是可爱的生物。
7. from the sublime to the ridiculous 各式各样都有，包罗万象，无奇不有

   People keep almost anything as a pet, ***from the sublime to the ridiculous***.

   人类几乎可以将任何东西都当成宠物，简直是无奇不有。
8. lizard /'lɪzəd; `lɪzɚd/ ***n.*** 蜥蜴
9. rabbit /'ræbɪt; `ræbɪt/ ***n.*** 兔子
10. guinea pig /'gɪnipɪg; `gɪnɪ,pɪg/ ***n.*** 天竺鼠，豚鼠
11. turtle /'tɜːtl; `tɝtl̩/ ***n.*** 乌龟
12. wild pig 野猪；山猪
13. keep a pet 饲养宠物

Keeping a pet can be fun.　饲养宠物会很好玩。

14. enjoy one's company　喜欢……的陪伴

I like to have a dog around my house because I just ***enjoy its company***.

我喜欢家里有一只狗，因为我就是喜欢有它陪伴。

15. abandon a pet　弃养宠物

16. irresponsible act　不负责的行为

Some people ***abandon*** their ***pets*** for some reason or other. That's an ***irresponsible act***.

有些人因为某些原因而弃养他们的宠物，那实在是一种不负责的行为。

17. pet owner　宠物饲主

18. a sense of responsibility　责任感

The ***pet owner*** needs to have ***a sense of responsibility***.

宠物饲主必须要有责任感。

19. in captivity　被关起来

Seeing animals ***in captivity*** in a zoo is safer than in a forest where they move freely.

观赏关在动物园里头的动物，比观赏在森林里自由活动的动物安全。

20. in one's natural habitat　在它们原本的栖息地

21. be exposed to sth.　暴露在某物面前

It's more natural to leave animals where they are supposed to be ***in their natural habitat***. But it could be quite dangerous for people to ***be exposed***, for example, ***to a lion*** or ***tiger*** in an open space.

能让动物待在它们原本的栖息地当然是比较合乎自然的，但是让人们暴露在有狮子或老虎这类动物的开放空间也会是相当危险的。

22. educational value　教育价值

The zoo is supposed to have an ***educational value***.

动物园应该是有教育价值的。

23. animal right activist　提倡动物权利的激进人士

Animal right activists say that it's inappropriate to use animals in scientific research.

动物权利保护者表示在科学研究中以动物为实验工具是不恰当的。

24. deprive ... of ...　剥夺……的……

I do not think it's fair to ***deprive*** many animals ***of*** life just for the sake of trying to improve one human life.

我认为只为了拯救一条人命而剥夺了许多动物的生命是不公平的。

25. conservation /ˌkɒnsəˈveɪʃən; ˌkɑnsə˞ˋveʃən/ ***n.*** （动植物、森林等的）保护

In order to save endangered species, we need to have some specific ***conservation*** programmes.

为拯救濒临绝种的动物，我们需要一些具体的保护计划。

26. raise the profile of ... 使……广为人知；引起大家对……的重视

27. advert /ˈædvɜːt; ˋædvɝt/ ***n.*** 广告（注：英式口语用法＝ advertisement）

28. campaign against ... 开展宣传活动反对……

We need to ***raise the profile of*** endangered species. ***Adverts campaigning against*** killing such species are effective, I believe.

我们需要引起大家对濒危物种的重视。我相信，反对猎杀这类动物的广告宣传活动就很有效。

29. shark fin 鱼翅

30. delicacy /ˈdelɪkəsi; ˋdɛlɪkəsɪ/ ***n.*** 佳肴

In China, the fins of sharks have long been considered a ***delicacy***.

在中国，鱼翅长久以来被视为一种佳肴。

31. Killing will stop when buying stops. 购买行为停止了，猎杀就会停止。

32. enforce stricter penalties 执行更严苛的处罚

It's necessary to ***enforce stricter penalties*** if anyone is found killing endangered animals or trading in any products derived from them.

假如发现有人捕杀濒危动物，或从事任何相关产品的交易，则有必要对其实施更严苛的处罚。

33. conquer nature 征服自然

We seem to think that we can always ***conquer nature***.

我们似乎认为人类总是可以征服大自然。

34. humble /ˈhʌmbəl; ˋhʌmbl̩/ ***adj.*** 谦卑的

Perhaps humans need to be ***humble*** in order to develop a good relationship with nature.

或许人类需要学会谦卑，才能和大自然和谐共处。

35. be subject to ... 受制于……；屈服于……

Even a large ship such as the Titanic ***is subject to*** the power of nature. Although it was believed to be "unsinkable", it eventually sank deep into the sea.

即使像“泰坦尼克号”这样的巨轮终究仍得屈服于大自然的威力。虽然大家都认为它是“永不沉没”的，然而最后还是沉入深海。

36. benign /bɪˈnaɪn; bɪˋnaɪn/ ***adj.*** 温和的；（肿瘤等）良性的

Nature is not always ***benign***, and we should acknowledge its power.

大自然并不总是温和的，我们应该承认它的力量。

37. irreversible /ˌɪrɪˈvɜːsəbəl; ˏɪrɪˋvɝsəbl̩/ ***adj.*** 无可挽回的

We should stop doing things to the earth that are ***irreversible***.

我们应该停止对地球做任何无可挽回的事。

38. ecosystem /ˈiːkəʊˌsɪstəm; ˋikoˏsɪstəm/ ***n.*** 生态系统

We should stop doing anything that changes the ***ecosystem*** of the planet.

我们应该停止一切会改变这个星球的生态系统的活动。

39. global warming 全球变暖

40. greenhouse effect 温室效应

Problems such as ***global warming*** and the ***greenhouse effect*** are getting serious.

全球变暖及温室效应这类问题日益严重。

QUESTION DATABASE 题库练习

个人陈述 (Individual Long Turn)

考官 Now please have a look at this card. This is your topic. I want you to talk about an animal you like best. You have one minute to prepare.

Talk about an animal you like best. You should say:

what it is
what it looks like
how often you see it
why you like it most.

INSTRUCTIONS

You will be asked to talk about the topic for one to two minutes.
You have one minute to think about what you are going to say.
You can make some notes to help you if you wish.

谈谈你最喜爱的动物，你应该谈到：

它是什么动物
它长什么样子
你多久会看到这种动物一次
你为什么最喜欢它。

【说明】：

针对这个话题作出一至两分钟的陈述。
你有一分钟的时间去思考你的陈述内容。
假如需要的话，你可以写下要点以帮助你组织陈述。

Sample Response

The animal I fancy most is the panda. It looks really special, with its black and white markings. It's a big animal with a slow walk. The panda is an endangered species that inhabits southern China, and there are two living in the zoo here. I see the panda about once a month in the zoo and I also see them on TV or in the newspapers from time to time. For me it's the best of animals for several reasons. First and foremost, it looks ever so cute! Just look at its eyes and the two big ears. It looks as if it were a cartoon figure coming to life. Of course, I am pleased that it's a flesh-and-blood creature, not a fanciful creation. Another reason why I like it is its gentle nature. It seldom attacks people. I remember vividly a TV programme I saw some time ago, made somewhere in Sichuan Province. Tourists were sitting next to a panda and having their photo taken with it. I suppose it stayed happy because they kept giving the animal its favourite food—bamboo leaves. That kept it busy, I suppose, which is why the tourists could apparently do anything they liked. For example, they were able to place their arms over its shoulders and even give it a hug. The panda was just too busy enjoying its feast to notice them!

回答范例

我最喜爱的动物是熊猫，它身上有着黑白交错的图案，看起来相当特别。它是一种体积庞大但走路缓慢的动物，栖息在中国南部，现在濒临绝种。这里的动物园里也养了两只大熊猫。我大概一个月就会去动物园看看，也会不时在电视或报纸上看到它们的踪影。熊猫之所以会成为我最喜欢的动物，有几个原因：首先，它看起来是如此可爱！只要看看它的眼睛及一对大耳朵，就会觉得它仿佛是卡通人物的化身。当然，我很高兴它是一种真实存在的生物，而不是幻想出来的。我喜爱熊猫的另一个原因是它们有着温驯的本性。它们很少会攻击人类。我还记得前阵子看过一个在四川省某地制作的节目，节目里，游客竟然可以跟一只熊猫坐在一起，并且与它合照。我想那可能是因为他们一直给它喂最爱的食物——竹叶的缘故吧。熊猫忙着吃，游客就能很轻易去做他们想做的事。例如：他们能够把手臂放在它的肩膀上，甚至拥抱它，而那只熊猫只是专注于享用大餐，根本没工夫理他们！

双向讨论 (Two-way Discussion)

◎ **Right, now let's talk about pets. What sorts of animals do people here like to keep as their pets?**

From the sublime to the ridiculous! Well, people will keep almost anything as a pet: dogs, cats, snakes, lizards, birds, rabbits, guinea pigs, turtles, monkeys, wild pigs and so on.

好，那现在让我们谈谈宠物。这里的人喜欢饲养哪一种宠物呢？

包罗万象，无奇不有！如狗、猫、蛇、蜥蜴、鸟、兔子、天竺鼠、乌龟、猴子、野猪等，人们几乎可把任何一种生物都当作宠物来饲养。

◎ **What do you think of keeping a pet?**

The idea of keeping a pet comes from a highly developed country or from a well-to-do family. I think it's a good thing to show affection for all living creatures. If you can afford to look after, say, a dog and you are willing to do it, then it seems that you can just enjoy its company and be friendly with him. I am always amazed at those people who treat their pet dogs or cats like their family members. They are lucky animals, aren't they? But I've also heard that some people abandon their pets for some reason or other. That's very bad and is quite an irresponsible act. So I think keeping a pet can be fun, but the pet owner needs to have a sense of responsibility.

你对饲养宠物有什么看法？

饲养宠物的观念来自高度发达的国家或富裕的家庭。我觉得能对所有生物表示关怀是很好的。假如你有能力照顾这些动物，比如一只狗，而且又愿意的话，那么你似乎就能享受它的陪伴，也会友善地对待它。有些人把他们所饲养的宠物狗或猫当成家人一般，我对他们总是赞叹不已，而那些动物本身也够幸运的，不是吗？但我也曾听说有些人因为某些原因而弃养他们的宠物，那实在是一种很糟糕又不负责的行为。所以，我认为饲养宠物可以是很有趣的，但作为主人，必须要有责任感才行。

◎ **Do you prefer to see animals in captivity in a zoo, or in a park or forest where they can move freely?**

I don't have any preference. You see, of course, it's more natural to leave animals where they are supposed to be in their natural habitat. But it could be quite dangerous for people to be exposed, for example, to a lion or tiger in an open space. They could get killed. Hmm ... as you know, the zoo is supposed to have an educational value. So far as I can tell, animals in captivity nowadays seem to live quite contented lives. So my point is that as long as they are well treated, it doesn't matter whether they are in a forest or in captivity.

你比较喜欢观赏关在动物园里的动物，还是可以在公园或森林里自由活动的动物？

我并没有特别偏好哪一种。你也知道，能让动物待在它们原本的栖息地当然是比较合乎自然的，但是让人们暴露在有狮子或老虎这类动物的开放空间也会是相当危险的，他们有可能因此丧命。嗯，就如你所知，动物园应有其教育作用。至少在我看来，那些被关在动物园里的动物似乎过得相当满足，所以我认为只要能受到妥善照顾，它们是否应该在森林里或被关起来也就不是那么重要了。

◎ **Animal right activists say that it's inappropriate to use animals in scientific research. What do you think?**

This is a difficult question. As a human, I find it hard to say it's inappropriate to use animals in scientific research, because what else can we use for such a purpose? To use humans in a scientific experiment that could result in death? On the other hand, I do not think it's fair to deprive many animals of life just for the sake of trying to improve one human life. However, if the result of scientific research was likely to benefit millions of people and save millions of human lives, the sacrifice of a few animals might seem worth it. Anyway, I am pleased that my profession does not involve the killing of animals.

动物权利保护者表示在科学研究上以动物为实验工具是不恰当的，你认为呢？

这个问题很难回答。身为人类，我很难说使用动物来做科学研究是不恰当的，因为除此之外我们还可以用什么呢？把人类作为可能导致人命的科学研究的实验工具吗？另一方面，我认为只为了拯救一条人命而剥夺许多动物的生命是不公平的。不过假如科学研究的结果可能有益于数百万人并挽救他们的性命，那么一些动物的牺牲似乎就值得了。不管怎样，我很庆幸我的职业并不会危及动物的生命。

◎ **Shall we move on and talk about conservation? What do you think we can do to save endangered species?**

Well, first of all, we need to raise the profile of endangered species. Adverts campaigning against killing such species are effective, I believe. For example, here in China, the fins of sharks have long been considered a delicacy. Despite this, however, not long ago I saw a TV commercial intended to discourage people from eating such food any more. Besides, there are really so many other choices of food. The advert showed the cruelty of killing a shark just to get its fins. The picture was disturbing and did succeed, I think, in communicating to people the fact that those who eat shark fins are indirectly involved in causing intense suffering and in killing. If no one wanted to buy or eat shark, no one would bother to kill it. You see, killing will stop when buying stops. Hmm... let me see if I can think of something else. Well, clearly it's necessary to enforce stricter penalties if anyone is found killing endangered animals or trading in any products derived from them.

让我们继续谈谈保护问题好吗？你认为我们有什么办法可以拯救濒临绝种的动物？

首先，我们需要引起大家对濒危物种的重视，我相信，像反对猎杀这类动物的广告宣传活动就很有效。例如，在中国，鱼翅长久以来被视为一种佳肴，尽管如此，不久前我就在电视上看到一则劝导大家不要再吃这类食物的公益广告。其实还有其他许多的食物可供选择，这则广告传达出只为了鲨鱼的鱼翅而猎杀它们是如何残忍，画面虽然血腥，但却成功地告诉那些食用鱼翅的人，其实他们是间接导致鲨鱼遭受极度痛苦与屠杀命运的凶手。假如没人愿意去购买或食用鲨鱼，也就不会有人想去捕杀它们。你瞧，购买行为停止了，猎杀就会停止。嗯……让我想想还能不能想到其他方面。哦！还有很明显的是，假如发现有人捕杀濒危动物，或从事任何相关产品的交易，则有必要对其实施更严苛的处罚。

◎ **What do you think is the ideal relationship between human beings and nature?**

The ideal relationship between human beings and nature? Hmm ... this is an interesting question indeed. Well, first of all, humans need to be humble. We seem to think that we can always conquer nature. The film *Titanic* is a perfect example. The ship was believed to be "unsinkable" at the time when it was constructed. It could be taken as a metaphor for modern technology. And yet eventually it was subject to the power of nature; the "unsinkable" ship sank deep... deep into the sea, and thousands of people died. Nature is not always benign, and I think we should acknowledge its power. For example, we should stop doing things to the earth that are irreversible; we should stop doing anything that changes the ecosystem of the planet. You see, nowadays, problems such as global warming and the greenhouse effect are getting serious. Well, we need to respect nature. Hmm ... I also think human beings can learn a lot from nature. For example, the taller the bamboo grows, the lower it bends. The bamboo provides a good lesson in humility for human beings. That's my opinion.

你认为人与自然的理想关系是什么样的?

理想的人与自然的关系?嗯……这是一个相当有趣的问题。首先,人类应该要谦卑,我们似乎认为人类总是可以征服大自然。电影“泰坦尼克号”就是一个很好的例子。当那艘巨轮被建造出来时,大家都认为它是“永不沉没”的,它可以被视为现代科技的象征。然而,它终究得屈服于大自然的威力,这艘号称“永不沉没”的巨轮就这样沉入了深深的……深深的海底,数以千计的人因此罹难。所以大自然并不总是温和的,我们应该承认它的力量。举例来说,我们应该停止对地球做任何不可挽回的事;我们应该停止一切会改变这个星球的生态系统的活动。你也知道,如今像全球变暖及温室效应这类的问题日益严重。我们需要尊重大自然。嗯,还有,我也认为人类可以从大自然中学到很多东西。例如:竹子长得愈高,垂得愈低。它为人类上了很好的一课——要学会谦卑。以上就是我个人的观点。

Chapter 3

考试第二、三部分题库：各类话题说不停

综合分类

10．媒体与社会篇

(Media and Society)

The Media

媒体

USEFUL EXPRESSIONS 实用表达

1. broadsheet /'brɔːdʃiːt; `brɔd,ʃit/ ***n.*** （尤指严肃的）宽幅报纸（有别于小版面的报纸，如周刊）

   The *Cankao Xiaoxi* is a popular ***broadsheet*** in China.

   《参考消息》这份报纸在中国颇受欢迎。

2. quality press 优质的报纸
3. domestic news 国内新闻
4. up-to-date ***adj.*** 最新的
5. feature article 特别报道
6. in-depth ***adj.*** 深度的

   Feature articles give ***in-depth*** reports on all sorts of topics, cultural or technological.

   特别报道能给予各种主题深度的报道，像是文化或科技方面的。

7. politics /'pɒlɪtɪks; `pɑlə,tɪks/ ***n.*** 政治
8. political stance 政治立场
9. ideological /ˌaɪdiə'lɒdʒɪkəl; ˌaɪdɪə`lɑdʒɪkl̩/ ***adj.*** 意识形态的

   It's very difficult to communicate with someone with a different ***political stance*** or a different ***ideological*** position.

   和一个与自己政治立场或意识形态不同的人沟通是很困难的。

10. broadcast /'brɔːdkɑːst; `brɔd,kæst/ ***n.*** & ***v.*** 广播

    Sometimes I listen to the radio ***broadcasts*** and read the news on the Internet.

    有时候我会听广播或者上网浏览新闻。

11. keep up with current affairs 掌握时事

    I read newspapers and watch TV news programmes to ***keep up with current affairs***.

    我通过阅读报纸和看电视新闻节目来掌握时事。

12. update /ʌp'deɪt; ʌp`det/ *v.* 更新

Internet news can be ***updated*** every minute or every hour.

网上的新闻每分钟或每小时便可更新一次。

13. top news story 重要新闻报道

You just log on to the Net and you can hear ***top news stories***.

你只要上网就可以收听重要新闻报道。

14. printed media 平面媒体，纸媒

Presenting news on TV makes more of an impact than the traditional ***printed media***.

在电视上呈现新闻比传统的平面媒体更具有影响力。

15. headline /'hedlaɪn; `hɛdˏlaɪn/ *n.* 标题

I sometimes buy a newspaper or magazine just because of its sensational ***headline***.

我有时候只是因为看到某个耸人听闻的标题就去买了某份报纸或杂志。

16. hit the front page headlines 成为头条新闻

The affair of a celebrity or the divorce story of a politician sometimes ***hits the front page headlines***.

名人的绯闻或是政治人物的离婚事件常常成为头条新闻。

17. coverage /'kʌvərɪdʒ; `kʌvərɪdʒ/ *n.* 新闻报道

The media can make an event important just by giving it so much ***coverage*** that you cannot ignore it.

媒体可通过令人无法忽视的大肆报道而让某件事变得异常重要。

18. forum /'fɔːrəm; `fɔrəm/ *n.* 论坛

The media offer a public ***forum*** where current affairs are made known and come under scrutiny.

媒体提供了一个公众论坛让时事可以广为人知，并受到公众的监察。

19. raise awareness of ... 提高对……的认识

The media can direct the attention of the public and ***raise awareness of*** some critical issues in society.

媒体可以引导大众的注意力并提高人们对某些重大社会问题的认识。

20. drug abuse 药物滥用

21. the gutter press 八卦杂志、媒体

22. tabloid /'tæblɔɪd; `tæblɔɪd/ *n.* 小报

23. weekly /'wiːkli; `wiklɪ/ ***n.*** 周刊
24. invade people's privacy 侵犯了别人的隐私权
25. the freedom of the press 新闻自由

Some ***tabloids invade people's privacy*** and then claim that ***the freedom of the press*** should be respected.

有些小报侵犯了别人的隐私权还宣称他们的新闻自由应受到尊重。

26. a hoard of paparazzi 一群狗仔队

Tabloids employ ***a hoard of paparazzi*** who are determined to get a story at any cost.

小报雇用了一群狗仔队，决心要不惜一切代价去挖别人的八卦。

27. be accused of libel 被控告毁谤

It comes as no surprise to me that tabloids ***are*** often ***accused of libel*** by angry politicians.

小报常被愤怒的政治人物控告毁谤，对此，我并不感到惊讶。

28. scandal /'skændl; `skændl̩/ ***n.*** 丑闻
29. peddle gossip 散布八卦

Some people just like ***scandal*** and ***peddle gossip***.

有些人就是喜欢谈丑闻，散布八卦。

30. censor /'sensə; `sɛnsɚ/ ***v.*** 审查（书报、杂志、影视节目等）

I think in principle the press should be ***censored***.

原则上，我认为所有出版物都该受审查。

31. censorship /'sensəʃɪp; `sɛnsɚʃɪp/ ***n.*** （书报、杂志、影视节目等的）审查（制度）

Censorship serves to remind the media that they should act within the principles of civilized behaviour.

审查制度的目的是提醒媒体，应遵守文明行为原则。

32. freedom of speech 言论自由

Freedom of speech doesn't mean that the newspapers should start thinking they can say anything they want without reaping the consequences.

言论自由并不代表报纸可以报道任何事而不需承担后果。

33. repressive /rɪ'presɪv; rɪ`prɛsɪv/ ***adj.*** 严苛的；镇压的
34. democracy /dɪ'mɒkrəsi; dɪ`mɑkrəsɪ/ ***n.*** 民主

Censorship should not be ***repressive***—that would be against the principles of ***democracy***.

审查制度不应该是压迫性的，否则便违反了民主的原则。

35. untruthful report　不实的报道

The press should be made aware of the consequences of giving ***untruthful reports***.

新闻业者应该清楚进行不实报道的后果。

36. objectivity /ˌɒbdʒekˈtɪvəti; ˌɑbdʒɛk`tɪvətɪ/ ***n.*** 客观性

37. objective /əbˈdʒektɪv; əb`dʒɛktɪv/ ***adj.*** 客观的

I personally dislike reports lacking in ***objectivity*** and liable to lead to disharmony between people, societies and countries.

我个人不喜欢缺乏客观性，并且可能导致人群、社会或国家间不和谐的报道。

38. journalist /ˈdʒɜːnəl-ɪst; `dʒɝnḷˌɪst/ ***n.*** 新闻工作者

A ***journalist*** should be properly trained in observation and in writing, so that his or her reports are factually accurate and easily understood by an ordinary person.

记者在观察与写作方面应当受到适当的训练，让他或她的报道能符合事实且容易被大众所理解。

39. in another person's shoes　站在他人立场

Journalists should be able to put themselves ***in another person's shoes***.

记者应能够站在他人立场来思考。

40. comment /ˈkɒment; `kɑmɛnt/ ***n.*** & ***v.*** 评论

41. subjective /səbˈdʒektɪv; səb`dʒɛktɪv/ ***adj.*** 主观的

42. one-sided ***adj.*** 维护某一方的；单方面的

Commenting presents us with value judgements which are often prejudiced, ***one-sided*** and ***subjective***.

评论会呈现给我们价值判断，而这些常常都是带有偏见的，维护某一方的，并且具有主观性。

QUESTION DATABASE 题库练习

个人陈述 (Individual Long Turn)

考官 Now please have a look at this card. This is your topic. I want you to talk about a newspaper that you read regularly or have read recently. You have one minute to prepare.

Talk about a newspaper that you read regularly or have read recently. You should say:

what it is
where you usually read it
what you like about it and why.

INSTRUCTIONS

You will be asked to talk about the topic for one to two minutes.
You have one minute to think about what you are going to say.
You can make some notes to help you if you wish.

谈一谈你常看或是最近看过的一份报纸，你应该谈到：

这是哪一份报纸
你通常是在哪里阅读
你喜欢它的哪个地方，为什么。

【说明】：

针对这个话题作出一至两分钟的陈述。
你有一分钟的时间去思考你的陈述内容。
假如需要的话，你可以写下要点以帮助你组织陈述。

Sample Response

The newspaper I read regularly is *Cankao Xiaoxi*, a popular broadsheet in China. I often read it at home after work. It appeals to me for several reasons. First and foremost, it belongs to the "quality press", so its standard should be above the average. Well, I also like the diversity of its contents. Apart from international and domestic news, it provides information on health issues, technology, tourism, etc. For example, I enjoy reading its section devoted to technology, where I acquire up-to-date information on cutting-edge technology. One more thing worth mentioning is its feature articles, which give in-depth reports on all sorts of topics.

回答范例

我时常看的是《参考消息》，这是在中国颇受欢迎的一份报纸，我常常是下班后回到家中才看的。它之所以吸引我，有以下几个原因。第一，也是最重要的，它是优质的报纸，所以它的水准比一般的报刊要高。再者，我也喜欢其内容的多元化。除了国内外新闻，它还提供了健康、科技、旅游等方面的资讯。例如，我很陶醉于阅读科技这一部分，从此处我可以获得最新的尖端科技资讯。还有一点值得一提的是它的特别报道，给予了各种主题深入的报道。

◎ **Do you usually discuss news stories with others?**

Yes, I do, sometimes with my friends and sometimes with my parents. Through the exchange of views and ideas, I usually come to see an event afresh. But I normally avoid talking about politics with someone I don't know well. You know, it's very difficult to communicate with someone with a different political stance or a different ideological position.

你常和他人讨论新闻吗？

是的，有时候会和朋友讨论，有时候是和父母。通过交流彼此的观点及意见，我对某一事件常能有新的看法。但是，我通常会避免和不太熟的人讨论政治，你也知道，和一个与你政治立场或意识形态不同的人沟通是很困难的。

双向讨论 (Two-way Discussion)

◎ **Do you subscribe to any newspapers or magazines?**

Yes, I subscribe to the daily newspaper, *Cankao Xiaoxi*.

你订阅报刊杂志吗？
是的，我订了日报《参考消息》。

◎ **Is reading newspapers the only way you have to keep up with current affairs?**

No, not really. I watch TV news programmes, too. And sometimes I listen to the radio broadcasts and read the news on the Internet.

阅读报纸是你掌握时事的唯一方法吗？
不，并不是这样。我也会看电视新闻节目，有时候我还会收听广播以及上网浏览新闻。

◎ **What's the difference between newspaper news and, say, Internet news?**

The difference between newspapers and Internet news? Hum, well, in terms of reporting style, newspaper news items are usually more detailed and analytical. Internet news tends to be very brief. Another difference is that Internet news can be updated every minute or every hour, but newspapers do that only on a daily basis. Some international broadcasting companies such as BBC and CNN offer free on-line news. You just log on to the Net and visit their websites, and you can hear top news stories and even watch news programmes on the Net. Seeing is believing, so that way of presenting news certainly makes more of an impact than the traditional printed media.

报纸和因特网上的新闻有什么不一样呢？
报纸和因特网上的新闻的不同之处？嗯，以报道的风格而言，报纸的新闻内容更详细且具有更强的分析性，而网络新闻偏向简短。另一个不同点是，网上的新闻可以每分钟或每小时就更新一次，但是报纸只能是每天更新。有些国外的广播公司，像 BBC 或 CNN 提供了免费的在线新闻，你只要上网，访问他们的网站，就可以收听重要新闻，甚至在网上收看新闻节目。眼见为实，所以用这种方式呈现新闻，当然比传统的平面媒体更具有影响力。

◎ **Would you buy a newspaper or magazine just because of its exciting or sensational headline?**

Well, I try not to, but sometimes I just can't help it. The media experts know what seizes the public's attention. Sometimes, they make an event seem tremendously important just by giving it so much coverage that you cannot ignore it. For example, the affair of a celebrity or the divorce story of a politician sometimes hits the front page headlines. I don't think that sort of thing deserves much attention at all.

你会只因为激动人心或耸人听闻的标题就买下某份报纸或杂志吗？

这个嘛，我尽量不这样做，但是有时候就是无法控制自己。媒体专家总是知道如何抓住公众的注意力。有时候他们可以使某事件变得异常重要，方法就是进行大肆的宣传报道，让你无法忽视它。例如，名人的绯闻或政治人物的离婚事件常常会成为头条新闻，我觉得这样的事情根本不值得这么多人去注意。

◎ **Apart from reporting what's new around the world, what role do you think the media should play?**

I think the media play an important and influential role. On the one hand, they offer a public forum where current affairs are made known and come under scrutiny. On the other hand, they can direct the attention of the public and raise awareness of some critical issues in society, be it someone in need of help or social problems such as drug abuse. Of course, the media also provide us with entertainment. Unfortunately, the gutter press is becoming popular here. They make money by exploiting people's lower nature.

除了报道全世界的新闻之外，你认为媒体还应该扮演什么角色？

我认为媒体扮演了很重要、具有影响力的角色。一方面，媒体提供了一个公众论坛让时事可以广为人知，并且受到公众的监察；另一方面，他们引导着大众的注意力并提高人们对一些重要社会问题的认识，比如有人需要帮助或如吸毒这样的社会问题。当然，媒体也提供娱乐。不幸的是，八卦刊物在这里越来越受欢迎，它们利用着人性的低层次趣味来赚钱。

◎ **Is there any tabloid in this country?**

Oh, yes. They are mostly weeklies.

在这个国家有小报吗?

哦，是的，它们大都以周刊的形式出版。

◎ **What do you think of tabloids?**

I wish they could be reduced to dust. They invade people's privacy and then claim that the freedom of the press should be respected. They employ a hoard of paparazzi who are determined to get a story at any cost. Maybe this is simply the price celebrities have to pay for their fame. It comes as no surprise to me that tabloids are often accused of libel by angry politicians. Anyway, I think tabloids will continue to exist, because there will always, I suppose, be people who like scandal and who peddle gossip. If politicians betray the public trust, that is a matter for the law, not for the tabloids.

你对小报有什么看法?

我希望它们能化为尘土。小报侵犯了别人的隐私权还宣称自己的新闻自由应受到尊重。它们雇用一群狗仔队，决心要不惜一切代价挖别人的八卦。也许这就是那些名人为其盛名所须付出的代价。这些小报常常被愤怒的政治人物控告诽谤，对此，我并不感到惊讶。不管如何，我觉得小报会继续存在，因为，我猜还是有人喜欢谈丑闻、散布八卦。即使政治人物背叛了人们对他们的信任，那也应归法律管辖，与小报无关。

◎ **Do you think the press should be censored?**

Yes, I think in principle it should. Although freedom of speech is important, that doesn't mean the newspapers should start thinking they can say anything they want without reaping the consequences. All actions have consequences, especially public ones. Censorship—and it should be made public when a newspaper is being censored—serves to remind the media that they should act within the principles of civilized behaviour. Of course, censorship should not be repressive—that would be against the principles of democracy. On the other hand, the press should be made aware of the consequences of giving untruthful reports, reports lacking in objectivity and liable to lead to disharmony and even violence between people, societies and countries.

你认为新闻应受到审查吗？

是的，原则上我认为这是应该的。虽然言论自由是重要的，但那并不表示报纸可以任意报道而不需承担后果。任何行为都有后果，尤其是公开的行为。审查制度是用来提醒媒体他们应遵守文明行为原则的，而当一份报纸受审时，应是公开的。当然，审查制度不应该是压迫性的，那便违反了民主的原则。另一方面，新闻业者应该清楚进行虚假的，不客观的，并且可能导致人群、社会或国家间产生不和谐甚至是暴力的报道的后果。

◎ **What qualities do you think a journalist should have?**

That's an interesting question! First of all, a journalist should be properly trained in observation and in writing, so that his or her reports are factually accurate and easily understood by an ordinary person. Also, they should have a sense of responsibility, so as to ensure that the content of their reports is well-founded and in the interests of social harmony and good citizenship. Then again, it's important that they try to be objective. That's very difficult, as we tend to see things from our own point of view and not from another's, but journalists should be able to put themselves in another person's shoes. They should also be able to tell the difference between reporting and commenting. Reporting is a matter of communicating the facts, but commenting presents us with value judgements which are often prejudiced, one-sided and subjective, which may misinform and mislead the reader.

你认为身为一名记者应具备哪些素质？

这是一个很有趣的问题！第一，记者在观察与写作方面应当受到适当的训练，如此一来他（她）的报道才能符合事实，并容易让一般人所理解。再者，他们必须有责任感，才能确保报道的内容是有根据的，并且有助于促进社会和谐和公民间的友好关系。还有，力求客观也很重要。这很难，因为我们常以自己的观点来看事物，而不是从别人的角度来看。但是，记者应该能够站在别人的立场来思考。此外，他们也需分辨报道和评论的不同。报道是在谈论事实，但是评论呈现给我们的是价值判断，而这些判断常常是带有偏见的，只维护某一方的，并且是主观的，可能会传递给读者错误的信息并误导他们。

Festivals

节日

USEFUL EXPRESSIONS 实用表达

1. Spring Festival = Chinese New Year 春节，中国新年
2. in the Chinese calendar = in the lunar calendar 农历，阴历

   The Spring Festival begins on New Year's Eve ***in the Chinese calendar***.

   春节从除夕夜开始。
3. close relations 亲人
4. spend time together 聚在一起

   It is one of the rare occasions when ***close relations spend*** quite a bit of ***time together***.

   这是一个难能可贵的场合，亲人们可以花一些时间团聚在一起。
5. atmosphere /'ætməsfɪə; `ætməs,fɪr/ ***n.*** 气氛

   The ***atmosphere*** of the festival is wonderful—really sweet and homely and full of good will.

   节日的气氛真的很美好——甜美、温馨、充满了祝福。
6. red envelope 红包
7. celebration /ˌselə'breɪʃən; ˌsɛlə`breʃən/ ***n.*** 庆祝
8. celebrate /'seləbreɪt; `sɛlə,bret/ ***v.*** 庆祝
9. exhibition /ˌeksə'bɪʃən; ˌɛksə`bɪʃən/ ***n.*** 展览

   There are numerous special ***celebrations*** and ***exhibitions*** in public places.

   有许多特别的庆祝活动和展览在公共场所举行。
10. be over the moon (about ...) 欣喜若狂

    Children ***are*** always ***over the moon*** when they receive "red envelopes" from their parents.

    当小孩子从父母那收到红包的时候，他们总是欣喜若狂的。
11. dancing-dragon and dancing-lion performances 舞龙舞狮的表演
12. a delightful break 愉快的休假
13. Mid-autumn Festival 中秋节

The Mid-autumn Festival is on the 15th of August in the Chinese calendar.

中秋节是在农历的八月十五。

14. Dragon Boat Festival　端午节
15. Lantern Festival　元宵节
16. be internationally recognized　国际皆知的

Christmas and Chinese New Year ***are internationally recognized*** festivals.

圣诞节和中国新年是国际皆知的节日。

17. time off　放假

A festival means not much more than "***time off***" to students.

对于学生而言，节日只是意味着放假而已。

18. underestimate /'ʌndər'estəmeɪt; `ʌndɚ`ɛstə,met/ ***v.*** 低估；忽视

I think the historical and cultural significance of festivals should not be ***underestimated***.

我认为我们不应该低估节日的历史与文化意义。

19. fall on ...　在……（天）

The Dragon Boat Festival ***falls on*** the fifth of May in the Chinese calendar.

端午节是在农历的五月初五。

20. commemorate /kə'meməreɪt; kə`mɛmə,ret/ ***v.*** 纪念

The Dragon Boat Festival ***commemorates*** a patriotic poet named Qu Yuan, who died of drowning.

端午节是为了纪念投河自尽的爱国诗人屈原。

21. dragon boat race　划龙舟比赛
22. Tomb Sweeping Festival　清明节
23. ancestor /'ænsəstə; `ænsɛstɚ/ ***n.*** 祖先

What we call "***Tomb Sweeping Festival***" is the time when people visit and clean the tombs of their ***ancestors***.

我们所说的清明节是指人们会在这时间去祭拜和打扫祖先的坟墓。

24. a manifestation of filial piety　孝道的展现
25. cherish /'tʃerɪʃ; `tʃɛrɪʃ/ ***v.*** 珍爱

The Tomb Sweeping Festival is ***a manifestation of filial piety***, which is so ***cherished*** by Chinese people.

清明节是孝道的一种展现，中国人对此相当重视。

26. be closely tied in with ... 和……息息相关

Festivals in this country ***are*** pretty ***closely tied in with*** its history and culture.

这个国家的节日通常和其历史与文化息息相关。

27. moon cake 月饼

When the Mid-autumn Festival approaches, there is a huge demand for ***moon cakes***.

中秋节快到的时候，月饼的需求量就会大大增加。

28. stimulate consumption 刺激消费

The festival ***stimulates consumption***.

节日可以刺激消费。

29. push cart food business 推手推车卖小吃的摊贩

Wherever there are crowds of people out of doors, there are small ***push cart food businesses*** on the streets.

在户外，只要是有人群的地方，在街上就可以看到卖小吃的摊贩。

30. commercial /kə'mɜːʃəl; kə`mɝʃəl/ ***adj.*** 商业化的

Festivals always have a tendency to turn a bit ***commercial***. I think that's inevitable.

节日通常都会有商业化的趋势，我认为那也是无法避免的。

QUESTION DATABASE 题库练习

个人陈述 (Individual Long Turn)

考官 Now please have a look at this card. This is your topic. I want you to talk about a festival you like best in your country. You have one minute to prepare.

Talk about a festival you like best in your country. You should say:

what it is
when it takes place
how it is special
what you think about it.

INSTRUCTIONS

You will be asked to talk about the topic for one to two minutes.
You have one minute to think about what you are going to say.
You can make some notes to help you if you wish.

谈谈你最喜欢的国内节日，你应该谈到：

那是什么节日
这节日在何时
这节日有什么特别的地方
你对这节日的看法。

【说明】：

针对这个话题作出一至两分钟的陈述。
你有一分钟的时间去思考你的陈述内容。
假如需要的话，你可以写下要点以帮助你组织陈述。

Sample Response

My favourite festival is the Chinese New Year or the Spring Festival. It begins on New Year's Eve in the Chinese calendar. It's special to the Chinese, just like Christmas is special to millions of people in the West. It's extraordinary in several ways. First and foremost, it's time for family members to get together. As you know, after a year's hard work, it is one of the rare occasions when close relations spend quite a bit of time together and share the ups and downs of their lives. The atmosphere is wonderful—really sweet and homely and full of good will. Then again, children enjoy the festival, because they receive from their parents a "red envelope", that is, extra pocket money. Finally, the cheerful atmosphere created by the end of the old year and the prospect of a new one can be felt when you walk in the streets. There are numerous special celebrations and exhibitions in public places such as cultural centres or department stores. You can see dancing-dragon and dancing-lion performances in many places. What do I think of it? Well, I like it very much. Although I am no longer over the moon about it, like I was when I was a kid, I still find it a delightful break.

回答范例

我最喜欢的节日是中国新年，也叫做春节。它从农历除夕夜开始。春节对中国人的特别意义就像是圣诞节对数百万的西方人一样。春节在某些方面是很特别的。首先，它是全家人团聚的时刻。如你所知，在一整年辛苦工作之后，这是一个难能可贵的场合，亲人们可以花一些时间团聚在一起，并且一起分享他们的人生经历。那种气氛真的很美好——甜美、温馨、充满了祝福。再者，小孩子非常喜欢这个节日，因为他们会从父母那儿收到“红包”，也就是额外的零用钱。最后，当你走在街上，你可感觉到岁末迎新的欢愉气氛。还有许多特别的庆祝活动和展览在公共场所举行，如在文化中心或百货公司。你可以在很多地方看到舞龙舞狮的表演。我对这节日的看法？嗯，我非常喜欢春节。虽然我不像小时候那样对它感到欣喜若狂，但我依然觉得这是一个令人愉快的节日。

◎ **Are there many festivals in this country?**

Oh, yes. For example, have you heard about the Mid-autumn Festival? It's on the 15th of August in the Chinese calendar. There are many other festivals here too: the Dragon Boat Festival, the Lantern Festival, the Tomb Sweeping Festival and so on.

在你的国家有很多节日吗？

是的。举例来说，你有没有听过中秋节？它是在农历八月十五。在我们国家还有很多其他节日，如端午节、元宵节和清明节等。

双向讨论 (Two-way Discussion)

◎ **Now, let's continue to talk about festivals. What festivals are internationally recognized?**

Internationally recognized festivals? Well, Christmas and Chinese New Year are two such examples. As you know, Christmas is celebrated in almost every part of the world, including many Asian countries. As for the Chinese New Year, wherever there are Chinese people, it is celebrated. I bet that China Town in London, in Birmingham or Manchester, or in Vancouver has something interesting going on during the Chinese New Year. I have also heard about the Edinburgh Festival; it's an arts festival, isn't it?

现在，让我们继续来谈谈节日。有哪些节日是国际皆知的呢？
国际皆知的节日啊？嗯，圣诞节和中国新年应该都是吧！就如你所知的，几乎世界各地包括很多亚洲国家都会庆祝圣诞节。而就中国新年来说，只要有华人的地方就会有庆祝中国新年的活动。我敢打赌，伦敦、伯明翰、曼彻斯特或温哥华的中国城在中国新年这段期间一定会举办一些有趣的活动。我也听过爱丁堡节，这是一个艺术节对吗？

◎ **What role do you think festivals play in society?**

Hmm... I think that students just like the fun of festivals—the great variety of colourful celebrations and unusual activities. So probably a festival means not much more than "time off" to them. However, I think the historical and cultural significance of festivals should not be underestimated. Take the Dragon Boat Festival here for instance. It falls on the fifth of May in the Chinese calendar. It commemorates a patriotic poet named Qu Yuan, who died of drowning. That's why nowadays it's celebrated on the river—with the dragon boat race. And we eat special food called "zongzi" on that day—glutinous rice wrapped in bamboo leaves. The food originates from the ancients' custom of dropping such food in the river so that the fish would eat the rice rather than Qu Yuan's body. Another festival worth mentioning is what we call "Tomb Sweeping Festival". As its name suggests, it's the time when people visit and clean the tombs of their ancestors. This festival certainly has its cultural significance, because it is a manifestation of filial piety, which is so cherished by Chinese people. So it seems to me that on the whole, festivals in this country are pretty closely tied in with its history and culture.

你认为节日在社会中扮演什么样的角色？

嗯……我想学生只是喜欢过节的乐趣，因为会有各式各样的庆祝与特别的活动。因此，节日对他们来说可能只是“放假”而已。然而，我认为我们不应该低估节日的历史与文化意义。以端午节来说，端午节是在农历的五月初五，是为了纪念投河自尽的爱国诗人屈原。这就是为什么现在我们在河上举办划龙舟比赛来庆祝端午节的原因。我们在那天会吃一种特别的食物“粽子”，它是一种用竹叶包着糯米制成的食物。这种食物起源于古代的风俗，人们把这种食物丢到河里喂鱼，这样鱼就不会去吃屈原的尸体。另一个值得一提的节日就是我们所说的“清明节”，顾名思义就是人们会在这时间去祭拜和打扫祖先的坟墓。这个节日当然有它的文化意义，因为它是孝道的一种展现，中国人对此相当重视。所以，在我看来，大致上，这个国家的节日和它的文化与历史息息相关。

◎ **Do you think the role of the festivals is changing?**

I don't think so. Children and young students might not be aware of the meaning of the festivals at first, but they'll be taught in school and will come to understand their cultural significance as they mature.

你是否认为节日所扮演的角色正在改变？

我不这么认为。一开始，小孩子还有年幼的学生可能不知道一些节日的意义，但是随着他们的长大成熟，他们会从课堂上学习并渐渐了解节日的文化意义。

◎ **Are some festivals too commercial these days?**

In a sense, yes. You see, from early December onward, decorations associated with Christmas are already on display in shops. Here in China, when the Mid-autumn Festival approaches, there is a huge demand for moon cakes. As you can well imagine, the bakery shops make a fortune out of this. So the good thing is that the festival stimulates consumption. This might be a sign of a healthy economy. I'm sure that shops welcome festivals of all kinds, because celebrations always attract people out on the streets and persuade them to buy things. You have probably noticed that wherever there are crowds of people out of doors, there are small push cart food businesses on the streets. Large numbers of hungry people give them a chance to make extra money. So festivals always have a tendency to turn a bit commercial. I think that's inevitable, but celebrations are still celebrations themselves.

现今是不是有一些节日太商业化了呢？

在某些层面是的。你知道的，从 12 月初我们就已经可以看到一些和圣诞节有关的装饰品展示在商店里面。在中国，当中秋节快要到的时候，市场对月饼的需求量总是大大增加。你可以想象，糕饼店一定因此而赚了很多钱。因此，就好的方面来说，节日可以刺激消费。这可能也是经济景气的象征。我敢确定店家一定很喜欢各种节日的到来，因为庆祝活动往往可以吸引街上来来往往的人群，并说服他们买一些东西。你可能也注意到了，在户外，只要是有人群的地方，在街上就可以看到卖小吃的摊贩。大批饥肠辘辘的行人给了他们多赚一些外快的机会。因此，节日通常都会有商业化的趋势。我认为那也是不可避免的，但是庆祝还是照样庆祝。

Religion and Cultural Impact
宗教与文化冲击

USEFUL EXPRESSIONS 实用表达

1. Buddhism /ˈbʊdɪzəm; `bʊdɪzəm/ ***n.*** 佛教
2. widespread /ˈwaɪdspred; `waɪd`sprɛd/ ***adj.*** 广泛盛行的

   Buddhism is ***widespread*** in this country.

   佛教在这个国家很盛行。
3. Buddhist /ˈbʊdɪst; `bʊdɪst/ ***n.*** 佛教徒 ***adj.*** 佛教的
4. recite Buddhist sutras 念诵佛经
5. Buddhist temple 寺院
6. Buddha /ˈbʊdə; `bʊdə/ ***n.*** 佛；佛陀
7. be convinced of sth. / be convinced that + 从句 深信某事

   I believe in Buddhism, because I ***am convinced of*** the teaching of the ***Buddha***.

   我信佛教，因为我深信佛陀的教导。
8. reincarnation /ˌriːɪnkɑːˈneɪʃən; ˌriɪnkar`neʃən/ ***n.*** 轮回转世
9. strive to do 努力去做……

   The idea of ***reincarnation*** makes people think about why they are the way they are and why they should ***strive to become*** better persons.

   轮回转世的观念让人们去思考自己的现世，思索为何他们应该努力去成为更好的人。
10. favourable rebirth 较好的来生
11. aspire to sth. / aspire to do 以某物为目标；立志要做……
12. enlightenment /ɪnˈlaɪtnmənt; ɪn`laɪtn̩mənt/ ***n.*** 开悟
13. for the sake of all sentient beings 为了（度化）众生
14. distant goal 一个遥远的目标

   Buddhists are supposed to ***aspire to enlightenment for the sake of all sentient beings***, but that seems a very far ***distant goal***.

佛教徒为了度化众生，应该以开悟为目标，但那似乎是一个非常遥远的目标。

15. compassion /kəm'pæʃən; kəm`pæʃən/ ***n.*** 怜悯；同情

16. wisdom /'wɪzdəm; `wɪzdəm/ ***n.*** 智慧

Another feature of Buddhism is its emphasis on both ***compassion*** and ***wisdom***.

佛教的另一个特色是慈悲与智慧并重。

17. penetrating insight into … 对……有深刻敏锐的见解

"Wisdom" refers to ***penetrating insight into*** the nature of existence, seeing things as they really are.

"智慧"是指对存在的本质洞若观火，看清事物的真实面目。

18. religious ceremony 宗教仪式

I sometimes attend ***religious ceremonies***.

我有时会参加宗教仪式。

19. meditation /ˌmedɪ'teɪʃən; ˌmɛdə`teʃən/ ***n.*** 冥想

I practise ***meditation*** in my own home sometimes.

有时我在家里进行冥想。

20. faith /feɪθ; feθ/ ***n.*** 信仰

One important aspect to ***faith*** is that you gain spiritual support from it.

信仰的其中一项重要特质就是：让人们获得精神上的支持。

21. Taoism /'taʊɪzəm; `taʊɪzəm/ ***n.*** 道教

22. Christianity /ˌkrɪsti'ænəti; ˌkrɪstʃɪ`ænətɪ/ ***n.*** 基督教

23. Islam /'ɪslɑːm; `ɪsləm/ ***n.*** 伊斯兰教

A small number of people in this country believe in ***Islam***.

在这个国家里有少数人信仰伊斯兰教。

24. compatible /kəm'pætəbəl; kəm`pætəbḷ/ ***adj.*** 相容的

Buddhism and Taoism are ***compatible***.

佛教和道教是相容的。

25. Taoist temple 道观

26. statue /'stætʃuː; `stætʃu/ ***n.*** 塑像

27. Bodhisattva /ˌbɒdɪ'sɑːtvə; bodɪ`sætvə/ ***n.*** 菩萨

28. indigenous /ɪn'dɪdʒɪnəs; ɪn`dɪdʒənəs/ ***adj.*** 源于当地的；本土的

Taoism is an ***indigenous*** Chinese religion and philosophy.

道教是一种源于中国本土的信仰和哲学。

29. take roots 生根；兴盛、盛行

Buddhism originates from ancient India, but it has ***taken roots*** in many Asian countries.

佛教源于古印度，但它已在许多亚洲国家盛行。

30. Taoist /'taʊɪst; `taʊɪst/ ***n.*** 道教徒 ***adj.*** 道教的

31. invisible spirit 看不见的灵魂

Taoism seems to believe in magic: for example, some ***Taoists*** claim that they can communicate with ***invisible "spirits"***.

道教似乎相信神迹灵异，譬如，有一些道教徒宣称他们能与看不到的“灵魂”互相沟通。

32. Buddhism sees all our experience as manifestations and interpretations of mind.

佛教视我们的一切体验为对意识的展现与诠释。

33. transform /træns'fɔːm; træns`fɔrm/ ***v.*** 使改变，使脱胎换骨

34. conduct my life in a worthwhile and fruitful way 以积极正面的态度掌握我的人生

I live happily, because I ***conduct my life in a worthwhile and fruitful way***.

我现在活得很快乐，因为我以积极正面的态度掌握我的人生。

35. cultivate /'kʌltɪveɪt; `kʌltə,vet/ ***v.*** 培养；耕耘

I try to ***cultivate*** compassion and wisdom.

我试着去培养慈悲心和智慧。

36. spiritual support 精神支柱

One important aspect of faith is that you gain ***spiritual support*** from it.

信仰的一个重要方面是你能从中获得精神支持。

37. cultural impact 文化冲击

Religion can make a ***cultural impact*** on a country.

宗教可以对一个国家造成文化冲击。

38. stimulate /'stɪmjʊleɪt; `stɪmjə,let/ ***v.*** 刺激；激起

39. different forms of artistic expression 不同的艺术表达形式

40. painting /'peɪntɪŋ; `pentɪŋ/ ***n.*** 绘画

41. sculpture /'skʌlptʃə; `skʌlptʃɚ/ ***n.*** 雕塑

42. poetry /'pəʊɪtri; `po·ɪtrɪ/ ***n.*** 诗歌
43. literature /'lɪtərətʃə; `lɪtərə,tʃur/ ***n.*** 文学
44. architecture /'ɑːkɪtektʃə; `ɑrkə,tɛktʃɚ/ ***n.*** 建筑

    Religion certainly ***stimulates*** many ***different forms of artistic expression***. You can see that influence at work in ***painting***, ***sculpture***, ***poetry***, ***literature*** and ***architecture***.

    宗教的确会激发多种多样的艺术表达形式。你可以在绘画、雕塑、诗歌、文学及建筑作品上窥见其影响力。

45. be amazed at … 对……感到惊奇；对……感到惊讶
46. gorgeous /'gɔːdʒəs; `gɔrdʒəs/ ***adj.*** 壮观的，极其漂亮的（注：英式口语用法）
47. cathedral /kə'θiːdrəl; kə`θidrəl/ ***n.*** 大教堂

    I ***am*** always ***amazed at*** these ***gorgeous cathedrals*** in the West.

    西方那些壮观的大教堂总令我惊叹不已。

48. exquisite /ɪk'skwɪzɪt; `ɛkskwɪzɪt/ ***adj.*** 精美的
49. be inspired by … 由……引发灵感

    Some of the most ***exquisite*** sculptures and buildings ***are inspired by*** Buddhism.

    那些雕工最为精细的雕塑和建筑中，有些正是因佛教而产生创作灵感的。

50. calligraphy /kə'lɪgrəfi; kə`lɪgrəfɪ/ ***n.*** 书法

    In this country, you'll find examples of ***calligraphy*** inspired by Buddhism.

    在这个国家，你可以发现一些受佛教思想启发而创作出来的书法作品。

51. be converted to 皈依（宗教）；转换成
52. religious denomination 某一宗教分支

    Some people ***are converted*** from one ***religious denomination*** to another, or even from one religion to another.

    有些人会从某一教派转换至另一派，甚至会改信另一种宗教。

53. I think everyone should have freedom of religious expression so long as it doesn't harm others.

    我认为只要不会伤害到其他人，每个人都有表达宗教信仰的自由。

54. a constraint on … = a restraint on … 对……的约束

    Some people think that religion is no more than ***a constraint on*** their lives. But it is far from being ***a restraint on*** one's freedom to live a good life.

    有些人认为宗教不过是他们人生中的枷锁。但是，它绝不会限制个人追求美好人

生的自由。

55. constricting /kən'strɪktɪŋ; kən`strɪktɪŋ/ ***adj.*** 约束的，限制的

56. be wary of … 对……存疑

Some people's experience of religion has been ***constricting***, so it's understandable that they ***are wary of*** it.

有一些人因为以往的宗教体验而觉得它约束很多，所以也就不难理解为什么他们会对宗教有所存疑。

57. an essential guideline for … 是……很重要的指导方针

58. spiritual development 精神发展

59. label /'leɪbəl; `lebḷ/ ***n.*** 标签

It would be a pity if religion became a ***label*** used to separate people, not to unite them.

如果宗教变成用来区别人们的标签，而不是来促进融合的话，那将会是很可惜的。

QUESTION DATABASE 题库练习

个人陈述 (Individual Long Turn)

考官 Now please have a look at this card. This is your topic. I want you to describe a religious faith you have or know about. You have one minute to prepare.

Describe a religious faith you have or know about. You should say:

what it is
how you came to know it
whether you believe in it
in what way it is special.

INSTRUCTIONS

You will be asked to talk about the topic for one to two minutes.
You have one minute to think about what you are going to say.
You can make some notes to help you if you wish.

请描述一个自己信仰的或所知的宗教。你应该谈到：

它是哪一类宗教
你是通过什么途径认识它的
你是否相信
它的与众不同之处。

【说明】：

针对这个话题作出一至两分钟的陈述。
你有一分钟的时间去思考你的陈述内容。
假如需要的话，你可以写下要点以帮助你组织陈述。

Sample Response

I am going to talk about Buddhism, which is widespread in this country. I came to know about it mainly through my parents; I was brought up in a Buddhist family. My mother used to recite Buddhist sutras regularly, and she still does. Do I believe in it? Yes, I do, because I am convinced of the teaching of the Buddha. I think it is special in many ways. First and foremost, there is the idea of reincarnation. It makes people think about why they are the way they are and why they should strive to become better persons. Good actions and skilful actions produce merit, and this results in favourable rebirth. Of course, Buddhists are really supposed to aspire to full enlightenment for the sake of all sentient beings, but that seems a very far distant goal. Another feature of Buddhism is its emphasis on both compassion and wisdom. To have compassion means to act so as not to harm any living things, including animals and insects. And "wisdom" refers to penetrating insight into the nature of existence, seeing things as they really are. With compassion, I learn to respect everything that lives. With wisdom, I learn to be contented and happy with what I have.

回答范例

我要来谈一谈佛教，它在这个国家是非常盛行的。因为从小生长在一个佛教家庭里，所以我主要是通过父母的引导来认识佛教的。我母亲过去时常诵经，直到现在她依然如此。至于我是否信仰该教，是的，我信仰，因为我深信佛陀的教导。我认为它在很多方面都是很特别的。首先，它有轮回转世的观念，这种观念让人们去思考自己的现世，思索为何他们应该努力去成为更好的人。今世行善积德来生定然不错。当然，所有的佛教徒为了度化众生，应该以开悟为目标，但那似乎是一个非常遥远的目标。佛教的另一个特色是慈悲与智慧两者并重。怀有一颗慈悲心是指不要伤害任何生命，包括动物及昆虫；而"智慧"指对存在的本质洞若观火，看清事物的真实面目。因为有着一颗慈悲心，我学会对每个生命的尊重；因为有着智慧，我学会对所拥有的一切感到知足与快乐。

◎ **Do you attend any religious ceremony?**

Occasionally I do. And I practise meditation in my own home sometimes.

你参与过任何宗教仪式吗？

偶尔会，有时我也会在家里进行冥想。

◎ **What are the other faiths that people here believe in?**

Apart from Buddhism, the popular ones are Taoism, Islam and Christianity.

在这里还有哪些其他宗教信仰？

在这个国家里除了佛教外，其他盛行的宗教还有道教、伊斯兰教和基督教。

双向讨论 (Two-way Discussion)

◎ **Right! Let's continue to talk about religion. How is Taoism different from Buddhism?**

How are they different from each other? Hum ... well, one difference is that Taoism is an indigenous Chinese religion and philosophy, but Buddhism originates from ancient India, although it has taken roots in many Asian countries. Then again, Taoism seems to believe in magic: for example, some Taoists claim that they can communicate with invisible "spirits". Buddhism, on the other hand, sees all our experience as manifestations and interpretations of mind. These are some of the differences.

好！那让我们继续谈谈宗教，道教与佛教有何不同？

它们之间有何差异？嗯……其中一个差异是道教是一种源于中国本土的信仰和哲学，而佛教源于古印度，尽管它已盛行于许多的亚洲国家。不只如此，道教似乎相信神迹灵异，譬如，有一些道教徒宣称他们能与看不到的“灵魂”互相沟通。另一方面来说，佛教却认为我们的一切体验都是对意识的展现与诠释。这些便是它们之间的一些差异。

◎ **What do you think is the significance of religion?**

As far as I can see, religion is not only a way of life but a way of transforming oneself and the world. I used to ask myself "What is the meaning of life?" To be successful? To make a name? To make a fortune? It seems to me that religion helps us to answer these questions. At least, my religion does! I live happily, because I conduct my life in a worthwhile and fruitful way. I try to cultivate compassion and wisdom. Hmm ... another important aspect of faith is that you can gain spiritual support from it.

你认为宗教有何重要性？

就我个人来看，宗教不只是一种生活方式，也是改变个人及世界的途径。我过去经常自问：“生命的意义是什么？”为了成功？或为了成名？还是为了致富？对我来说，宗教似乎帮助我们解答了这些问题，至少我的信仰的确帮助我解答了这些疑问！我现在活得很快乐，因为我以积极正面的态度掌握我的人生。我试着去培养慈悲心和智慧。嗯……另外，很重要的一点就是你可以获得精神上的支持。

◎ **What kind of cultural impact do you think a religion can have on a country?**

Cultural impact? I assume you mean ... on art or music and things like that? Hmm, well, religion certainly stimulates many different forms of artistic expression. You can see that influence at work in painting, sculpture, poetry, literature and architecture. And here in this country, you'll find some of the most exquisite sculptures and buildings and examples of calligraphy are inspired by Buddhism.

你认为宗教对一个国家会造成什么文化冲击？

文化冲击？我想你是指……艺术或音乐之类的吧？嗯……宗教的确会激发多种多样的艺术表达形式。你可以在绘画、雕塑、诗歌、文学及建筑作品上窥见其影响力。而在这个国家，你会发现，那些最为精美的雕塑、建筑及书法作品中，有些正是因佛教而产生创作灵感的。

◎ **Some people think religion is no more than a constraint on their lives. What do you think?**

Well, to start with, everyone is free to decide whether or not they want to live their life with faith in something higher. But of course that faith finds expression in all sorts of ways. Some people live their lives according to the faith of their parents, others are converted from one religious denomination to another, or even from one religion to another. I think everyone should have freedom of religious expression so long as it doesn't harm others. Unfortunately, though, some people's experience of religion has been constricting, so it's understandable that they are wary of it. Such people may choose not to have a religion at all. However, I find that religion, far from being a restraint on one's freedom to live a good life, is an essential guideline for one's spiritual development. Don't you think everyone should be responsible for his own or her own actions?（注：though 在英语口语中可当副词，意思是"然而"、"尽管如此"）

有些人认为宗教不过是他们人生中的枷锁。你认为呢？

首先，每个人都有自由去选择他们的人生是否要有一些较高层次的信仰，但是，信仰当然有很多的表现方式。有些人遵从父母的信仰，有些人则会改信另一教派，甚至会改信另一种宗教。我认为，在不伤害他人的前提下，每个人都有表达宗教信仰的自由。然而不幸的是，有些人因为以往的宗教体验觉得它约束很多，所以也就不难理解为什么他们会对宗教有所存疑，像这样的人可能就会选择不去信仰任何宗教。但是我觉得宗教信仰绝没有限制个人追求美好人生的自由，相反，它是指导个人提升精神境界的重要方针。难道你不认为每个人都应对自己的作为负责吗？

◎ **Do you feel uneasy with people with a different faith?**

No, not at all. Indeed, I believe dialogue between religions can help bring about mutual understanding. It would be a pity if religion became a label used to separate people, not to unite them. Whenever I hear news about confrontations between different religions or denominations, I feel very sad. You see, religion is supposed to bring peace and harmony to the world. So I feel there's really no limit to my developing friendships with those of different religions and faiths, as long as they respect and are willing to seriously consider the truths which are seen and cherished by my religion, my faith.

你和不同信仰的人在一起时会感到不自在吗？

不，一点也不会。我相信宗教之间的对话能增进彼此的了解，如果宗教变成被用来区别人们的标签而不是促进融合的话，那将会是很可惜的。每当听到关于不同的宗教或教派之间产生冲突的新闻，我就会感到很难过，因为宗教原本是应该为世界带来和平与和谐的。因此我觉得只要他们能够尊重，并且愿意去思考我的宗教信仰所珍视的真理，那么与不同信仰的人建立友情，真的是没有任何限制的。

Chapter 4

实战测验：仿真考场验证成效

IELTS Speaking Test 1

（此练习的第一部分特别适合学生或刚毕业的考生；第二部分和第三部分则不限）

第一部分

Can you tell me your full name?

Can I see your identification?（注：identification 指准考证、身份证件等）

Do you work or are you a student?

Do you enjoy your study?

What's your favourite subject?

Will you continue to explore this area of study?

What do you do in your spare time?

How did you become interested in doing that?

Let's talk about school life. Do you live in a dormitory?

What is your student accommodation like?

How about the student-teacher relationships in your Institute?

第二部分

Now please have a look at this card. This is your topic. I want you to describe your favourite city or town in China. You have one minute to prepare.

Describe your favourite city or town in China. You should say:

where it is
how long you have stayed there
in what way it is special or famous
why you like it best.

INSTRUCTIONS

You will be asked to talk about the topic for one to two minutes.
You have one minute to think about what you are going to say.
You can make some notes to help you if you wish.

Where were you originally from?

Do you prefer to live in a city or a town?

第三部分

Right! Let's talk about city. How would you compare your hometown with your favourite city?

What are the advantages and disadvantages of living in a city?

Apart from providing a living environment, what other functions or services do you think a city or town should provide?

What changes have taken place recently in this city?

What do you think of these changes?

In what direction do you expect the city to develop in the future?

IELTS Speaking Test 2

（此练习的第一部分特别适合有工作经验的社会人士；第二部分和第三部分则不限）

第一部分

How shall I call you?

Can I see your identification?（注：identification 指准考证、身份证件等）

Can you tell me something about your educational background?

Do you work or are you a student?

How do you like your present job?

What do you find is the most difficult part of your job?

Is this the only job you have ever had?

What qualities do you think one should develop in order to have a successful career in your profession?

Let's move on to talk about music. Do you favour any particular type of music?

What is the significance of music?

Do you yourself play any instrument?

How would you characterize the traditional music of your country?

第二部分

Now please have a look at this card. This is your topic. I want you to describe your experience with the Internet. You have one minute to prepare.

> Describe your experience with the Internet. You should say:
>
> where you usually use it
> when you started using it
> what role it plays in your life
> what you think of it.
>
> **INSTRUCTIONS**
>
> You will be asked to talk about the topic for one to two minutes.
> You have one minute to think about what you are going to say.
> You can make some notes to help you if you wish.

How often do you go on-line?

Do you read any computer magazines to keep yourself informed of the latest development of computer technology?

第三部分

Right! Let's talk about computer technology. Do you think you can do without computers?

Do you think the advantages of the equipment you use often outweigh its disadvantages?

What impact does the Internet have on society?

How do you compare emails with traditional letters?

In what direction do you think the Internet will change?

Do you think the development of science and technology has made our lives better?

What do you think of the idea of virtual reality?

IELTS Speaking Test 3

（此练习的第一部分特别适合准备移民的考生；第二部分和第三部分则不限）

第一部分

Can you tell me your full name?

Can I see your identification?（注：identification 指准考证、身份证件等）

What kind of house do you live in?

Could you tell me about your room? What is it like?

Do you work or are you a student?

Could you talk about your past working experience?

Why did you move from your former job to the present one?

How do you feel about the change of job?

Why do you want to take IELTS?

What is so special about that country that you have decided to move there?

Do you have any plan for the future?

Let's talk about living environment. What are some of the factors that people would consider when they move from one place to another?

What is your ideal living environment?

What do you think of the transport in this country?

第二部分

Now please have a look at this card. This is your topic. I want you to describe your perfect holiday. You have one minute to prepare.

> Describe your perfect holiday. You should say:
>
> where you want to spend it
> when you will take the holiday
> with whom you will go
> why it is a perfect holiday for you.
>
> **INSTRUCTIONS**
> You will be asked to talk about the topic for one to two minutes.
> You have one minute to think about what you are going to say.
> You can make some notes to help you if you wish.

Did you ever have such a holiday?

Is there any other place you fancy if you can afford to go there?

第三部分

Now, let's talk about holiday and tourism. Is it a common practice for people in this country to spend their holidays abroad?

What do you think of this trend?

Do you think the ways people here spend their holidays have changed, say, over the past 30 years? What changes have taken place?

Do you think tourism in this country is flourishing or deteriorating?

What could best be done to boost the tourist industry of this country?

Do you prefer to travel alone or with someone? Why?

What are the advantages and disadvantages of travelling alone?

IELTS Speaking Test 4

第一部分

Could you tell me your name?

Can I see your identification?（注：identification 指准考证、身份证件等）

Do you work or are you a student?

Where did you do your first degree?

Do you enjoy your study?

What do you do in your spare time?

What would you suggest that people see or do when visiting this city?

Let's talk about recreational facilities. What common recreational facilities are available here?（注：recreational facilities 指娱乐场所、设施，如 parks, KTV shops, Internet café 等）

What do you think of them?

Do you think the way people find entertainment in this country has changed?

第二部分

Now please have a look at this card. This is your topic. I want you to talk about a good friend of yours. You have one minute to prepare.

Talk about a good friend of yours. You should say:

who the person is

how long you have known each other

how you came to know each other

why the person is special to you.

INSTRUCTIONS

You will be asked to talk about the topic for one to two minutes.

You have one minute to think about what you are going to say.

You can make some notes to help you if you wish.

Do you have many friends?

How do you usually make friends?

第三部分

Now, let's talk about friendship. What do you think is the significance of friendship?

Everyone makes friends at different stages of his or her life. Are your childhood friends different from those you make, say, when you are a college student?

How about the friends you make at work? Are they, again, different from your university friends?

What qualities do you think real friendship should have?

Do you think one should be selective in making friends?

Chapter 5

口语材料练听力：考生验证的彪悍听力复习法

IELTS

虽然本书的主要目的是为准备雅思考试口语部分的考生提供一些指南，但因为本书的对话皆为英文，且含有不同的题材，故也**可当作听力练习的辅导用书**。

以下列出雅思听力考试常见题型的应试技巧及练习题。这些练习的内容皆取自本书的对话，熟悉题型并做完以下六组练习题后，可**自行选听**本书的任何对话或独述**来练习做笔记、写关键词，**以便训练自己写答案的速度。

Exercise

01 填表格题型

SKILLS

1. 快速画出各项标题及**关键词**。
2. 根据标题及关键词，心里先**预期**（anticipate）要填什么答案。如本练习题第（1）题答案可能是某某 College 或 University；(2) – (5) 必是学科名称。
3. 听时，注意对话**一问一答**的结构。对话中的**问题**提醒考生谈及**何项标题**，而对话中的**回应**即是**答案**所在。
4. 有些号码如会员号码（membership No.）、驾照号码（driver's licence No.）、车号（car No.）等可能含字母（如 M99656），不要遗漏。

Questions 1-7

Complete the form below.

*Write **NO MORE THAN THREE WORDS** for each answer.*

Educational Background

Name of School/Institute: **(1)** ....

Major Subject of Study: **(2)** ....

Favourite Course (Now): **(3)** English ....

Favourite Course in the Past: **(4)** ....

Difficult Course: **(5)** ....

Club Attended: **(6)** ....

Significance of the Club: play and share the interest

(7) ....

Exercise

02 分类题型

SKILLS

1. **熟悉分类方式**。例如此题将说话者对种种食物的意见分成“赞同”（in favour）、“反对”（against）及“并无强烈看法”等三种。
2. 快速画出各项**标题及关键词**。
3. 不管任何听力的题型，都要**抓住意思、态度，试卷中出现的语句未必和听到的语句一模一样**。如试卷上写着 people nowadays are more aware of ... 而实际听到的句子是 people are thinking with increased awareness about ...

Questions 1-6

What is the male speaker's opinion on the following points?

Write **A** if he is in favour

Write **B** if he has no strong opinion either way

Write **C** if he is against

People nowadays are more aware of healthy food than before.	**(1)** ....
Fast food is becoming popular.	**(2)** ....
Organic foods are healthful to humans.	**(3)** ....
Genetically modified foods are natural.	**(4)** ....
GM foods can have a harmful effect on humans.	**(5)** ....
Customers have no right to know whether a product is GM food.	**(6)** ....

Exercise

03 完成句子的填空题型

SKILLS

1. 画出各句的**关键词**。
2. 答案要让句子**合乎语法**，如：

   The students feel __________ .（答案必须是形容词或名词）

   There are four __________ .（答案必须是名词且是复数形式）

   The city is __________ than before.（答案必须是比较级）
3. **抓住意思、态度，试卷中出现的语句未必和听到的语句一模一样。**
4. 注意字数的限制（no more than three words）。

Questions 1-6

Complete the sentences below. Write ***NO MORE THAN THREE WORDS*** *for each answer.*

Public transport of the city is ....**(1)**..........than before, but there is no ....**(2)**.......... in this city yet.

One of the advantages of using public transport is that it reduces the number of ....**(3)**.......... .

Another advantage is that it is ....**(4)**.......... than using a car.

The downside is that it is not always ....**(5)**..........; what's more, you need to ....**(6)**.......... .

Exercise

04 只写关键词的填空题型（类似笔记纲要）

SKILLS

1. 快速画出各项**标题**及**关键词**。
2. **同时注意两道题（或更多）**，特别是**属于同一标题、项目的问题**，讲话者可能会一次说完，例如：

   Contributing factors:

   - economic development
   - ____________________
   - industrial expansion
   - ____________________

3. 属于**同一项目的笔记**，要填入的词语，须**属相同结构**。（例如：上面四点皆是名词短语）。
4. 属于**同一项目的笔记**，常出现的**标志性词语**有：also; ... as well; ... and ...; both ... and ...; first, second, third 等，暗示另一要点。
5. 利用**转折词**辅助理解。如 well, next, now, OK, right, then again, finally 等词会用于**不同项目或标题间**，故听到这些词，要自动往**下一题、下一项目**看。又如 for instance 及 for example 等词会用于说明**同一项目或标题**。又如 however 及 on the other hand 等词后面提及的是**对照**的观点且**必是要点**。

Language Classroom

How do Children Learn a Foreign Language?

Aspects of language children can pick up naturally:

- new words
- (1) ....
- (2) ....

Language environment: only (3) .... language is spoken

Main methods:

- playing
- (4) ....

Focus: speaking and listening

How do Adults Learn a Foreign Language?

Language environment: (5) .... can be spoken

Difficult to change their (6) .... or pronunciation

The purposes of leaning a foreign language:

- go sightseeing
- (7).........................
- study abroad

The Best Principle: (8) ....

Should One's First Language be Used in a Language Classroom?

No: using the foreign language forces learners to use the new language

Yes: using the first language helps (9) ....

In principle, one's native language used when it is (10) ....

Exercise

05 多选题题型

SKILLS

1. 快速掌握问题。
2. 画出各答案的**关键词**。
3. 注意答案的区别，若有两答案相反，则可能其中之一是正确答案。如：本练习题（3-5）题的 A 与 C 相反。

Questions 1-2

Circle **Two** letters **A-E**.

What does the female speaker say about her style of dress at work?

A. She looks neat and graceful.

B. She dresses in a particular way.

C. She likes to combine different colours.

D. She does not think it is important to be style conscious.

E. She likes all sorts of fashionable clothes, including outlandish ones.

Questions 3-5

Circle **Three** letters **A-F**.

What does the male speaker say about his style of dress at work?

A. He dresses casually.

B. He puts on sandals and shorts sometimes.

C. He dresses conservatively.

D. He wears different colours of ties.

E. He usually wears a suit.

F. He dresses in a way similar to the style of his business friends from abroad.

Exercise

06 简答题题型

SKILLS

1. 圈出问什么，如 where, when, how often, how long, what 及 why 等，并画出其他**关键词**。
2. 根据所问及关键词，心里先**预期**（anticipate）听时要掌握什么信息。如：问 where，则答案必是某地方；问 how long，则答案必是一段时间（如 fifty minutes 或 three years）。
3. 注意字数的限制。
4. 不管任何题型，问题的顺序大多与所听内容的顺序一致，但会有少数题目例外。

*Write **NO MORE THAN THREE WORDS** for each answer.*

1. What is the speaker's favourite animal?

   ....

2. In which part of the world does the animal normally live?

   ....

3. How often does the speaker see the animal in the zoo?

   ....

4. What is the food that the animal likes to eat?

   ....

5. How does the speaker characterize the nature of the animal?

   ....

听力原文 (TAPESCRIPTS)

EX 01

You'll hear a conversation about university life. You have some time to look at questions 1-7. As you listen, answer questions 1-7.

Man: Are you a student or do you work?

Woman: I am a student studying at Peking University. *Q1*

Man: What do you study?

Woman: I am doing a major in Education. *Q2*

Man: What is your favourite subject?

Woman: My favourite subject! Well, if I had to choose just one, it would be a course called English Reading and Conversation. The *Q3* reason why I like that one best is that I have benefited a lot from it. For example, I've learned some very useful reading skills, developed more efficient learning methods and improved my oral English.

Man: How about your favourite subject when you were in primary school and in secondary school?

Woman: My favourite subject in primary school? Gosh, that's a long time ago! Let me think about it. I think it was Music. I have been fond of music ever since I was little. I used to play the *Q4* flute, the Chinese flute, in primary school. Then I became interested in English when I was in high school. I wasn't the best student of English in my class, but I have improved my English comprehension, vocabulary and conversational abilities a lot since then.

Man: What is your school life like?

Woman: During the day, most of my time is spent attending lectures and doing my homework. In the evening, I sometimes join in group activities or just chat with a few of my friends. Like most students nowadays, I spend time surfing the Net. I try to find a balance between study and play. I try to be nice to myself although I have not forgotten my duty as a student.

Man: I wonder if you have the experience where you are not interested in a course but you have to study it?

Woman: Yes, I have. For example, a year ago, I had to take a course in Accounting, but I found it difficult, so difficult that I managed to achieve only a borderline grade. Maybe that's not where my potential lies. *Q5*

Man: Do you join any extracurricular activities? Why?

Woman: I participate in a guitar club in my college. I play my guitar there almost every week. I joined it because I love music and I like to make friends there. Being in this club means a lot to me. It's a situation where I can play and share impressions with other music lovers. What's more, I'm learning how to communicate better. *Q6* *Q7*

EX 02

You'll hear a conversation about food and eating habits. You have some time to look at questions 1-6. As you listen, answer questions 1-6.

Woman: Now, let's talk about eating habits. Do you think the eating habits practised in this country have changed over the years?

Man: Hmm ... yes, I think so. One big difference is that there are many fast food restaurants. As you know, hamburgers and fried chicken are high in calories and cholesterol, but many youngsters and children just fancy them. On the other hand,I've noticed a totally different trend—some people are thinking with increased awareness about healthy food. *Q1*

For example, more and more people are becoming vegetarian, because eating too much meat can block the walls of the arteries and even cause heart problems. And then there's the question of compassion. More people are becoming sensitive to the ethical issues concerning the slaughter of animals. And then again, a growing number of people here eat raw organic foods. Using a blender, they just mix organic vegetables and fruits. They believe such a diet has healing effects.

Woman: What do you think of the change?

Man: Well, I have mixed feelings. I think it's a real shame that fast food is becoming so popular. I've noticed that there are more and more children who are overweight. This certainly has a lot to do with it. On the other hand, I think it's good that we are more aware of the importance of eating healthy foods such as fruits, vegetables and organic foods. At least we are becoming more alert to the need for a balanced diet, with sufficient quantities of different food groups such as protein, minerals, fibre, vitamins, etc. *Q2* *Q3*

Woman: Are organic foods popular in this country?

Man: They're getting popular. There are an increasing number of "health shops" selling organic foods and all sorts of dietary supplements. So yes, I think they are indeed growing popular. Though organic foods are expensive, those who can afford them consider health more important than price.

Woman: What do you think of genetically modified foods?

Man: GM foods? Well, I've got quite a lot to say about this. If I had a choice, I'd prefer not to buy them. As I see it, they are definitely not 100% natural. Plant cells have evolved through interaction with the environment—with the soil and other plants and insects and animals—over millions of years. The naturally-evolved composition of the plant cell over long periods of time *Q4* is then suddenly altered by scientific means.

So how GM plants will affect the rest of life is actually unknown. And once GM seeds are planted and germinated, they are bound to spread all over the world by wind, birds, insects and so on. Though scientists claim that GM foods are "safe", they cannot really be completely sure of their effects on human, animal and plant life over a long period. And these products have already appeared on our market shelves. I think they should be clearly labeled as such. Recently a well-known soya milk product here was criticized because it used GM soya beans, but it didn't specify this detail on the package. Consumers should be at least informed of that so that they can choose whether or not they want to buy a GM food. *Q5* *Q5* *Q6*

EX 03

You'll hear a conversation about public transport. You have some time to look at questions 1-6. As you listen, answer questions 1-6.

Man: Right! What do you think of the public transport of this city?

Woman: It's much better and more convenient than it used to be, because buses run more frequently than before. Also, there are more bus routes these days. However, I think public transport here still leaves something to be desired. When I was studying in Beijing, I took the metro quite often and I found it really handy. But we don't have metro in this city. It's a pity. *Q1* *Q2*

Man: What are the advantages and disadvantages of using public transport?

Woman:	Let me talk about the advantages first. It helps reduce the number of private vehicles on the road. So an efficient public transport system reduces traffic density, which has the knock-on effect of making the remaining traffic flow more easily. Another good thing I can think of is that ... it is a much cheaper means of transport than private ownership of a vehicle, at least for the individual. Then again, it is less polluting, both in terms of noise and of exhaust emission, than private transport. As to its disadvantages, well, I'd like to point out several things. First of all, it's not always comfortable or even convenient. You may have to put up with standing in a queue, or squash up amongst others, especially at peak hours. Another disadvantage is that you will often have to wait. And if you are in a hurry and have to wait, you will probably feel very restless and frustrated. This is my experience, anyway.	*Q3* *Q4* *Q5* *Q6*

EX 04

You'll hear a talk about learning foreign languages. You have some time to look at questions 1-10. As you listen, answer questions 1-10.

Woman:	Should there be any difference in the ways children and adults learn a foreign language?	
Man:	If you ask me, my answer is yes! Children pick up languages quite naturally. They are able to pick up new words, intonations and speech patterns very easily. So it's a good idea for children to learn a foreign language by introducing them as early as possible to an environment where the target language alone is spoken. And their learning can well be combined with playing and singing. Speaking and	*Q1-2* *Q3* *Q4*

listening should be the chief method of a language learning programme for children. For adults, well, things may be quite different. Take my father for example. I don't think he would succeed in learning English, and certainly wouldn't enjoy it, if he heard no explanations at all in Chinese in a language class. In terms of learning environment, adults, especially those at the beginner level, might find it really daunting to have to speak in a situation where their mother tongue is not *Q5* spoken at all. Then again, the way in which adults pronounce words tends to become fixed rather early on; then they find it difficult to change their accent or pronunciation. Generally *Q6* speaking, adult learners are quite a heterogeneous lot. They learn foreign languages for various reasons and with varying degrees of proficiency. For instance, some learn so that they can go sightseeing, some want to gain promotion, others *Q7* want to study abroad, etc. It's hard to generalize what is the best learning strategy for them, because it depends on their purpose and on their motivation. However, I do believe that practice makes perfect. This principle applies to learners of all *Q8* ages and of all levels.

Woman: Do you think one's first language should be used in a language classroom?

Man: Well, if possible it should be kept to a minimum. Creating a totally new language environment for learners can force them, as it were, to use the language they're learning. On the other hand, using one's own, one's first language in a foreign language classroom helps slow learners understand the *Q9* lesson better. But I still think one's mother tongue is best used only when it's absolutely necessary. *Q10*

EX 05

You'll hear two speakers describing how they usually dress when going to work. You have some time to look at questions 1-5. As you listen, answer questions 1-5.

I'd like to tell you the sort of styles I like to wear when I go to work. I often wear a blouse and a skirt, but sometimes a dress or a matching outfit. I don't need to dress in any particular way, but one thing I think is important is to look as neat and graceful and bright and fresh as possible, and to give expression to how I feel. I like to dress in all sorts of different ways—variety is the spice of life. I combine different colours and choose all sorts of patterns and cuts. What do I think about all this? Well, I think it's important to dress tastefully, and I believe I do. This is important nowadays, especially with all this talk of the "total look" in fashion designs. But I don't like the outlandish styles that some avant-garde designers create nowadays. I love the different forms of natural beauty we see all around us—in flowers, in plants, in ancient buildings and even in the sky and clouds. There's so much beauty and subtlety in these things. And yes, I am style conscious; I feel that wearing stylish clothes is a way of adding to the beauty in the world. *Q1* *Q2*

I'm going to tell you how I normally dress for work. I usually dress quite conservatively, wearing a shirt with a tie. I don't normally wear a suit unless it's cold, or when I have to attend, say, an important event such as an office reception party. My basic style at work doesn't change much, but the different colours of my shirts and ties add a bit of variety to it. Why do I dress this way? Well, it's a practice encouraged and adopted by my company. We have to deal with business associates from abroad who are formally dressed. And I think it's important to show them that we care about their visits by dressing in a way that's not too different from theirs. In any case I think dressing formally is an act of politeness. Imagine what would happen if I put on sandals and shorts to see a significant business client! He might imagine I wasn't taking him seriously. So I consider my style of dress at work is both appropriate and necessary. *Q3* *Q4* *Q5*

EX 06

You'll hear a talk about animals. You have some time to look at questions 1-5. As you listen, answer questions 1-5.

The animal I fancy most is the panda. It looks really special, with its black and white markings. It's a big animal with a slow walk. The panda is an endangered species that inhabits southern China, and there are two living in the zoo here. I see the panda about once a month in the zoo and I also see them on TV or in the newspapers from time to time. For me it's the best of animals for several reasons. First and foremost, it looks ever so cute! Just look at its eyes and the two big ears. It looks as if it were a cartoon figure coming to life. Of course, I am pleased that it's a flesh-and-blood creature, not a fanciful creation. Another reason why I like it is its gentle nature. It seldom attacks people. I remember vividly a TV programme I saw some time ago, made somewhere in Sichuan Province. Tourists were sitting next to a panda and having their photo taken with it. I suppose it stayed happy because they kept giving the animal its favourite food—bamboo leaves. That kept it busy, I suppose, which is why the tourists could apparently do anything they liked. For example, they were able to place their arms over its shoulders and even give it a hug. The panda was just too busy enjoying its feast to notice them!

Q1 Q2 Q3 Q4 Q5

听力练习答案 (Answer Key)

EX 01

(1) Peking University
(2) Education
(3) Reading and Conversation
(4) Music
(5) Accounting
(6) guitar (club)
(7) learn to communicate 或 communicate better

EX 02

(1) A (2) C (3) A (4) C (5) B (6) C

EX 03

(1) better 或 more convenient
(2) metro
(3) private vehicles
(4) cheaper 或 less polluting
(5) comfortable or convenient
(6) wait

EX 04

(1) intonations

(2) speech patterns

(3) target

(4) singing

(5) mother tongue 或 first language 或 native language

(6) accent

(7) gain promotion

(8) Practice makes perfect.

(9) slow learners 或 understand lessons better

(10) (absolutely) necessary 或 essential

EX 05

1-2 A C

3-5 C D F

EX 06

1. (the) panda 或 pandas
2. (southern) China
3. once a month
4. bamboo leaves
5. gentle (nature)